Developmental
Perspectives
on Motivation

Volume 40 of

the Nebraska Symposium

on Motivation

University of Nebraska Press

Lincoln and London 1993

Nebraska Symposium on Motivation 1992

Developmental Perspectives on Motivation

Richard Dienstbier
Janis E. Jacobs

Series Editor
Volume Editor

Presenters
Richard M. Ryan

Professor of Psychology and Director of Clinical Training, University of Rochester

Mihaly Csikszentmihalyi

Professor of Psychology and Education, University of Chicago

Kevin Rathunde

Assistant Professor of Human Development and Family Studies, University of Utah

Susan Harter

Professor of Psychology, University of Denver

Jacquelynne S. Eccles

Professor of Psychology, Universities of Colorado and Michigan; Chair, Combined Program in Education and Psychology, University of Michigan

Laura L. Carstensen

Professor of Psychology, Stanford University

Nebraska Symposium on Motivation 1992 is Volume 40 in the series CURRENT THEORY AND RESEARCH IN MOTIVATION

"The Library of Congress has cataloged
this serial publication as follows:"
Nebraska Symposium on Motivation.
Nebraska Symposium on Motivation.
[Papers] v. [1]–1953–
Lincoln, University of Nebraska Press.
v. illus., diagrs. 22cm. annual.
Vol. 1 issued by the symposium under
its earlier name: Current Theory and
Research in Motivation.
Symposia sponsored by the Dept. of
Psychology of the University of Nebraska.
1. Motivation (Psychology)
BF683.N4   159.4082   53-11655
Library of Congress

Preface

The volume editor for this 40th edition of the Nebraska Symposium on Motivation is Janis E. Jacobs. Her responsibilities have exceeded those of previous volume editors, for several labor-intensive procedural changes were tried under Jan's guidance. Those modifications allowed more people from outside Nebraska and the surrounding area to participate and have changed the structure of this volume. They are mentioned here to fully credit Jan for her efforts, but also to alert our readers, all of whom are our potential Symposium guests, that we have endeavored to make your coming to the Symposium more possible and more rewarding.

In past years we divided our contributors into two sessions, one in the fall and one in the spring. With this Symposium we consolidated all activities into one session. Additionally, this year we invited posters on topics relevant to the main theme of this volume, so that guests from outside our geographical area could travel to the Symposium as participants. Both of those modifications were experimental during this first session, but they were obviously successful and will be continued. Thus the new section in this volume containing the abstracts of those posters represents a change that will be repeated in future volumes. Jan planned those new activities as well as performing the usual volume editor's responsibilities of planning the volume, drawing together the contributors, and coordinating all aspects of the editing. My thanks to our contributors for the excellent chapters developed and delivered in timely fashion and to Jan for her editorial excellence in seeing the volume through to its completion.

The Symposium series is supported largely by funds donated in memory of Professor Harry K. Wolfe to the University of Nebraska Foundation by the late Professor Cora L. Friedline. This Symposium volume, like those of the recent past, is dedicated to the memory of Professor Wolfe, who brought psychology to the University of Nebraska. After studying with Wilhelm Wundt, Professor Wolfe returned to this, his native state, to establish the first undergraduate laboratory of psychology in the nation. As a student at Nebraska, Professor Friedline studies psychology under Professor Wolfe.

We are grateful to the late Professor Friedline for her bequest and to the University of Nebraska Foundation for continued financial support for the series.

RICHARD A. DIENSTBIER
Series Editor

Contents

Introduction

Janis E. Jacobs
University of Nebraska–Lincoln

This volume marks the 40th anniversary of the Nebraska Symposium on Motivation, and with it a renewed commitment to the Symposium's original focus on motivation. Although we may reemphas-
ize the topic, it is clear that motivation, as an area of study, has
changed dramatically over the past 40 years. Although motivation
has remained an important theme, it has had to share the stage with
other important topics as the field of psychology has expanded. In
addition, the concept of motivation has been applied to many diverse areas, has been defined and measured in a variety of ways, and
has been used as both description and explanation for a number of
social, cognitive, and emotional outcomes. In short, the study of
motivation has become more complex and diverse, so that, while re-
emphasizing it means that all volumes will have motivation as the
underlying theme, it also means the inclusion of a richer, more varied array of topics than was possible 40 years ago.

Some of the changes just attributed to the field of motivation,
such as greater diversity and complexity, parallel the changes we
study in developmental psychology. Thus the theme of "developmental perspectives" seems a particularly fitting issue to herald the
Symposium's renewed interest in motivation. In developmental
psychology we study most of the same phenomena studied in other

areas of psychology, but with a focus on changes across the life span. Much of the interest in the developmental aspects of motivation begins with the problem cases—the capable adolescent who is not motivated to achieve in school or the child whose motivation is undermined by a poor self-concept. Thus the questions we ask about motivation are often guided by an interest in predicting (and even changing) developmental outcomes based on our knowledge of the ways various biological and experiential factors affect development. How is motivation maintained and transformed across the life span and across tasks? What personal characteristics and what task-specific features affect motivation? How does the level of development interact with the environment to hinder or enhance motivation? These and other questions provide the basis for developmental research in this area.

Surprisingly, within developmental psychology, motivation is seldom seen as a subject area of its own. The topic is unlikely to be found as a chapter heading in introductory textbooks in developmental psychology or as part of a core curriculum for graduate students. However, this does not mean that there is little interest in the development of motivation. It means, instead, that the topic has become integrated into a number of diverse areas. As motivational concepts have been applied to more areas, our thinking about them has expanded and become broader and richer.

My goal in assembling the chapters in this volume was not only to present the best current work in the area, but to foster integrative thinking by bringing together diverse approaches to conceptualizing and studying the topic. To this end, I tried to represent different periods of the life span, influences from various sources, and both emotional and cognitive components of motivation that are important for development. In other words, I wanted to provide a look at the breadth and diversity of research on motivation, extending the more traditional area of achievement motivation to include some new perspectives from outside developmental psychology that I believe are important for the growth of motivation. The obvious danger in looking for unique perspectives is that the chapters might have nothing in common and would fail to form a coherent picture. I do not think that has happened in this case. Although the authors who contributed to this volume come from different subdisciplines and from different perspectives within psychology, there were numerous overlapping themes. The most notable of these were: (1) an emphasis on the self (whether labelled the I-self, the core self, or self-perceptions); (2) an emphasis on the internal (e.g., intrinsic motivation, flow) and external (e.g., family, schools) factors that affect developing motivations; and (3) an emphasis on the choices that may result from one's cognitive, social, or emotional motivations.

The opening chapter by Richard M. Ryan places the entire volume in context by giving historical and theoretical perspectives on development and developmental models that may be used to understand motivation. His viewpoint is that of both a clinician and a researcher as he discusses his own work on autonomy and factors that facilitate or undermine intrinsic motivation. In general, this chapter proposes an integrative approach that expands on an organismic view by including social contexts that support the expression of autonomy, competence, and relatedness in shaping what Ryan calls the core self.

Mihalyi Csikszentmihalyi and Kevin Rathunde also focus on intrinsic motivation, but they are most interested in the motivation that emerges from the sense of satisfaction, or flow, that comes with full involvement with an activity. They advocate using ongoing, moment-to-moment sampling to explore motivation as it occurs, and their research using the experience sampling method (ESM) typifies this view. After discussing research conducted over several years and with diverse samples, they highlight a longitudinal study of the flow experiences of adolescents. The chapter concludes by asking what experiences an environment (particularly families) should provide for children so that they develop complex and conscious motivational systems that will lead to full involvement in activities, and thereby to more productive lives.

The chapter by Susan Harter picks up the theme of the self system, begun in Ryan's chapter, and contrasts the I-self and the me-self by reviewing the models of William James and Charles Cooley. She then reviews her own research with diverse samples from early childhood through adulthood, discussing points of convergence with those models. Her work indicates that self-esteem is related to social support and to competence in important domains; these constructs, in turn, are good predictors of mood state. In addition, an unexpectedly high relation between self-evaluation of physical appearance and self-esteem causes her to consider the liabilities of the "looking-glass self" and to suggest a more Eastern philosophy, focusing on the I-self.

Although the previous chapters all mention the importance of social contexts, Jacquelynne S. Eccles *stresses* the link between the social contexts of family and school and the motivational constructs related to achievement and activity choice. She presents the complex general expectancy-value framework that she is known for and fills out more of the details with recent empirical work. The chapter is divided into two parts. The first part describes how parental practices early on and through adolescence lead to gender-differentiated choices that may alter males' and females' motivations, interests, self-perceptions, and activities. The second half describes how the lack of fit between adolescent development and schools, as well as parent and teacher expectations, may lead all students to experience lowered motivation (particularly in achievement) during adolescence. This chapter provides many research examples that corroborate the points made in the earlier chapters about supportive and nonsupportive social contexts.

The chapter by Laura L. Carstensen maintains Eccles's focus on the importance of activity choice but is concerned with a later point in the life span, when social contact declines. Although Carstensen does not talk about motivation in the traditional sense, and does not even use the word very much, she is clearly talking about social-emotional motivation for activity selection. She suggests that people become increasingly discriminating in their social partners as they age, as a result of changing social motivations. This chapter complements the others by concentrating on another part of the life span (although some of her work extends down to adolescence) and by contrasting with the more cognitive models offered earlier. Carstensen contends that emotions are the organizing, and thus motivating, force for choices about how and with whom to spend time.

To highlight the reemphasis on motivation this year, we changed the format of the Symposium as well. In previous years speakers have given their presentations at two different times during the year, although the papers have always been published as a single volume. Beginning with this year, we invited all the speakers to present at the same conference rather than having two meetings. This enabled a discussant to comment on all the papers while speakers were present to interact. That commentary, provided by

Ryan, is presented as the last chapter in this volume. The other change in format that is noteworthy was the addition of a poster session during the Symposium. Researchers from around the country were invited to share poster presentations of their latest work, and the abstracts for the posters are included at the end of this volume.

Acknowledgments

I want to thank the people whose efforts were instrumental in conducting the Symposium. My colleagues at the University of Nebraska, Calvin Garbin and Heidi Inderbitzen-Pisaruk, helped with the extra work associated with the addition of the poster session this year. Richard Dienstbier, series editor, proved an invaluable resource as I came to him with endless questions throughout the year. Claudia Price-Decker took care of all the organizational details from beginning to end, so that the entire event went smoothly. Graduate students Robin Beyer, Laura Finken, Mary Fran Flood, Alice Ganzel, Andrea Geiler, Patricia Hashima, Rodger Narloch, and Nina Pitman took on a variety of tasks that made the Symposium a reality. Finally, I want to thank the contributors, who delivered well-organized and interesting talks, cheerfully maintained the rigorous pace I set during the conference, and promptly turned in well-crafted manuscripts for publication here.

Agency and Organization: Intrinsic Motivation, Autonomy, and the Self in Psychological Development

Richard M. Ryan
University of Rochester

The term *development*, which is the theme of this 1992 Symposium, connotes a kind of change that is unique to living things. It pertains to an internal principle through which an entity expands and elaborates itself while at the same time preserving its integrity and cohesion (Jacob, 1973; Varela, 1979). This internal principle is described by the concept of *organization*. Once alive, organisms are ever attempting to "overtake themselves," as Jean Piaget (1971) described it. This organizational feature or attribute of development is an aspect of the more general tendency of life to move toward greater variability, flexibility, and higher-order processes (Nicolis & Prigogine, 1977). So widely accepted is the idea that living things tend toward greater organization that organismic and systems perspectives have become paradigmatic in biology (Lazlo, 1987; Mayr, 1982; Rosenberg, 1985; von Bertalanffy, 1968).

The idea of a biologically based organizational propensity has been widely adopted in structural approaches to cognitive development. Heinz Werner (1948) argued in his orthogenetic model that development proceeds in the direction of differentiation and hierarchic integration. Piaget (1971) similarly depicted cognitive development in terms of progressive elaboration of individual structures and their increasing organization through "reciprocal assimilation."

Ego psychologists such as Loevinger (1976) view the ego as a synthetic process that, following Freud (1923/1962), "aims at complicating life, and at the same time . . . preserving it" (p. 30). This synthetic function results in a series of stagelike equilibrations that describe growth in individual personality organization.

More recently the new paradigms in developmental psychopathology conceptualize many pathological phenomena in terms of disruptions of normal organization or ontogenetic processes. In these approaches both organic and environmental (interpersonal) factors can interrupt the natural integrative tendency of development and result in less organized, adaptive configurations of functioning (see Cicchetti, 1990).

Finally, a number of organismic theories in the fields of clinical and personality psychology also assume developmental trajectories toward greater organization. Kurt Goldstein (1939) postulated a general need among organisms to realize potential and achieve wholeness in functioning. Jung (1951/1959) portrayed the development of the psyche in terms of differentiation and individuation, guided by the integrative function of the self. Carl Rogers (1963) argued that the basic principle of life is actualization, which for him involves the differentiation of organs and functions, and their integration, resulting in an overall thrust away from heteronomy and toward autonomy. Andras Angyal (1965) described life as a process of "self-expansion" in the directions of both increased self-regulation and homonomy. The developmental assumptions of these theories are also reflected in their conceptualizations of personality growth and therapy. For the theorists mentioned, therapy entails mobilizing healing forces that are believed to reside within the individual. These "forces" refer back, of course, to the tendency toward organization, actualization, and wholeness.

In most of these perspectives the concept of organization serves not only as a trajectory or goal of development, but also as a basic explanatory principle of the process of development—a kind of prime mover. In terms of a trajectory, organization models suggest that psychological development proceeds toward increased autonomy or self-regulation (as opposed to heteronomy) and toward increased unity or integration in functioning. In terms of a process conception, organizational perspectives typically assume that the movement toward integration and order occurs "naturally," which is to say that it appears to be an "automatic" feature of organisms. For example, in his model of cognitive development, Piaget (1952) argued that it is simply the inherent tendency of structures to elaborate themselves through further functioning (Flavell, 1963). We do not ask what motivates a seed to grow, so why should we ask this of developmental processes in the realm of psychology? As Piaget (1971) puts it, organization is such a basic attribute of life that it cannot be further defined or reduced. Similarly, structural approaches to personality development such as Jane Loevinger's (1976) focus mainly on the residue of the organizational processes rather than on their energetic bases. The ego's synthetic activity is assumed to create a pattern of personality stages that is relatively invariant across individuals and cultures (Loevinger & Blasi, 1991). However, the motivational bases of the real-life activities that produce such equilibrations receive little attention compared with the detailed assessments of the formal properties of the progressive stages her theory posits. Finally, humanistic approaches conceive of actualization as "the very nature of the process called life" (Rogers, 1963, p. 3) and thus view it as a fundamental and irreducible motivational force.

Significant risks are involved in positing irreducible or inherent directional processes in development. Chief among such risks, in my view, is that explanations of development in terms of an innate or invariant trajectory can obscure the dialectical relationship between the developing person and the social context in which such development is embedded. Social environments clearly can either facilitate or forestall organization and activity and accordingly exert a major impact on developmental rate and on the degree of integration the individual achieves. Organismic views are too often insulated from a *social* psychology of development, that is, from an examination of social forces as they act upon, and sometimes redirect, the organizational tendencies that nature provides.

An associated risk of organizational viewpoints is their tendency to imply a passive subject who is "lived" by his or her organizational tendencies. The assumption of an automatic tendency toward differentiation and integration reifies development, making *it* the "actor" within an individual over time. But phenomenological accounts suggest that development is an active process of engaging one's internal and external environments. Most integration occurs through activity, and accordingly, the work (and play) of development is done in each case by an agent or subject who either tackles challenges or balks and stutters. Thus, from the subjective viewpoint negotiating the trials and tasks of development is hardly automatic or unproblematic. Differentiation and synthesis involve activity, effort, and sometimes courage.

Put more specifically, explaining psychological development merely in terms of a propensity toward organization can obscure the *agency* that at each moment along the way enacts learning, change, and new syntheses. An abstract developmental principle removes the subject from the activity of integration. Even if development, on average, may be described by a relatively invariant sequence of stages (Loevinger, 1976) or by processes "inherent in structures" (Piaget, 1952), it is still done by some*one* through moment-to-moment intentions, willing, and motives. An understanding of the process of development is enriched by focusing on the being-in-context that *does* the developing. This requires, however, shifting one's view to consider what Michael Polanyi (1958, p. 336) so aptly described as that "active center operating unspecifiably in all animals" from which activity proceeds.

Other authors have made these critical points concerning organismic theories in somewhat different ways. On the issue of obscuring the social context of development, Broughton and Zahaykevich (1988) maintain that focusing on the "natural" process of synthesis within the individual minimizes one's attention to conflictual and oppressive aspects of culture, resulting in a psychology of conformity. Dannefer (1984) suggests that organismic approaches are "reductionistic" in that they explain behavior at the individual and biological levels and thus ignore the influence of socioeconomic forces on development and organization. Wapner, Ciottone, Hornstein, McNeil, and Pacheco (1983) argue that the morphogenetic emphasis of developmental theory needs to be complemented by an ideographic analysis of concrete sociohistorical agents who are obliged to deal with various cultural stresses and strains. These critical perspectives suggest that a focus on the inner forces of development is often associated with an underemphasis on the dynamic effects of "outer" structures on development and ignores the types of content that a culture may offer for assimilation or integration by the individual.

With regard to the obscuring of agency, Blasi (1976) argues that the "intrinsic" properties of personality and their role in functioning, particularly the issues of freedom and consciousness, are lost in purely structural perspectives. Kaplan (1983) states that development always implicates *agents* who are using or constructing "means" to attain "ends." He maintains that there is no development without an agency that realizes it. Quite recently Vandenberg (1991) has argued that structural and constructivist models of development typically fail to address the existential concerns and realities of the developing subject. These and other thinkers view development as dependent on activity, and thus as involving agency and enactment.[1]

In the motivational work that my colleagues and I at Rochester[2] have undertaken, we have tried to place the concept of agency back into the study of action and organization, as well as to provide a dialectical viewpoint on the social psychology of development. To do so we begin with an acknowledgment that there is an active center of initiation and spontaneous engagement with the surround, namely the *self*. The self, at least as I use the term here, is both the agent that integrates and the structure to which new functions, values, and propensities are integrated (Ryan, 1991). The core sense of self is thus the phenomenal correspondent to the organization function that is described in biological and structural theories.

When activity proceeds from the self, we describe it as *self-regulated* or *autonomous*, which means that activity is (relatively) consistent with and proceeds coherently from the core organization. In this view the self in self-regulation is an emergent of organizational processes, and the sense of autonomy we possess pertains to whether our activity flows from this emergent center of activity as opposed to some other locus.

Whether activity is experienced as stemming from the self is of great psychological significance to the individual. Self-regulated activity is experienced as coherent and vital. This vitality is exuded because individuals, in self-regulated activity, operate from the energetic center of animate existence and thus tap the springs of their own living nature. Coherence follows insofar as self-regulated or autonomous action is integrated—it reflects the coming together of the self in action. Such feelings are the phenomenological accompaniments of actions that reflect the core self.

This concept of autonomy also bears significantly on theories of relatedness and attachments between people. I will argue that a central dimension that defines the quality of relatedness between individuals is the degree to which each experiences the other as accepting and supporting the core self. In early relationships the quality of attachment is thus hypothesized to relate to how sensitive and responsive caregivers are to spontaneous signals and initiatives that emanate from the infant's core self. The quality of adult relationships can similarly be understood in terms of a mutuality of autonomy, involving contact with and openness to each other's selves. In either case, relatedness fundamentally requires the reception and support of the self, and such relationships facilitate development and organization. The self is what relates and is related to in authentic interpersonal transactions.

Clinicians like myself are apt to consider the construct of a core self or organization central to their understanding of personality change and pathology. Most of the concerns that occupy clients involve the regulation of behavior and affect by external or intrapsychic forces that are not well integrated or under their control. They have lost a sense of self in relationships or in behavior. Such concerns reverberate throughout clinical literature, in which constructs concerning the true versus the false self (Horney, 1950; Winnicott, 1965) or integrated versus introjected regulation (Meissner, 1981; Schafer, 1968) abound. Much of the work of therapy involves the recovery (or acquisition) of autonomy and integration with respect to significant life issues.

In clinical work the "nonautomatic" nature of organization and integration in development is particularly apparent. If the unity of behavior and attitudes were easy or "natural," then autonomy and integration would be the common outcome for individuals, whereas splitting, defensiveness, and conflict would be a rarity. Instead, we find many people who have faced circumstances and experiences that are not readily "reciprocally assimilated" to one another or brought into harmony within oneself. Other people have given up their autonomy and self to preserve connections with others. Still others are obstructed from self-realization and relatedness by overpowering economic and social forces affecting them, their families, and their communities.

So pervasive is fragmentation that a number of theorists have raised serious doubts concerning the viability of any unity or integration hypotheses (e.g., Dennett, 1985; Hilgard, 1977; Meissner, 1988; Minsky, 1982). Others continue to place important emphasis on synthetic or integrative tendencies (Deci & Ryan, 1985b; Loevinger, 1976; Popper & Eccles, 1977; Westen, 1985). Greenwald (1982, p. 157) summarized the ambivalence of the field in stating that "if there is a position on the unity issue . . . it is that unity of the person is not to be taken for granted."

Unity is not to be taken for granted. But assuming an organizational tendency toward unification and integration in personality does not particularly contradict evidence that disintegration, dissociation, self-deception, and inconsistency are common in human action and personality. Such departures from integrity become understandable when the organizational function is seen in its dialectical role with respect to an environment that is not always conducive to assimilation and integration. If families and culture supply contradictory values or provide conditions that disrupt rather than nourish the natural psychological functions, then fragmentation will be a common result. The very fact that achieving psychic harmony is so difficult in contemporary society suggests that we need to examine the interpersonal and cultural conditions under which organizational tendencies are either encouraged or stunted and blocked.

Another reason why instances of dissociation, nonregulation, or other forms of disunity do not necessarily contradict organizational perspectives derives from understanding that the self, as an organization, never encompasses the psyche as a whole—it is only an aspect of it. Thus there are many psychological events that are not capable of ready assimilation within self structure, and there is situational variation in how active the self is in regulating experience. There are also realms of human experience that defy symbolization and can escape even one's sincere efforts to assimilate them. This is only to say that although the self is a synthetic function, it can never, even in ideal circumstances, achieve complete synthesis. The self must thus be understood as a central but not all-encompassing aspect of the person. As Broughton (1991) puts it, the self is not "all there is" in mental and social life, but it strives to be so. It is, however, a significant focus of developmental study because of its role in initiating and regulating action and experience and its phenomenological salience from the standpoint of the actor.

In the remainder of this essay I examine more closely the connections between organization, autonomy, and the self in development. In particular I will be concerned with the role of autonomy in the kinds of actions on which development depends. I begin by reflecting on what is meant by autonomy or self-regulation, focusing particularly on the phenomenological connections between the sense of self and the experience of autonomy. I will then turn to empirical studies that examine the functional significance of autonomy in development and personality.

Autonomy and Heteronomy in Relation to the Self

The term *autonomy* literally means "self-governing" and therefore implies regulation by the self. Its opposite, heteronomy, refers to regulation from outside the self, by alien or external forces. Comprehension of the phenomenal experience of autonomy versus heteronomy is thus relevant for understanding what it means for behavior or experience to emanate from, or to express, the self.

One of the earliest theorists who explored the phenomenology of autonomy was Alexander Pfander (1908/1967). Using methods drawn from Brentano and Husserl, Pfander distinguished between self-determined acts—those that reflect one's *will*—and other forms of striving or motivation. According to Pfander, acts of will are distinguished phenomenally because they are experienced "precisely not as an occurrence caused by a different agent but as an initial act of the ego-center itself" (p. 20). Although inner impulses or external pressures may supply "grounds" for willing, the act of will or self-determination requires an *endorsement* of the behavior that might follow from these grounds by the self or "ego-center." Insofar as one's actions are perceived to be engendered by forces outside the self (ego-center) or are not fully condoned or endorsed by the self, then willing or self-determination is not in evidence.

Paul Ricoeur (1966) ventured further into the same territory in his *Freedom and Nature*. Like Pfander, he ascertained that the terms will and autonomy refer to acts that are fully endorsed by the self. However, autonomy need not entail a literal absence of strong pressures, grounds, or even mandates to act in a specific way. One can be willful and free even under pressure to act in certain ways, provided one *concurs with* or *accepts* the mandates in a personal sense. Influences and inputs to my behavior must *engender in me* reasons for acting in concert with them, otherwise my behavior is not self-determined. Thus one is autonomous to the extent that one willfully consents or is truly receptive to motives, obligations, or inducements.

Accordingly, autonomy or will (here used interchangeably) pertains to acts that are experienced as freely done and endorsed by the self. This of course applies to behaviors that are easily chosen (playing tennis might typically be autonomous, since it is unconflicted fun and expresses a self interest) as well as to more difficult choices such as forgoing fun to work on a valued volunteer task. Here the self endorses and enacts the behavior because of its fittingness and coherence with one's inner organization of values and personal commitments. In either case, the self phenomenologically underlies actions that seem to have the character of volition or inner commitment. Autonomy is also a relevant dimension in analyzing one's response to environmental pressures and rewards. If I comply with pressure or force without the full consent of the self, then my behavior, by these definitions, is not autonomous. However, I can also "willingly" behave as I am pressured to do and thus, in such assent, experience autonomy. Finally, phenomenological analysis suggests that autonomy or self-determination can be threatened by factors both within and without. Just as an external authority may coerce one, so can an inner impulse or drive. One can locate the cause of one's behavior in a desire or impulse that "lies outside the self"— that one feels compelled to follow—and thus not feel self-determined when acting on it.

Existentially oriented theorists distinguish between authentic and inauthentic actions using definitions akin to those of phenomenologists. The term *authentic* means literally "really proceeding from its reputed source or author" (cf. Wild, 1965). Authentic actions are those that one identifies as proceeding from the self, and for which one takes responsibility. A person's actions, even intentional ones, are inauthentic if they are experienced as not truly reflecting or emanating from the self (e.g., Kierkegaard 1849/1968).

The importance of such phenomenological analyses lies in their locating the definitions of self-determination or autonomy in a subjective framework. They specify that for an act to be autonomous it must be "endorsed" by the self or experienced as one's own doing. Autonomous acts are also integral to the person, reflecting the relative unity of the self "behind" one's actions. They convey how the senses of ownership, authenticity, responsibility, and choice are all entailed in autonomy.

In a recent analytic approach to the philosophy of autonomy, Dworkin (1988) arrived at considerations similar to those derived from existential phenomenology. Dworkin (like Ricoeur) argues that autonomy does not entail "being subject to no external influences" (e.g., parents, teachers, public figures). As Dworkin points out, there is no possible world that is free of external influences. The issue is whether my following such influences reflects mere obedience or coercion rather than a reflective valuing of the direction or guidance these inputs provide. It is in one's subjective assent to some influences and not others that the question of autonomy becomes meaningful. Similarly, Dworkin argues that autonomy does not necessarily mean behaving without constraint. Clearly, one can act in accord with certain constraints and in doing so still be autonomous. I may feel constrained in stopping for a particular red light, but at the same time I may assent to the idea that traffic laws are useful in ensuring my safety and everyone else's. I therefore consent to follow them, and in doing so have lost no autonomy. Indeed, I enact my autonomy with this *higher-order*, reflective commitment. For Dworkin, in fact, autonomy entails endorsement of one's actions at the highest order of reflection.

From a psychological viewpoint this process of reflective appraisal from a higher order that Dworkin and others cite is similar to what Søren Kierkegaard (1849/1968) referred to as *relating the self to the self*. It means taking stock of or *interest in* one's feelings, evaluations, choices, and actions and, in doing so, organizing and regulating them from the standpoint of the whole. This is an essential aspect of synthetic process involved in progressive self-regulation. In order to synthesize, or bring into unity, a possible action, value, or belief, one must both acknowledge and evaluate it from the standpoint of the self (see also Blasi, 1984). Reconciling and coordinating values, beliefs, and potential actions with respect to the self entails taking an interest in them, and such reflective interest is typically incited or catalyzed only under specific conditions.

FROM PHENOMENOLOGY TO ATTRIBUTION: PERCEIVED LOCUS OF CAUSALITY

The philosophical traditions reviewed above are relatively divorced from the literature of empirical psychology. Yet, as often happens, philosophical issues enter psychology through a side door. Distinctions concerning authentic and autonomous actions were smuggled into the mainstream through just such a side entrance by Fritz Heider (1958) and Richard deCharms (1968) with their formulations of "naive" psychology. Heider, in fact, was conversant with phenomenological methods and may have derived some of his thinking from that tradition (Spiegelberg, 1972).

Heider felt that people, in the process of understanding their own and others' behavior, are centrally concerned with the "causes" of action. To describe how such causes are phenomenally encoded, he introduced the construct of *perceived locus of causality*. According to Heider, actions and outcomes could be perceived either as personally caused or as a result of nonintentional or impersonal causes. The critical feature of personal causation is *intentionality*, which implies that both ability and effort toward some end are evinced. In contrast, impersonal causation is marked by an absence of control or initiation with regard to actions or outcomes. Heider's distinction has become important in the literature of interpersonal perception, in which people's inferences about the motives and intentions of others are examined.

A decade later, deCharms (1968) extended and applied Heider's work in his book *Personal Causation*. He argued that intentional action is itself not always free or self-initiated. In fact, we often perform intentional actions precisely because we feel pressured or coerced to do so by external agents. The policeman *makes* me slow down to 55 miles per hour, or my boss *forces* me to take on an extra task at work. Both the speed change and the task done in these examples represent intentional acts—but neither is necessarily done autonomously.

To clarify the differences between freely performed and heteronomous intentional actions, deCharms proposed a further distinction that applied *within* the category of intentionality or personal causation. He argued that intentional acts can be accompanied by either an *internal* or an *external perceived locus of causality* (PLOC). The former connotes actions that are volitional, in which one experiences oneself as an "origin" of action, whereas the latter represents instances in which one is a "pawn" to pressures or inducements, even though one intends to perform the action.

DeCharms (1968) also pointed out that there is an enormous difference between interpersonal attributions regarding perceived locus of causality and personal knowledge concerning this issue. The central difference is that in interpersonal attribution one lacks direct access to the internal states of others and must make inferences based on external conditions surrounding action. By contrast, individuals know the motivational status of their own behavior directly, because they themselves enact it. Thus one does not typically need to "observe" one's own behavior to know whether an act is intentional and whether it is autonomous. I have personal knowledge of autonomy, insofar as my autonomous act is something I organize and authenticate in the context of behaving (Ryan & Connell, 1989).

The difference between these two types of intentional behavior—with an internal versus an external PLOC—is exemplified in everyday occurrences. For example, a worker may intentionally proceed to her job each morning. She may feel compelled to work by financial stress or need or by social pressures of one sort or another. In this case she may lack a sense of volition, working only because she "has to." She experiences herself as a *pawn* in deCharms's terminology. In a second case, however, imagine a person who "wants" to go to work—who feels enjoyment, challenge, and a sense of commitment to her work. She sees her work as an expression of herself. Here she is an *origin,* and she perceives her efforts as emanating from an internal locus of causality—the self. In these examples the contrast between origin and pawn is akin to the distinction between alienated labor and autonomous labor.

To show the real-life impact of such alienation, Ryan and Grolnick (1986) used a measure developed by deCharms (1976) to assess children's perceptions of their classroom climate along a dimension ranging from origin to pawn. They found that students who experienced the classroom as more pawnlike evinced less curiosity, desire for challenge, and independent mastery orientation than students who viewed their classroom climate as having more of an "origin" character. Being in an atmosphere that was conducive to an external perceived locus of causality led to a less active, less mastery-motivated mind-set and, we suggest, to less expression of the assimilative integrative tendency that is natural to learners. In a separate part of this study, students who rated their current classroom climate as more pawn-oriented also wrote projective stories about a neutral classroom scene that depicted more authority, rebellion, and control than students in "origin" climates. This suggested that children "internalize" a set of expectations concerning social contexts and motivation and apply or generalize it to new situations.

As this study illustrates, the perceived locus of causality construct offers an operational route into the issues of agency and self-determination versus heteronomy. By instantiating conditions that add salience to external forces or reasons for acting, presumably the PLOC can be shifted from internal to external, thus creating the experience of being a pawn. Conversely, conditions that conduce to choice and volition should facilitate a more internal PLOC, or a sense of autonomy.

An internal perceived locus of causality refers to initiation and organization of behavior by the self. Typically the contrast with self-regulation is external regulation, that is, when other people regulate one's actions. It is also common that *inner* forces, such as drives and impulses, can be the cause or impetus to action without the "endorsement" or support of the self, indeed, without even the sense of intentionality. Thus, for example, a person who was impulsively aggressive after drinking alcohol claims the next day, "I was not myself." By this he means that his actions did not reflect his self organization; they occurred without self-regulation. Much of the struggle for autonomy, in fact, concerns gaining regulatory control or management over inner wishes and drives as well as over outer regulations and commands. Thus there are forces that are external to the self at both its "internal" and its "external" boundaries (Greenspan, 1979).

We have used this construct of perceived locus of causality to organize a variety of empirical projects that examine the functional effects of autonomy versus heteronomy on behavior, learning, and personality development. We do not see the issue of autonomy as merely an attributional issue, however. Rather, we view the sense of autonomy as reflecting a *quality of behavior* that is meaningful throughout development and applies to activity in all domains. Autonomy is not primarily a cognitive process, nor is it well defined as a concept or representation. It is a hypothetical variable we use to understand the dynamics of behavioral regulation, and we attribute to it a *functional significance* (Deci & Ryan, 1985b), whether or not it explicitly enters awareness.

WHAT AUTONOMY IS NOT: A DISCURSION

Having discussed both structurally and phenomenologically what autonomy is, it seems worth a brief digression to examine some concepts that are often confused with autonomy, or particular uses of the concept of autonomy that are inconsistent with the current formulation. I will argue that autonomy is not a stage; is not reducible to self-efficacy; and is not equivalent to "independence" or detachment. I take up these issues in turn.

Autonomy is not a stage. Autonomy, when viewed as a sense of volition and choice resulting from the integration of regulatory processes, is an ongoing issue throughout the life span. Behavior at all levels of development reflects either more or less autonomy—it is more or less self-regulated. The form and content of autonomous action will vary, however, at different developmental stages. Several authors stress the salience of autonomy at specific points in development, suggesting that these life periods are particularly critical.

Perhaps the best-known theory in which autonomy is regarded as a specific stage is that of Erik Erikson (1950). Erikson modified and expanded Freud's (1913/1959) theory of psychosexual development by reformulating the theory in interpersonal rather than libidinal terms and by differentiating new stages of adult development. In his formulation, Erikson delineates the second and third years of a child's life as representing the crucial stage for the development of autonomy. He suggests that if allowed a gradual experience of increasing autonomy and choice a child develops a sense of pride and confidence, whereas a child who continually faces rigid dominance or evaluation will instead develop a sense of shame and doubt.

Piaget (1967) discussed the concept of will, suggesting that it is a regulatory process that comes into existence during middle childhood in relation to moral issues. For a child of that age, morality is gradually shifting from being based wholly on authority to being determined more by mutuality and consent. The shift away from exclusive reliance on authority necessitates the development of internal regulatory processes that will, in the words of Piaget, allow a morally superior principle to win a conflict with a morally inferior drive.

Adolescence has also been widely characterized as an important phase in the development of autonomy (e.g., A. Freud, 1958; Steinberg & Silverberg, 1986). The teenager is gradually individuating from parental direction and guidance, facing the challenge of developing the types of internal regulatory processes that constitute mature self-direction and judgment (Ryan & Lynch, 1989).

Finally, Loevinger (1976) reserves the term *autonomous* to describe her fifth stage of ego development. This stage is characterized by a capacity to acknowledge and cope with ambiguity and conflict and to project less of one's inner conflict onto external figures. The autonomous person recognizes other people's needs for autonomy and is able to see individual motives as products of differences in experience. An autonomous level of ego development is rarely achieved before adulthood, and the modal individual in American culture may not reach it at all.

In each of these cases the significance of autonomy at various phases of development is underscored. However, that issues of autonomy figure heavily in each of these conceptualizations suggests that its dynamics affect development at every level. Thus in infancy autonomy concerns the consolidation of a sense of self and the emergence of a sense of initiative and trust. For toddlers the prominent issue may be assimilating social practices while preserving initiative, and in middle childhood and early adolescence the struggle for autonomy may be more concerned with sorting out what is one's own from prescribed moral concerns. In adolescence autonomy may take the form of negotiating increasing self-direction while maintaining one's connections with caregivers. At every level of development the social tasks and the competencies brought to them differ, but at all levels the degree to which regulation is assumed by the self or located in external sources is at issue. Thus each of these stage-oriented conceptions describes issues related to perceived locus of causality, though that issue is applied to different contents and plays out in different contexts.

In our conception, the issue of autonomy is psychologically relevant from the very beginning of life. A sense of a core self appears, by sound empirical accounts, to be central to activity and organization in the human infant quite soon after birth. It is, as Stern (1985) argues, a "first order of business" for the infant to develop this core sense of self. He suggests that the kinds of experiences required to consolidate a core self are amply provided in early development, such that the sense of self is generally integrated in the first half year of life in humans. He also maintains that though this core self is *not* a mental concept or a representation of oneself in awareness, however, it is accompanied by a sense of both coherence and volition (initiation). Thus very young infants show evidence of "knowing" which actions emerge from the self and which ones do not.

Crockenberg and Litman (1990) argued that autonomy is important in late infancy and to toddlers as well. They distinguish compliance from autonomy, arguing that autonomy reflects a "willing engagement" on the part of the child, whereas compliance occurs through fear or force. Clearly, here the consideration that underlies their distinction is the internal perceived locus of causality of the child.

This core sense of self continues to be involved in the progressive ordering of experience and is by no means a static or fixed organization. With development, the sense of self—and also one's purposes and values that organize behavior—becomes more elaborate and changes in content. In addition, the conditions required to nourish and enhance the core self and its autonomous functioning vary with development. It is these changing dynamics of autonomy throughout the life span that suggest autonomy should be construed as a quality of behavior rather than as a specific stage of development in which the issue is settled once and for all.

Autonomy is not self-efficacy. Bandura (1989) has articulated a "social-cognitive" theory of *agency* that is built on his earlier construct of self-efficacy. In Bandura's model, motivation is ultimately explained by the idea that "people strive to gain anticipated beneficial outcomes and to forestall aversive ones" (p. 1180). This striving is influenced by self-efficacy, which entails feeling able to perform the activities connected with such outcomes. One exercises agency, in Bandura's view, by envisioning the likely outcomes of prospective actions.

The equating of agency with the rather restricted notion of self-efficacy is particularly problematic. The belief that one can successfully perform an action and thus obtain an outcome does not address the question of why one might perform the action in the first place. And it is this "why" question that is the very crux of the issues of autonomy and agency, and of motivation more generally (Ryan & Connell, 1989). An obedient but competent slave could be self-efficacious ("I can competently do what he tells me and thus obtain a reward or avoid punishment") and thus would be "agentic" in this social-cognitive model. There is simply no view here of an integrated organization of purposes, and no theoretical position on what is meant by the idea of self, so that agency becomes merely a statement about outcome-oriented beliefs and capabilities.

Competence and efficacy do figure importantly in the issue of agency, but more complexly than considered in social-cognitive theory. All intentional actions have as their prerequisite some form of efficacy beliefs. As Heider (1958) stated long ago, one must believe one "can" do something to be motivated to do it. But true agency requires more than mere ability or efficacy. The true agent feels volitional in action, viewing action as having an internal locus of causality. Thus the most efficacious pawn—whether a success-driven stockbroker or a highly introjected achiever—is not an agent unless his or her actions are experienced as authentic and autonomous. Bandura, however, writes off the concept of autonomy as meaningless by defining it as action that is "entirely independent" (1989, p. 1175) of the environment. The issue of relative assent, consent, or volition with respect to an "environment" is thus disregarded without serious analysis.

Not only does the definition of agency as self-efficacy ignore the issue of autonomy, it also bespeaks a conformist ideology, fitting perfectly with postindustrial economic organizations (Ryan, 1991). In social-cognitive theories (e.g., Bandura, 1989; Locke & Latham, 1990) behavior is ultimately regulated by rewards and approvals, and the "agentic" person is the one who can set the right goals and grab them up most efficiently. No matter that the efficacious character might be type A, greedy, conflicted, or alienated from inner needs. In this weltanschauung, effectiveness at obtaining rewards and approval becomes elevated to a developmental ideal.

In a more extreme, but more internally consistent argument,

B. F. Skinner (1971) denied any credibility to ideas of autonomy and agency. He argued that we speak of autonomy primarily when we are ignorant of the actual factors that control behavior. Thus, "If we do not know why a person acts as he does, we attribute his behavior to him" (p. 53). In his theory, control over action is tautologically defined as external to the organism, and whatever unity or organization appears in action must in principle be due to the unity and organization of the contingencies in the environment.

Like Bandura, Skinner pits the idea of "the external" against the concept of autonomy, and thus he can dismiss this most difficult yet crucial construct for a human psychology. In contrast to their views, I suggest that the issue of autonomy does not primarily concern whether external contingencies and circumstances influence behavior, but rather involves whether the behavior that occurs in the context of an environment is experienced as emanating from or congruent with the self. Behaviorisms and neobehaviorisms, built as they are on efficient causal foundations rather than organismic principles, simply cannot adequately address whether the locus of regulation resides within one's developing self-organization or outside it. They thus ignore the phenomenological and functional effects that follow from this difference.

Autonomy is not independence. In common usage, and in some theories, independence is equated with autonomy. Obviously, dictionary definitions of these two terms overlap. However, I suggest that there are at least some meanings of autonomy and independence that can be distinguished, and that such differentiation is crucial for developmental theory.

Independence refers primarily to not relying on others for the fulfillment of needs. One is therefore independent to the extent that one is self-reliant. Conversely, dependence in human relationships involves having one's needs provided for by another. Infants are highly dependent on their parents for the gratification of their needs. In growing older, a child becomes less dependent on others for those same needs—he or she acquires new skills and functions that can sustain and protect the organism and the self—but significant elements of dependence will remain. Dependence throughout the life span is both natural and appropriate; it is the specific provi-

sions for which one relies on others that change considerably with development.

Insofar as we have defined autonomy as a sense of volition, it is clear that a person can be dependent in a relationship yet not necessarily lack autonomy (Memmi, 1984). One can be happily and unconflictually provided for, experiencing a sense of choice about it. Alternatively, of course, a person can feel controlled or coerced in the context of dependence. Providers, for example, may use their position to control behavior in the dependent, and thus their provisions can come to be viewed as instruments of subjugation or control. Here dependence may take on an external perceived locus of causality: "I take from them, but I don't like it."

Independence, defined as lack of reliance on others, can also be characterized by either autonomy or control. One can be quite volitional in one's independence from another, fully choosing to do for oneself. But being independent does not ensure autonomy, as when one feels forced by others to assume some independent functions. A teenager, for instance, may want to earn his own spending money, and the independence is initiated from within. But he may also get a job because he feels humiliated by asking his parents for help. Here he works because he has to, and the perceived locus of causality for the "independent" behavior will be external.

Although independence and autonomy are analytically and operationally separable, they are often dynamically related. Most human needs are met in the context of interdependencies, and these interdependencies do not in themselves threaten autonomy. On the contrary, most of us desire interdependencies; we would not choose to be wholly self-reliant. Dependency and control are easily fused, however, so that people often find the road to freedom may require relinquishing reliance on certain others.

There is another way the development of independence and the issue of autonomy are intertwined. As I have already argued, the organizational propensity entails individuals' continually exercising and elaborating their functioning, and this results in the acquisition of new capabilities and areas of independence (White, 1963). The one-year-old *wants* to walk to the car (rather than be carried), the two-year-old *wants* to dress herself (rather than be dressed). These expressions of desire to do for oneself emanate from the core self

and can be either supported or ignored by caregivers. Caregivers are thus in a position to support developing autonomy—that is, volition and intentionality—when they support self-initiated independence. However, there is always a judgment to be made about the dependent's readiness to be self-reliant with respect to a given activity. Premature pressure toward self-reliance or thwarting of initiative toward self-reliance both represent dynamic situations where issues of autonomy and independence become separable and sometimes stand in opposition.

Autonomy is not detachment. Several theories view the development of autonomy in terms of relinquishing attachments to others. This is particularly true of some approaches to adolescent development, where autonomy is construed in terms of breaking ties with the family (e.g., A. Freud, 1958; Blos, 1962; Steinberg and Silverberg, 1986). Presumably such detachment sets the stage for establishing extrafamilial attachments and for greater self-direction.

I have argued both theoretically (Ryan, 1991) and empirically (Ryan & Lynch, 1989) that autonomy and detachment are not equivalent. One can be attached to another quite volitionally, just as previously I pointed out that one can be autonomously dependent or interdependent. Furthermore, there is no evidence that adolescents who detach from parents are more autonomous as a result. On the contrary, detachment from parents in adolescence typically results in less optimal circumstances for developing self-direction and autonomy. Detached adolescents are more susceptible to conformity and less able to form mature relationships with others (see Ryan & Lynch, 1989).

Good-quality attachments to others not only do not prevent autonomy, they facilitate it. In a secure attachment the other person is attuned to and receptive of one's self. This resonation and attunement help the individual to be more aware of his or her own needs and desires as well as their effects on others. Such attachments enhance rather than detract from self-determination. Conversely, relationships in which there is not support for or receptivity to self-expression and autonomy are likely to be insecure. Excessive control or neglect of the inner self by significant others leads to the need either to detach (as in the rebellious or isolated adolescent) or to insecurely cling to and comply with attachment figures (as in the inse-

cure, enmeshed adolescent). In these latter cases, conflicts between relatedness needs and the overall thrust toward autonomy in functioning come into unnecessary conflict. Thus, although attachment and autonomy can conflict, in optimal circumstances they support one another.

The Effect of Variations in Autonomy on Behaviors related to Organization

Having defined autonomy both positively (in phenomenological terms) and negatively (in terms of what it is not), I now turn to the *functional* impact of autonomy in development. I will rely heavily on empirical investigations of autonomy with regard to types of behavior that are crucial to organization and development. In particular I will examine two processes intricately associated with organizational propensities, namely intrinsic motivation and internalization. Intrinsic motivation concerns the active, exploratory, challenge-seeking nature of individuals, which plays a crucial role in the acquisition and elaboration of structures and functions. Internalization refers to the assimilation of external regulations and values and their integration into the self.

THE SELF AND AUTONOMY IN INTRINSIC MOTIVATION

Intrinsic motivation is defined as doing something "for its own sake," for example, out of curiosity, from a sense of challenge, or for the inherent satisfactions that accompany the activity. Intrinsic motivation emerged as a specific construct in post-Hullian experimental work in the 1950s, when it was noticed that animals would spontaneously explore, manipulate, and examine novel aspects of their surround without any reinforcement, and sometimes in spite of aversive consequences.

Robert White (1959, 1963) used the term *effectance motivation* to describe this phenomenon, noting that there seemed to be a spontaneous need for organisms to "have an effect" on their environment and to experience an inherent pleasure or interest in the exercise of their skills and capacities. He also attempted to conceptualize a bridge between animal and human psychologies by articulating the common character of their spontaneous effectance-related action. White's work brought into focus the significant developmental role of intrinsic motivation, in that the progressive elaboration of functions is energized by this endogenous need (see also Flavell, 1977).

DeCharms (1968), building on White's ideas, suggested further that intrinsic or effectance motivation is evinced only when one experiences an internal locus of causality. He argued that the desire to be a causal agent or an "origin" is a primary motivational propensity and that being intrinsically motivated requires that one's behavior originate from the self. Exploration, curiosity, creativity, and spontaneous interest are all characterized by deCharms as self-determined, and he hypothesized that factors that detract from a sense of self-determination will diminish the occurrence of these types of behavior.

Deci (1975) and Deci and Ryan (1980, 1985b, 1987, 1991) drew on the theories of White and deCharms in formulating a functional theory of intrinsic motivation. In their cognitive evaluation theory they proposed that inputs or conditions that foster *perceived competence* and *perceived autonomy* enhance intrinsic motivation. Furthermore, they argue that competence feedback will not promote intrinsic motivation unless it occurs in a context that affords autonomy, thus differentiating their approach from theories that emphasize only competence and optimal challenge in the analysis of intrinsic motivation. To be intrinsically motivated, one must feel that one's competent actions come from the self.[3]

Deci (1971) accomplished the first test of the hypothesis that conditions conducive to a perceived external locus of causality would "undermine" intrinsic motivation. He gave college students a monetary reward for doing an interesting puzzle-solving activity, hypothesizing that this would lead them to experience an external locus of causality. Relative to unrewarded subjects, rewarded participants evinced significantly less interest and persistence at the task during a subsequent free-choice period where they were unrestricted in their choice of activity.

As the subsequent literature has developed, it has been shown that the effects of rewards on intrinsic motivation vary considerably. Such variations are largely a function of the degree to which rewards are perceived as supporting or threatening self-determination. Rewards that are salient as controls over behavior have a deleterious effect on intrinsic motivation, whereas those used in noncontrolling ways (e.g., to acknowledge competence) do not necessarily undermine intrinsic motivation (see Ryan, Mims, & Koestner, 1983). Thus rewards are undermining primarily when they detract from the individual's sense of autonomy and initiative.

Theoretically, such activities as creative work, interested exploration, or curious problem solving are natural expressions of the organizational tendency of the self. They are thus experienced as autonomous by our current definition. When rewards are used by others as tools for promoting certain behaviors, however, the perceived locus of behavioral regulation shifts away from the self and to the rewarder. Rewards thus pull one away from the organization of activity by the self, and behavior is seen as "determined" by exogenous forces.

This describes on a psychological level what many social critics refer to as *alienation*. To be alienated means to have one's activity subjugated. One no longer acts from one's own center but is regulated by a source alien to the self. To the extent that rewards are used in a way that specifies such external control, they will produce a sense of alienation and drive out any intrinsic motivation that might otherwise have been present.

Danner and Lonky (1981) provided a classic demonstration of the link between intrinsic motivation, rewards, and perceived locus of causality in cognitive development. They preclassified children on a variety of Piagetian tasks, then showed that when children were left free to work on such tasks without external direction (using a free-choice paradigm) they spontaneously chose tasks that were just beyond their current levels of ability. However, Danner and Lonky also showed in the same experimental setting that children who were rewarded for task engagement were more likely to select nonchallenging tasks—that is, they chose tasks within their already established range of skills. They interpreted their findings within the framework of cognitive evaluation theory (Deci & Ryan, 1980), arguing that behaviors that stretch and elaborate existing schemata are more likely to occur when conditions facilitate an internal perceived locus of causality.

Rewards obviously instantiate only one type of strategy people use to control others' behavior and thus are only one way to undermine intrinsic motivation. A variety of experimental studies using varied tasks and age groups have identified other factors that promote a perceived external locus of causality and reduce intrinsic motivation, including threats of punishment (Deci & Cascio, 1972); awards and prizes (Harackiewicz, 1979; Lepper, Greene, & Nisbett, 1973); controlling praise (Ryan, Mims, & Koestner, 1983); externally set deadlines (Amabile, DeJong, & Lepper, 1976); surveillance (Plant & Ryan, 1985); evaluations (Amabile, 1979; Benware & Deci, 1984), and numerous other factors. Such studies have been widely replicated and reviewed (see Deci & Ryan, 1987; Koestner, & McClelland, 1990). In all these studies, subjects' spontaneous interests and actions were made less likely to occur by contexts that conveyed pressure to behave in specified ways. Conversely, conditions affording choice (Zuckerman, Porac, Lathin, Smith, & Deci, 1978) and support for autonomy (Grolnick, Frodi, & Bridges, 1984; Koestner, Ryan, Bernieri, & Holt, 1984) sustain and enhance intrinsic motivation.

The significance of these studies lies in what they can tell us about how to motivate or promote development. Many well-intentioned people believe in and extensively use external controls to foster learning or developmental change, without realizing that such factors often have unintended deleterious consequences. In fact, some research suggests that adults typically endorse a heavy use of controls and rewards to motivate children's intrinsic interest (Boggiano, Barrett, Weiher, McClelland, & Lusk, 1987). Attempts to instill learning and change using such strategies often paradoxically interfere with the intrinsic growth forces that more typically inspire development and interest.

Deci, Schwartz, Scheinman, and Ryan (1981) tested the hypothesis that adults' beliefs and assumptions about how to motivate children could affect developing mastery motivation. Before an academic year began they assessed teachers' values and orientations concerning how to motivate children along a dimension ranging from autonomy-supportive to controlling. Eight weeks into the school year, students in the classrooms of more controlling teachers were found to be lower on measures of mastery motivation and perceived competence than those in classrooms of more autonomy-supportive teachers. These children were less eager to learn, less interested in challenge, and less self-directed in their mastery attempts than children exposed to autonomy-supportive teachers. They also reported lower self-esteem than children in an autonomy-supportive context. This study suggests that the ideology adults hold about how children grow and learn does in fact affect how they grow and learn. Adults who treat children as origins facilitate intrinsic motivation, whereas those who focus on external control produce alienated and less challenge-seeking "pawns."

This literature on intrinsic motivation has important implications for developmental theory. First, it demonstrates that using external pressures to "push" development along typically backfires by undermining the spontaneous organismic tendency that more naturally underlies growth. Second, it bespeaks the inner initiative that underlies organismic development and the fact that it is nurtured under conditions supportive of autonomy. Elkind (1971) took a similar position in an earlier Nebraska Symposium. He argued that cognitive growth cycles are motivated by what he labeled *intrinsic growth forces*. Whereas cognitive growth largely depends on intrinsic motivation, however, performance using existing competencies usually occurs because of extrinsic factors. Cognitive growth, that is, typically is not promoted by external prods, though such prods certainly can lead to actions of an extrinsic sort.

The literature on the "undermining" of intrinsic motivation can be most meaningfully interpreted through a dialectical model of developmental processes. We assume there is an innate and vital movement in the direction of assimilation and synthesis that is typified in spontaneous, intrinsically motivated activities. However, this activity meets with various inputs and obstacles that are largely a function of social relationships in which the individual is embedded. These obstacles and inputs can either forestall or encourage further activity and organization, such that the residue of development (i.e., the structures, competencies, and functions that evolve) represent the synthesis of culture and nature in interaction. The human agent is of course the fulcrum of this interaction.

At this point there is a plethora of studies demonstrating the negative impact of external controls on mastery or intrinsically motivated activity. The few studies reviewed here are merely illustrative (see Ryan & Stiller, 1991, for a more extensive review). The point to be gleaned from them is that the kinds of behaviors associated with cognitive growth are facilitated by conditions that support autonomy, are inhibited by factors that lead to a perception of being controlled or pressured, and tend to be experienced by the actor as emanating from the self—that is, they have an internal perceived locus of causality.

EGO INVOLVEMENT, AUTONOMY, AND INTRINSIC MOTIVATION

About a decade ago, I became interested in why so much of the heteronomous regulation that occurred in my clients and in my students (and, needless to say, in myself) was not so much a function of external events as of internal ones. People's internalized ideals, standards, "shoulds," and "have tos" often seem to enslave them and pressure them at least as powerfully as any external agent could. These same internalized controls often appeared to be inimical to further development, killing intrinsic interest, rigidifying values, and foreclosing alternative directions for growth and change. A student could lose all the fun of learning under the self-held gun of achievement standards; a client could shy away from desired relationships under the self-scrutiny of concern with appearance; an athlete could come to find sports participation onerous under the yoke of performance pressure.

Most such cases of "internally controlling" dynamics have at least one feature in common: Individuals see their own worth or "esteemability" as contingent on attaining certain outcomes. This common feature I labeled "ego involvement" after discovering that it had been well described as early as 1947 by the social psychologists Sherif and Cantril. I reasoned that if ego involvement represented an internal form of heteronomy, and if intrinsic motivation would be expressed only when one was acting autonomously, then ego involvement would be just as obstructive to intrinsic motivation as any external control.

In the first experiment testing this (Ryan, 1982), I led students to believe that their performance on a simple hidden-figures test might reflect their intelligence. Other students were simply given a description of the task without the tie to intelligence. Results showed that even though all subjects received positive feedback on their performance, those who received the ego involvement induction lost a significant degree of their intrinsic motivation for the task. A number of subsequent experiments with varied tasks and age groups have obtained results consistent with this formulation (Butler, 1987; Koestner, Zuckerman, & Koestner, 1987; Plant & Ryan, 1985; Ryan, Koestner, & Deci, 1991; and others). It seems that the spontaneous activity of the self can be quashed when one regulates action "in order to" attain some outcome that one's self-esteem hinges on.

An important aspect of this research is the clarification of the idea of "internal" in the locus of causality construct. Ego-involvements represent internal but heteronomous pressures that disrupt autonomy. Thus, although ego involvements, being intrapsychic forces, are internal to the person, they are "external" to the self. They therefore have an external perceived locus of causality (deCharms, 1968) and can be as coercive (or compelling) as any external regulator.

In educational settings ego involvement is a pervasive phenomenon implicitly and explicitly fostered by teachers, parents, and the evaluative "motivational" structures that are widely employed. This ego involving atmosphere, in turn, has a lot to do with why the "natural" tendency to assimilate and learn goes awry in schools (Nicholls, 1984; Ryan, Connell, & Deci, 1985). It seems that perceiving one's self-worth as contingent on attaining specified performance outcomes can affect not only one's interest in learning but also its quality.

Recent experiments, in fact, suggest that depth of processing and conceptual integration of new inputs is obstructed by ego involvement. For example, an experimental study of children's learning (Grolnick & Ryan, 1987) examined how variations in control versus autonomy support affected not only children's interest but also the quality of their learning. Results showed that learning that occurred under ego-involving pressures (grades) was less integrative or conceptual (and more "rote" oriented) than learning that occurred under noncontrolling conditions. A number of additional studies have similarly shown that ego involvement can result in more superficial processing, more rigid learning sets, less challenge seeking, and less long-term memory in learning settings (see Ryan & Stiller, 1991, for a review).

Although the focus of the ego involvement literature has tended to be on educational processes, it is equally clear that this phenomenon extends to many domains. Ego involvement can have as its content one's appearance, one's wealth, one's achievement, one's status, or a variety of other concerns (Ryan & Deci, 1989). To the extent that one has come to believe one's worth is related to such outcomes, ego involvement and its associated heteronomy, internal pressure, and disruptive effects on intrinsic motivation will be in evidence.

To what social factors can we attribute the etiology and pervasiveness of ego involvement? I argue that ego involvement is inevitable wherever social structures, or the people who internalize them, contingently value and esteem individuals based on some specified attribute. Thus if school systems or parents implicitly define as "better" children who are smarter and more efficacious, then children will come to base their own sense of worth on this contingent standard. In a similar way, other forms of ego involvement are hatched. Young girls come to see both from others and from the mass media that their worth in the eyes of others is contingent on their looks (Henley, 1977). Both girls and boys can be led to believe it is wealth that "makes it" and that possessions define one's adequacy. In these cases the internalization of contingent evaluation in the form of ego involvement is the inevitable next step. Looking deeper, we can also examine how the socioeconomic structure of society generates and supports the ethics of ego involvement. Here we can also see how the psychology of ego involvement is compatible with the ideology of self-efficacy (e.g., Bandura, 1989; Locke & Latham, 1990). Social-cognitive "agents" can establish their worth by competently pursuing the "right" outcomes. The exclusive focus on outcome efficacy precludes critical analysis of why one seeks those outcomes or whether their pursuit is congruent with autonomy and integration.

THE SELF AND AUTONOMY IN INTERNALIZATION

Research on ego involvement led directly to another much more important domain of inquiry, one that I believe subsumes the idea of ego involvement. This domain concerns the assimilation of new forms of behavioral regulation that are not inherent in the organism but are socially transmitted. This process of assimilation is referred to in several theoretical perspectives as *internalization*. Internalization on the most global level can be described as the transformation of external controls and regulations into internal ones. More fundamentally, it means transmuting heteronomous demands into autonomous ones where possible (Deci & Ryan, 1985b; Ryan, Connell, & Deci, 1985).

Internalization is clearly implicated in most conceptions of development that are based on the organizational perspective. Internalization represents the organism's acquisition of internal regulations to replace external ones. Internalization has adaptive consequences (the organism anticipates and "fits" with the surround) and also results in greater coordination and unity between people. Internalization, that is, holds together the fabric of culture by weaving in the organization of the individual (Parsons, 1952; Ryan, Connell, & Grolnick, 1992). Thus internalization pertains to both individual and social organization.

It is also clear that internalization assumes many forms. Some internalizations are of the same nature as described in ego involvement, in that a person can "take on" a regulation or an idea about how to behave in order to preserve a sense of worth. A child may learn to stay neat even while playing outside if he has felt the pain of rejection or disapproval from a parent when he "looked a mess." To the extent that he has internalized this parental attitude and value structure, he will act to stay neat and clean even when away from the parent—say in a day-care setting where that same attitude is not held by adults. If we examine what motivates the child (from a phenomenological or dynamic viewpoint), we see that he has come to conceive of messiness as "bad" and sees himself as less estimable if he gets dirty. The behavior is thus internalized—it is independently maintained by the child—through an internalization of the contingent approval that was originally externally applied. One part of himself now oversees and evaluates behavior as the parent originally did. We label this internally controlling type of internalization *introjection* (Deci & Ryan, 1985b; Ryan et al., 1985; Ryan & Connell, 1989).

Not all internalization bears the mark of such self-splitting and esteem-related contingency, however. In another form of internalization, which we refer to as *identification,* an adopted value or regulation is motivated by an appreciation of the importance or *worth of the behavior* (or outcomes associated with it) rather than the *worth of the child* for doing it. This seemingly subtle difference in motivation is hugely different in terms of intrapsychic experience and functional consequences.

In our conceptualization, both introjection and ego involvement represent partial internalizations. The source of regulation is internal to the person but remains external to the self. It thus retains a character of heteronomy with respect to the self because it is not fully organized or assimilated as one's own value. By contrast, identification represents a fuller assimilation of values or regulations insofar as they are interpreted as one's own. Really, both introjection and identification represent points along a continuum of internalization that runs from external regulation to fully integrated self-regulation, or from heteronomy to autonomy.

Ryan and Connell (1989) attempted to empirically demonstrate the continuum of internalization and its character in terms of relative autonomy. They sampled children's reasons for acting in two domains: achievement (e.g., doing homework) and pro-social behavior (e.g., inhibiting aggression). Children were given reasons for performing behaviors in these two areas that were categorized a priori into four types. *External* reasons described doing the target activities to comply with authorities or because they "had to"; *introjected* reasons pertained to performing the behavior to gain approval from self and others or to avoid guilt and "feeling bad" about themselves; reasons subsumed under *identification* entailed endorsing the value or importance of the activity; and *intrinsic* reasons involved doing the activity for fun or enjoyment. It was hypothesized and found that such reasons could be mathematically described by a quasi-simplex or "ordered correlation" pattern in which the categories fell along a continuum of relative autonomy.

In a cross-sectional study of internalization, Chandler and Connell (1987) examined the motivational basis for both intrinsically motivated activities and activities that were more uninteresting and socially mandated. Behaviors in the former category included play and games; activities in the latter category included such things as doing chores, brushing teeth, or doing homework. They found that games and play were done "for fun" throughout their sampled age groups. By contrast, socially mandated activities tended to be done, according to younger subjects, for external reasons such as avoiding punishment or following parents' directions. With increasing age, however, these nonintrinsically motivated behaviors were more frequently reported to be performed because they were important to or valued by the children themselves. These results supported the view that development entails an increasing internalization to the self of that which is originally externally prescribed. We view such internalization as an aspect of an overall tendency to move away from heteronomy toward autonomy by assimilating regulations into the self.

In recent studies variations in the degree to which behavioral regulations are internalized to the self have been shown to have a strong impact on mental health. Ryan, Rigby, and King (1992) examined introjection versus identification with regard to religious beliefs and practices in various adult Christian samples. In general, they found that whereas introjection was associated with poorer personal adjustment (more anxiety, depression, and lower self-worth), identification with religious beliefs was positively correlated with better mental health and adjustment. This suggests, again, that *how* a set of values or regulations is internalized or anchored in the self has a functional effect on the overall integrity and well-being of the individual. Similar results were obtained by O'Connor and Vallerand (1990), who employed a simplex model to study religious motivation in the elderly. In their sample more fully internalized religious motivation was associated with greater well-being and life satisfaction. Other studies in different domains of internalization show similar patterns of results, including school motivation (Ryan & Connell, 1989; Vallerand & Bissonnette, 1992), leisure motivation (Pelletier, Vallerand, Blais, & Briere, 1990), and treatment motivation (Plant, 1990).

What are the social-contextual conditions that foster this integration process? Our first hypothesis stems from our metatheoretical understanding of organization and its relation to internalization. We suggest that whereas behaviors related to the values and regulations one internalizes are not themselves intrinsically motivated, the *process* of integrating external regulations into the self *is* intrinsically motivated. *Internalization is part of the overall thrust of development toward assimilation to the self.* Thus conditions of autonomy support should encourage fuller assimilation of conveyed regulations and values of this type. Second, we hypothesize that one motive clearly implicated in internalization is *relatedness* (Ryan, 1991). The more closely related one feels to socializing others, the more likely it is that internalization will occur. We have begun to empirically test these theoretical assumptions in several ways.

In a field study examining some of these hypotheses, Grolnick and Ryan (1989) interviewed parents about their motivational techniques with regard to school behaviors. Parents who were rated as more "controlling" versus "autonomy supportive" had children who reported less internalization of school-related values. Teachers reported similarly less self-motivation in the children of more controlling parents and more problems in their behavioral self-regulation in school. An interesting side benefit of such internalization dynamics was that the children who had more autonomy-supportive parents (and accordingly more identification with school-relevant values) had better objective achievement outcomes as well. Another finding from this study was that maternal involvement—the dedication of time and resources to child rearing—was associated with better school-related outcomes. Thus an environment characterized by support for autonomy and by maternal care maximized internalization and adjustment to the extrafamilial domain of school.

More recently, children's *perceptions* of parents' autonomy support and involvement were shown to predict both children's internalization of academic values and their perceived competence. In turn these motivationally relevant variables predicted objective achievement outcomes (Grolnick, Ryan, & Deci, 1991). In this study, children's degree of internalized motivation and sense of competence mediated between the perceived parental environment and performance. This again speaks to the functional significance of the social context in facilitating internalization of socially transmitted values. In this case it appears that children will more actively internalize parental values when they do not feel overly controlled while they are learning them.

An intriguing experimental study suggests a similar point. Maccoby and Martin (1983) hypothesized that reciprocal relationships between parents and children (where each has some negotiating power and voice) would be more likely to produce children who would "accept" influence from the parents, such as adhering to parents' requests. Parpal and Maccoby (1985) then tested this assumption by instructing mothers in an experimental study to either allow their children control during a play period or not. Children who had been allowed some control were more likely to subsequently comply with the request to pick up toys than ones who were not afforded control over their play.

The crucial point here is that internalization, in which external practices, regulations, and values are adopted as one's own, can be understood in terms of autonomy. The more fully internalized a regulation, the more it is experienced as reflecting the self. Furthermore, the process of internalization is itself intrinsically motivated, and it is furthered by contexts that afford support for autonomy.

A final point is that a consideration of internalization shows that cultural prescriptions are "taken in" to various degrees. We suggest that some regulations and values can never be fully internalized (although they may be introjected). Thus the idea of internalization allows us to examine the congruence of cultural transmissions with the human nature that assimilates them. Although the "telos" of internalization is the integration of culture and self, mere compliance with culture is not necessarily a desirable developmental end.

Autonomy in Human Relationships

During the same period when experimental psychologists were grappling with the concept of an organismic need for effectance and autonomy represented in intrinsic motivation, another non-drive-based organismic need was being studied. John Bowlby (1969), Harry Harlow (1958), and others argued for recognizing a primary need for relatedness as a basic organismic attribute. As Bowlby (1988, p. 3) put it, "The propensity to make strong emotional bonds to particular individuals [is] a basic component of human nature." The need for relatedness is also expressed by object-relations theorists who, following W. Ronald Fairbairn (1954), proposed that people are innately "object seeking," meaning that we naturally seek connection and relatedness with others.

The recognition on the psychological level of an intrinsic need for relatedness faced opposition similar to that faced by other intrinsic motives. Alternative reinforcement and drive-based explanations had to be countered, and investigations of the functional impact of object-seeking motives had to be provided. Early work by Harry Harlow, René Spitz, Mary Ainsworth, and others accomplished much of this, showing that the propensity to form bonds with others was "neither subordinate to nor derivative from food and sex" (Bowlby, 1988, p. 3).

My interest in the current thesis concerns not so much the history of this work as how the apparently intrinsic need for relatedness[4] connects with the concept of autonomy. That is, my focus will be on the impact that attachment and relatedness have on the development of autonomy, and on the meaning of autonomy in the context of adult relationships. Finally, I will examine the contrast between the core self as reflected in autonomy and the concept of the looking-glass self of symbolic interactionism.

Autonomy and attachment. Human attachments are the major context of development, and they represent the earliest and most pervasive environmental influence on organizational processes and autonomy. The earliest relationships with caregivers provide the cradle for nascent self-organization and the nourishment for its development. The importance of this interpersonal context for self-development and integrative capacities cannot be overstated. Let us now consider the qualities that make an attachment facilitative for the self and those that interfere with the expression of that active center.

The neonate begins early on sorting out and integrating "self invariants" into a stable self-organization (Stern, 1985). This task is made optimal because the nascent self structure of the infant "shares in" the self-organization of the caretakers, who anticipate needs and regulate stimulation. Consolidation of the self is facilitated as well by complex integrative capacities infants possess, which have only recently become recognized (see, e.g., Papousek & Papousek, 1987). Integration occurs primarily through activity, however, and the growth of self-regulation therefore depends on a more or less responsive world that acknowledges and supports activity.

In this regard, note that most conceptualizations of the caregiving environment that produces a secure attachment in infancy prominently include the idea of support for such autonomous initiations. As Bretherton (1987, p. 1075) states, "In the framework of attachment theory, maternal respect for the child's autonomy is an aspect of sensitivity to the infant's signals." Failure to respect or respond to signals as they emanate from the infant thus disrupts attachment and has consequences for the infant's further self-development.

One immediate consequence of insensitivity is its disruption of the "attachment-exploration balance." Secure infants can more safely use the caregiver as a base from which to freely explore the environment or to engage in play, manipulation, and other spontaneous assimilative adventures (Sroufe & Waters, 1977). Grolnick, Frodi, and Bridges (1984), for example, examined the relation between behavioral ratings of maternal autonomy support and mastery motivation in a sample of one-year-olds. Their results showed that infants whose mothers were more autonomy supportive were more persistent at the mastery task.

Such findings show how autonomy support may be related to organizational development. The infant whose initiations and signals are acknowledged and responded to develops more initiative and vitality in exploring his or her world. As Sroufe (1990, p. 298) suggests, children with histories of secure attachment are more likely to be "independent, resourceful, curious, and confident in their approach to the environment." In our terms, infants who have been supported in developing a sense of autonomy and initiative are more mastery oriented or intrinsically motivated in a variety of situations.

Besides attachment theory, other perspectives on early self-development also emphasize the issue of support for the infant's nascent autonomy. Winnicott (1965), for example, stresses the need for caregivers to create a "facilitating environment" that includes both responsive caregiving and sensitivity to the infant's initiations. For Winnicott, a facilitating environment enables the infant to express his or her *true self*, the original sense of organization and aliveness. Winnicott's concept of true self is akin to the core self I have described as an emergent organization—a center of spontaneity and vitality. Responsiveness to signals from the infant and lack of intrusion during periods of quiescence result in the strengthening of the true self, and along with it the sense of being real. However, with surplus intrusions or demands from the caregiver the infant must reorganize the world in accord with something external, and this compliant reorganization is referred to by Winnicott as the *false self*: putting forth what one is not in order to preserve contact and support. For Winnicott, the false self serves primarily as protection for the true self. One puts up a false front in order to adapt to or satisfy others to whom one needs to stay connected.

Behrends and Blatt (1985), in their psychoanalytically oriented developmental theory, argue that optimal relationships are those that involve emotional closeness and support within a context of encouragement for "one's efforts at individuation and autonomy" (p. 20). They apply this model not only in infancy but across child and adolescent development. For them, as for Winnicott, the development of self is aided by empathic, sensitive caregiving that draws forth communication and affords acknowledgment and support.

Each of these approaches recognizes a nascent self that requires a responsive and encouraging caregiving environment in order to gain strength and coherence. This responsiveness to the self of the infant is what we would call autonomy support, and it reflects the caregiver's capacity to take on the child's internal frame of reference in organizing responses and provisions.

The role of autonomy support in sustaining attachment goes beyond infancy and in part explains the figures to whom children attach, whom they model, and whose lessons they internalize. In later relationships we predict that, as in infancy, when adults provide autonomy support and nurturance (involvement) they draw forth a sense of relatedness and facilitate the development and integration of the child's self.

We have tested this formulation in a few studies to date. Avery and Ryan (1988) examined object representations in a middle childhood sample using a projective procedure developed by Blatt, Chevron, Quinlan, and Wein (1981). Avery and Ryan found that "good" objects (those perceived as nurturant and positive) were described on independent self-report surveys as parents who were "involved" and "autonomy supportive." Grolnick and Ryan (1989), in their interview study discussed earlier, showed similarly that maternal involvement and autonomy support were pivotal predictors of adjustment, internalization, and achievement in middle childhood.

More recently, Ryan, Stiller, and Lynch (1992) explored how the experienced quality of relatedness to parents, teachers, and friends was connected with motivational and adjustment outcomes in a junior-high-school sample. They found that the internalization of school-related values was uniquely and independently associated with the perceived quality of parent and teacher relationships, whereas relatedness to friends was not systematically connected to these outcomes. Here socializing adults are more likely to successfully transmit their values if children feel secure and identify with them. Furthermore, as Ryan and Lynch (1989) had previously shown, students who felt detached from adults fared less well on indexes of self-regulation, again showing that autonomy and relatedness typically are complementary rather than antithetical constructs. Most notable for our present focus is that the general quality of relationship, as perceived by the child, was found to be largely a function of the perceived autonomy support and involvement of parents or teachers.

In all these studies it appears that what makes a relationship secure and facilitating is that the adult provides real resources for the still developing child, in the context of supporting the child's autonomy. For us that specifically means acknowledging and being responsive to the child's core self and encouraging a perceived internal locus of causality for action. Parents, teachers, and other caregivers who offer these psychological provisions also have as a result a stronger bond of attachment between them and the children they care for. We recognize as well that though autonomy and "ego strength" are heavily shaped by processes occurring in infancy, relationships with significant others continue to affect motivation, autonomy, and organization throughout development. Relationships contribute *situationally* as well as developmentally to one's autonomy, integrity, and coherence.

The dynamics of autonomy and relatedness. We have seen in the research and theory described above that the regulation of behavior is often based in an external perceived locus of causality. This means that the impetus or basis for acting stems from outside the self. When we further examine the factors that lead people to behave other than autonomously, we find that in most cases it is *the regard or approval of other people* that they seek.

A few case examples may help to illustrate. Case A: A seemingly buoyant child acts "happy" all the time to sustain his parents' affects and thus his own self-approval. Surrounding affective expression lies an introjection based on the perceived contingency of parental approval or responsiveness, such that the child constricts the range of affects available to the self, giving up some internal signals to maintain relatedness. Case B: A financially successful man continues to pursue further wealth, giving up his true interests to make more money. We find underneath this that money is a surrogate for parental approval. Case C: A client engages in self-destructive patterns of dieting in order to appear attractive and "under control" to others from her past and present. In doing so she lives up to her mother's standards, with regard to which she must be vigilant and unfailing. In these examples, the disruption of autonomy comes about because of the perceived contingent regard of others. They illustrate that, dynamically, people will often forgo autonomy (give up a part of the self) in order to preserve relatedness.

In many situations, then, the intrinsic needs for autonomy and for relatedness are placed in opposition to one another. One can give up autonomy to secure regard or approval from an attachment figure. This is the case in introjected internalizations, where one preserves a sense of approval and esteemability by compliantly doing what one "should." Alternatively, one can give up relatedness to preserve autonomy. Teenagers, for example, may detach themselves from parents who are too controlling and thus retain a sense of individuality, but they forgo the support and guidance parents can offer during a critical developmental passage. It is particularly interesting to note that when a person forgoes satisfaction of one need for the other the degree or quality of both autonomy and relatedness suffers. The quality of the relatedness one achieves by complying with others' demands (thus giving up autonomy) lacks the characteristics of high-quality relatedness, namely the sense of mutuality and the experience of one's true self relating to another. Similarly, as shown by Ryan and Lynch (1989), when people forsake relationships to gain autonomy, they are likely to end up with independence or detachment but not a real sense of personal autonomy.

In optimal development neither autonomy nor relatedness is forgone. In what circumstances can this happen? First and foremost, it requires parents who do not make relatedness contingent on specified kinds of behavior. They convey a noncontingent love for their child and a willingness to care for and nurture their dependent while giving support for the ever growing range of autonomous decision making the child exhibits. In fact we suggest that, insofar as parents are both autonomy supportive and involved, children can remain securely attached throughout development— they will see no need to detach in order to individuate. Thus we predict both the development of intrapersonal integration (autonomy) and the development of mutually satisfying interpersonal relations (homonomy) in the context of such parental provisions.

Autonomy in adult relationships. The role of autonomy support in caregiving relationships is clearly crucial. Autonomy support translates into sensitivity and responsiveness and helps strengthen self in the dependent. But what is the role of autonomy in mature relationships that are characterized by interdependence and equality rather than unilateral dependence?

Autonomy in adult relationships concerns, in part, the authenticity of the relationship. In other words, autonomy in relationships concerns what one relates to in the other, and how. An authentic relationship between people involves the self of each, rather than just any connection between people. Each person is capable of understanding and strives to understand the world of his of her partner from the partner's internal frame of reference. Each is receptive of and acknowledges disclosed experience and encourages self-expression, meaning what one really feels, believes, and is. Furthermore, in authentic relationships one does not attempt to make the other be or behave in specified ways. Together the mutual perspective sharing and support for autonomy create conditions ripe for a meeting of the hearts, a true relatedness. Insofar as these qualities of addressing each other are shared, the condition of "mutuality of autonomy" described in object-relations theory has been achieved (Ryan, 1989).

One factor contributing to whether a relationship will be authentic concerns *why* each partner is relating to the other. This issue of why one relates to another can be addressed in terms of one's reasons for relating and their perceived locus of causality. I may relate to someone, say a boss or a customer, because I "have to." Rewards, promotions, or other instrumental gains can be had from "relating." Here the "locus of causality" lies in external inducements, and the relationship is "extrinsically motivated." I may relate to others, say a parent or an in-law, because I would feel guilty if I did not. Such an internally controlling motivation also represents an external locus of causality. Whatever the impetus, to the degree that I relate to another without full volition and autonomy, my relating is inauthentic. Alternatively, I can be relating for authentic purposes such as the intrinsic satisfactions inherent in connecting, sharing, and being with another, or because I value some aspects of the relationship. Relating would thus have an internal perceived locus of causality and be authentic—it would come from the self.

Several recent studies support the view that the "why" of relationships affects their quality and security. Blais, Sabourin, Boucher, and Vallerand (1990) applied self-determination theory to a model of couple happiness. To do so they developed a measure of the relative autonomy of each partner's motives for sustaining the relationship. Using this survey, they then showed that marital satisfaction and happiness were largely a function of how much autonomy the participants expressed. The more autonomous the participation of the partners, the greater the perception of cohesion, affectivity, and positive dyadic interactions. In a similar vein, Rempel, Holmes, and Zanna (1985) showed that the belief that one's partner is "intrinsically" motivated was associated with increased emotional security in the relationship. In these studies, the perception that relatedness is authentic bespeaks its quality and translates into security and satisfaction.

There are clearly many relationships in which one does not communicate authentically. Much day-to-day interaction is made up of such relating. It would certainly be difficult to be real and authentic in every encounter, whereas wearing a persona fit for each occasion can be highly adaptive. However, the need for relatedness suggests that there must be some interactions where authentic relating happens if the self is to feel sustained, enhanced, and coherent. In cases where such contact with significant others does not occur, usually one experiences too little sensitivity to one's frame of reference to risk exposure, or else one feels pressure and control to be or to feel certain ways. Accordingly, one attempts to relate through a false self (Winnicott, 1965), so as to protect the core self from vulnerability, rejection, or merely frustration. Thus is described the absence of authenticity or self-engagement in relationships—the inability or unwillingness to be who one is in the context of others.

Authentic relatedness describes a particular type of human interaction, one in which there is freedom and openness between selves. Such relatedness between adults reflects a mutuality of autonomy and expresses the object-seeking, emotionally bonding nature that makes us human. Humans need such relatedness throughout the life span. Whether in a dependent or interdependent position, each of us both thrives and coheres best in the context of others who can reach and acknowledge our self. The need for sensitive partners continues beyond the early "attachment" years, as long as a vital core self persists in reaching beyond itself to others.

HOW DOES THE CORE SELF COMPARE WITH THE LOOKING-GLASS SELF?

Much of the developmental literature on the self pertains not at all to my concerns with autonomy and authenticity. For the most part, developmental psychologists have focused on the self not as a center of synthesis or organization, but rather as a concept or representation. In this approach the self is "acquired" at about 20 months of age, when there is evidence of a clear awareness of self as an object in the world, separate from others. By contrast, the self at the center of the present theory is not a mere concept, but rather is a process. The self as conceptualized here thus predates self-awareness, being manifest in synthetic or integrative activities inherent in the organism and evident from birth. How then do theories of self-concept compare with an organismic conception of self and of autonomy?

The theoretical framework for much of the literature on self-concept is derived from *symbolic interactionism*, and the idea of the *looking-glass self* (Cooley, 1902). Harter (1988, p. 51) describes the idea of the looking-glass self succinctly: "The significant others in one's life become social mirrors, as it were, and one gazes into these mirrors in order to determine others' opinions of oneself. One then adopts this opinion in forming one's self definition." Self-concepts are thus understood as internalizations of other people's appraisals. This framework suggests that our perceptions of how valuable or competent we are in the eyes of others are used to organize behavior, and further that we possess a powerful set of motives to maintain self-esteem either by eliciting positive appraisals from others or by avoiding negative ones.

Theories that emphasize the looking-glass self accordingly place considerable emphasis on public aspects of the self, since these are the primary bases on which others' opinions are formed. Self-concept formation depends heavily on social comparisons of competencies, achievements, appearance, status, and other issues where external feedback is provided. It is, after all, the external view of the self that is ultimately internalized.

One can see immediately that the looking-glass self is in stark contrast to the core self examined in this essay. Whereas the core self is innate and emergent, albeit dependent on a social environment, the looking-glass self is socially imputed; whereas the sense of self entailed by the core self concerns the degree to which one initiates and organizes action, the sense of self in the looking-glass model is externally derived; whereas the core self is defined by its subjectivity, the looking-glass self is the self as object (Deci & Ryan, 1991; Ryan, 1991).

The looking-glass self of Charles Cooley (1902) parallels William James's description of the "social self." James (1890, p. 294) argued that a person has as many social selves as "there are distinct groups of persons about whose opinion he cares." It is because these others' opinions matter that one's behavior can be regulated in order to affect their appraisal. This alteration of behavior, I maintain, can reflect either more or less autonomy. That is, either one believes the opinions and appraisals of others and can endorse and embrace them as also one's own, or one can merely conform with them to avoid disapproval.

Generally speaking, behavior that reflects the social self represents an adaptation to the individuals and groups with whom one interacts. However, the specific form such adaptation often takes is a heightened concern with what others might think of oneself (Cooley, 1902; Webster & Sobieszek, 1974). Specifically, the gaze into the looking glass typically entails experiencing the self as an "object" from the perspective of the other. One becomes *self-conscious*, or "objectively" (Duval & Wicklund, 1972) or "publicly" (Carver & Scheier, 1981) self-aware. Although this objectifying self-consciousness can be a source of useful information or feedback, it more typically represents a heteronomous factor in the organization of action, fostering conformity and lack of self-expression.

If this reasoning is correct, then conditions that give rise to this objectifying self-consciousness should promote an external perceived locus of causality. Accordingly, we hypothesized that in a situation where one was intrinsically motivated, the induction of public self-consciousness would undermine autonomy and thus motivation. Plant and Ryan (1985) tested this by placing subjects in conditions that typically enhance public self-consciousness (in a room with a mirror in front of them or under video camera surveillance) and comparing them with subjects not exposed to a catalyst of public self-focus. They found that both situational and dispositional public self-consciousness undermined intrinsic motivation. They interpreted this as showing that the regulation of self through the (projected) eyes of others is inimical to autonomy and thus to intrinsic motivation, which depends upon autonomy. This finding is consistent with a plethora of studies showing that surveillance, evaluation, and contingent praise from others tend to disrupt intrinsic motivation insofar as they reflect regulation for the other rather than self-regulation.

In a recent study, Ryan and Kuczkowski (in press) examined the imaginary audience phenomenon (Elkind & Bowen, 1979) in a cross-sectional adolescent sample. The imaginary audience is a form of objective self-awareness that reaches its height after early adolescence. We suggested that while the imaginary audience experience is a normal developmental process, it nonetheless serves to constrain or inhibit self-expression. In this study we found, as expected, that individual differences in the salience of the imaginary audience were positively correlated with public self-consciousness as traditionally measured. More important, both the imaginary audience and public self-consciousness constructs predicted lower public individuation (Maslach, Stapp, & Santee, 1985). That is, adolescents who were most concerned with others' views of the self were least willing to stand out from the crowd, or to be nonconforming. This again suggested that concern with the looking-glass self is frequently antagonistic to autonomy.

Public self-awareness is a prototypical "state" version of the Coolean self. The publicly self-aware person is always checking and adjusting his or her behavior with respect to projections about what others think. Self-consciousness is thus a form of ego involvement in the sense that self-esteem hinges on one's presumed impression in the eyes of others. This formulation is consistent with evidence that when made publicly self-aware, people are more likely to conform, wear makeup, or make other adjustments that might gain the regard of others (Carver & Scheier, 1981). In addition, public self-awareness has been associated with a controlling style of self-regulation in adulthood (Deci & Ryan, 1985a). When one's self-esteem becomes contingent on the inferred appraisals of others, the possibility of acting contrary to the self (inauthentically) is maximized. In short, it seems that when the interpersonal context offers only contingent approval, so that people must be content with relatedness that is not accompanied by autonomy support, their development is likely to be characterized by the emergence of a strong, unintegrated social self that in turn perpetuates public self-consciousness.

The general point here is that when the looking-glass self is the focus of concern, the core self is often subjugated to it. Yet this need not be the case. Decentering one's perception, viewing oneself "as if" from the outside, and taking stock of others' appraisals of oneself can all be helpful inputs into self-regulation. Insofar as concern with the regard of others is preeminent, however, external regulation becomes the predominant trend in personality, and the integration of the self is hampered.

The conditions of the current culture potentiate this antagonism. To the extent that modern economic conditions increasingly pressure people toward individualism, self-sufficiency, and self-interest, there is increased concern with the relative standing of each "me" compared with others (Derber, 1979). One's value becomes a function of how one is packaged and presented and can be likened to a commodity in a marketplace where the currency is approval and regard. Individuals become preoccupied with enhancing the visible self, spending energy and time on appearance, possessions, and status building. One must purchase the right clothes, own the fashionable car, develop the right body type and the impressive self-presentation. These motives represent the myriad ego involvements that I previously showed represent heteronomy rather than autonomy. Approval and esteem can thus become alienating forces, forming the basis for a cultural narcissism so aptly described by one of my colleagues at Rochester (Lasch, 1978). Given these conditions, it should not be surprising that Loevinger (1976) finds the modal level of ego development among American adults to be conformity, marked by preoccupation with appearance and regulation by socially prescribed roles and attitudes. We again see how cultural and interpersonal contexts dynamically affect autonomy and integration in individual development.

Certain groups are hardest hit by such cultural conditions. Foreman (1978), for example, argues that the focus on the self as object has been particularly oppressive to women. She suggests that women exist in the mode of "being-for-others," obtaining a sense of worth through the projected lens of the other. Thus women's self-conceptions are frequently based on others' reactions and needs, often to the neglect of their own development. Women's preoccupation with the appraisals and values of others is also reflected in excessive focus on body, appearance, and styles—all of which address only externalized self-definitions (Eichenbaum & Orbach, 1983).

Lerner (1988) suggests that the preoccupation with being-for-others lies at the heart of many clinical problems brought to her by adult women. She views her work, in part, as helping clients toward increased autonomy. In this struggle she argues that autonomy requires that "we determine our own choices, decide our own risks, and assume primary responsibility for our own growth and development" (p. 64). Much of that work means facing the loss of self-definitions based on the love and approval of others and moving toward mutuality and equality. This in part requires reexamining the relations of contingent regard experienced early in life, as well as relying less on the looking glass in current behavior.

The existence of a looking-glass psychology thus exists in some relation to a psychology of the core self I have outlined, but the relation is a complex one. The core self and the internalized social self are neither essentially compatible nor contradictory. In development, however, social contexts can either be oriented so as to strengthen and reinforce the need to be checking the looking glass and regulating the self through the eyes of others, or alternatively can provide enough unconditional regard and autonomy support so that the core self can be enhanced. Ultimately, the core self must synthesize and integrate the various "mes" that interactions within the social world precipitate if they are to be used as input into *self-*regulation rather than as a basis for nonautonomous regulation. Whereas developmental psychologists have paid considerable attention to the nature of internalized appraisals, less consideration has been placed on how the mes can be reconstructed into an order and congruence with the core self that would constitute autonomy.

Toward a Synthetic View of Agency in Development

Living things share an organizational propensity that is the defining feature of development. Organismic theories in psychology acknowledge this and place organization at the core of their models. In many of these theories this organizational propensity is assumed to be automatic, and theorists have been content to focus on the structural products that result from it rather than on the dynamics of its exercise. My goal has been to challenge this contentment in two ways: by arguing first that many developmental processes in the psychological sphere are mediated by behavior and thus require an agent, and second that the dynamics of agency can be explicated by a consistent theory of autonomy.

I have placed the role of agency in development in the hands of a core self. In forwarding this view, I argued that the core self is not a mere representation or a concept, but rather corresponds to an active center of organization, one that concerns assimilating and integrating one's experience with inner and outer worlds. Autonomy, accordingly, entails the experience of regulation or endorsement of behavior by this self, which means that behavior fits or is congruent with psychological organization. Thus the self has both a phenomenological referent in the idea of autonomy and a structural referent vis-à-vis organization.

There appear to be two directions that the core self takes. On the one hand, self-organization proceeds toward differentiation and integration within the individual, a process poetically described by Varela, Maturana, and Uribe (1974) as *autopoiesis,* or "self-creation." But the other thrust is toward the *relatedness* and integration of the individual with others (Angyal, 1965; Ryan, 1991). It appears that the development and well-being of the core self depend heavily on the success of the organization in progressing in both directions, without forgoing one for the other. On the level of psychological development, the dual directions of the organizational tendency are expressed in dynamic relations between intrinsic needs for autonomy and relatedness. In this essay I have focused primarily on autonomy, but its embeddedness in relational dynamics necessarily brings both organizational tendencies to the fore.

These dynamics of relatedness and autonomy tell us much

about the social psychology of development. We see that in most circumstances the kinds of behaviors that concern developmentalists, such as intrinsic motivation and processes of internalization, are spontaneous functions of the individual. However, these spontaneous growth-related activities are enhanced and sustained by autonomy support and relatedness. Considerable research suggests that development is something that typically cannot be controlled, imputed, reinforced, or shaped; rather, it must be afforded, facilitated, catalyzed, guided, and supported. Growing out of motivational work on these developmental processes is thus a model of facilitating interpersonal environments based on autonomy support and relatedness that has application in domains ranging from education to psychotherapy.

The spontaneous nature of development involves assimilation and integration. Not only does one assimilate new stimuli, new skills, and new knowledge, one also assimilates ways of living with others. This assimilation of ambient, culturally accepted forms of life is a process of internalization to the self. The more fully internalized something is, the more it reflects autonomy, whereas partial assimilations remain heteronomous. Examination of social development, then, must be accompanied by a concern for the degree of internalization reflected in socialized actions. How autonomous such actions are can be explained both by the process through which internalization is achieved and by the nature of the content and practices that culture transmits. In the dialectic viewpoint of self-determination theory (Deci & Ryan, 1985b, 1991) not just anything can be taken in, and the humanity of a given cultural milieu can be judged both by the assimilability of its teachings and by the methods through which it transmits those teachings.

More generally, the developmental psychology of human beings cannot, in the present view, be divorced from the perspective of the life sciences (Ryan, 1991). Once we recognize that we are products of evolution on both biological and cultural levels, we see that our sense of self is not created ex nihilo. On the contrary, from the very beginning we operate from a regulatory center that tends toward greater organization. In cognitive and social development, actualization of that tendency depends heavily upon particular social conditions. Social contexts that support the expression of autonomy, competence, and relatedness provide the psychological nutriments that ultimately afford individuals a sense of unity and coherence. It is also within such environments that individuals are most likely to integrate practices important to the community and develop authentic attachments with others.

NOTES

1. The structure of the problem regarding organization principles and the agency that often "carries them out" is parallel to the Kierkegaardian critique of Hegel. For Hegel the development of the individual, the culture, and history is explained as necessity by the dialectical laws of the Spirit. But according to Kierkegaard these developments are made possible only by human action, which he describes as the "secret agent" of cultural and individual change (Kierkegaard, 1844, CD).

2. I take responsibility, but not full credit, for the viewpoints expressed here. Self-determination theory is a profoundly collaborative product between myself and Ed Deci. Wendy Grolnick of Clark University has made substantial contributions both theoretically and empirically. James Connell (Public Private Ventures in Philadelphia), Richard Koestner (McGill University), and Robert Vallerand (University of Quebec, Montreal) each have added their own unique perspectives. The members of the Motivation Research Group at Rochester continually inspire changes in the theory. Preparation of this chapter was supported by grants from NICHD (HD19914) and NIMH (MH18922).

3. A number of studies have supported the cognitive evaluation theory propositions concerning the effects of feedback and level of challenge on intrinsic motivation. However the focus on autonomy in this chapter precludes coverage of this important area. See Koestner and McClelland (1990) for a recent review of relevant research.

4. Self-determination theory (Deci & Ryan, 1991; Ryan, 1991) posits three fundamental or intrinsic psychological needs that underlie development—namely, autonomy, competence, and relatedness. The emphasis of this essay on agency in development has led me to focus primarily on autonomy, to the relative neglect of relatedness.

REFERENCES

Amabile, T. M. (1979). Effects of external evaluations on artistic creativity. *Journal of Personality and Social Psychology, 37*, 221–233.

Amabile, T. M., DeJong, W., & Lepper, M. R. (1976). Effects of externally imposed deadlines on subsequent intrinsic motivation. *Journal of Personality and Social Psychology, 34*, 92–98.

Angyal, A. (1965). *Neurosis and treatment: A holistic theory.* New York: John Wiley.

Avery, R. R., & Ryan, R. M. (1988). Object relations and ego development: Comparison and correlates in middle childhood. *Journal of Personality, 56,* 547–569.

Bandura, A. (1989). Human agency in social cognitive theory. *American Psychologist, 44,* 1175–1184.

Behrends, R. S., & Blatt, J. S. (1985). Internalization and psychological development through the life cycle. *Psychoanalytic Study of the Child, 40,* 11–39.

Benware, C., & Deci, E. L. (1984). Quality of learning with an active versus passive motivational set. *American Educational Research Journal, 21,* 755–765.

Blais, M. R., Sabourin, S., Boucher, C., & Vallerand, R. J. (1990). Toward a motivational model of couple happiness. *Journal of Personality and Social Psychology, 59,* 1021–1031.

Blasi, A. (1976). Concept of development in personality theory. In J. Loevinger, *Ego development* (pp. 29–53). San Francisco: Jossey-Bass.

Blasi, A. (1984). Autonomy in obedience: The development of distancing in socialized action. Published in German in W. Edelstein & J. Habermas (Eds.), *Soziale Interaktion und Soziales Verstehen* (pp. 300–347). Frankfurt: Suhrkamp.

Blatt, S. J., Chevron, E. S., Quinlan, D. M., & Wein, S. (1981). *The assessment of qualitative and structural dimensions of object representation.* Unpublished manuscript, Yale University.

Blos, P. (1962). *On adolescence: A psychoanalytic interpretation.* Glencoe, IL: Free Press.

Boggiano, A. K., Barrett, M., Weiher, A. W., McClelland, G. H., & Lusk, C. M. (1987). Use of the maximal-operant principle to motivate children's intrinsic interest. *Journal of Personality and Social Psychology, 53,* 866–879.

Bowlby, J. (1969). *Attachment.* New York: Basic Books.

Bowlby, J. (1988). Developmental psychiatry comes of age. *American Journal of Psychiatry, 145,* 1–10.

Bretherton, I. (1987). New perspectives on attachment relations: Security, communication and internal working models. In J. Osofsky (Ed.), *Handbook of infant development* (pp. 1061–1100). New York: John Wiley.

Broughton, J. M. (1991). *Structure, anti-structure and non-structure in "personality."* Unpublished manuscript, Columbia University.

Broughton, J. M., & Zahaykevich, M. K. (1988). Ego and ideology: A critical review of Loevinger's theory. In D. K. Lapsley & F. C. Power (Eds.), *Self, ego, and identity.* New York: Springer-Verlag.

Butler, R. (1987). Task-involving and ego-involving properties of evaluation: Effects of different feedback conditions on motivational perceptions, interest, and performance. *Journal of Educational Psychology, 79,* 474–482.

Carver, C. S., & Scheier, M. F. (1981). *Attention and self-regulation: A control theory approach to human behavior.* New York: Springer-Verlag.

Chandler, C. L., & Connell, J. P. (1987). Children's intrinsic, extrinsic and internalized motivation: A developmental study of children's reasons for liked and disliked behaviours. *British Journal of Developmental Psychology, 5*, 357–365.

Cicchetti, D. (1990). The organization and coherence of socioemotional, cognitive, and representational development: Illustrations through a developmental psychopathology perspective on Down syndrome and child maltreatment. In R. A. Thompson (Ed.), *Nebraska symposium on motivation, 1988* (pp. 259–366). Lincoln: University of Nebraska Press.

Cooley, C. (1902). *Human nature and the social order.* New York: Charles Scribner's Sons.

Crockenberg, S., & Litman, C. (1990). Autonomy as competence in 2-year-olds: Maternal correlates of child defiance, compliance, and self-assertion. *Developmental Psychology, 26*, 961–971.

Dannefer, D. (1984). Adult development and social theory: A paradigmatic reappraisal. *American Sociological Review, 49*, 100–116.

Danner, F. W., & Lonky, E. (1981). A cognitive-developmental approach to the effects of rewards on intrinsic motivation. *Child Development, 52*, 1043–1052.

deCharms, R. (1968). *Personal causation: The internal affective determinants of behavior.* New York: Academic Press.

deCharms, R. (1976). *Enhancing motivation: Change in the classroom.* New York: Irvington.

Deci, E. L. (1971). Effects of externally mediated rewards on intrinsic motivation. *Journal of Personality and Social Psychology, 18*, 105–115.

Deci, E. L. (1975). *Intrinsic motivation.* New York: Plenum Press.

Deci, E. L., & Cascio, W. F. (1972, April). *Changes in intrinsic motivation as a function of negative feedback and threats.* Paper presented at the meeting of the Eastern Psychological Association, Boston.

Deci, E. L., & Ryan, R. M. (1980). The empirical exploration of intrinsic motivational processes. In L. Berkowitz (Ed.), *Advances in experimental social psychology* (Vol. 13, pp. 39–80). New York: Academic Press.

Deci, E. L., & Ryan, R. M. (1985a). The general causality orientations scale: Self-determination in personality. *Journal of Research in Personality, 19*, 109–134.

Deci, E. L., & Ryan, R. M. (1985b). *Intrinsic motivation and self-determination in human behavior.* New York: Plenum Press.

Deci, E. L., & Ryan, R. M. (1987). The support of autonomy and the control of behavior. *Journal of Personality and Social Psychology, 53*, 1024–1037.

Deci, E. L., & Ryan, R. M. (1991). A motivational approach to self: Integration in personality. In R. Dienstbier (Ed.), *Nebraska symposium on motivation, 1990* (pp. 237–288). Lincoln: University of Nebraska Press.

Deci, E. L., Schwartz, A. J., Sheinman, L., & Ryan, R. M. (1981). An instrument to assess adults' orientations toward control versus autonomy with children: Reflections on intrinsic motivation and perceived competence. *Journal of Educational Psychology, 73*, 642–650.

Dennett, D. C. (1985). *Elbow room: The varieties of free will worth wanting.* Cambridge: MIT Press.

Derber, C. (1979). *The pursuit of attention: Power and individualism in everyday life.* Oxford: Oxford University Press.

Duval, S., & Wicklund, R. A. (1972). *A theory of objective self-awareness.* New York: Academic Press.

Dworkin, G. (1988). *The theory and practice of autonomy.* New York: Cambridge University Press.

Eichenbaum, L., & Orbach, S. (1983). *Understanding women: A femininist and psychoanalytic approach.* New York: Basic Books.

Elkind, D. (1971). Cognitive growth cycles in mental development. In J. K. Cole (Ed.), *Nebraska symposium on motivation, 1970* (pp. 1–31). Lincoln: University of Nebraska Press.

Elkind, D., & Bowen, R. (1979). Imaginary audience behavior in children and adolescents. *Developmental Psychology, 15,* 38–44.

Erikson, E. H. (1950). *Childhood and society.* New York: Norton.

Fairbairn, W. R. D. (1954). *An object-relations theory of the personality.* New York: Basic Books.

Flavell, J. (1963). *The developmental psychology of Jean Piaget.* New York: Van Nostrand.

Flavell, J. (1977). *Cognitive development.* Englewood Cliffs, NJ: Prentice-Hall.

Foreman, A. (1978). *Femininity as alienation.* Dallas: Pluto Press.

Freud, A. (1958). Adolescence. In R. S. Eissler, A. Freud, H. Hartmann, & M. Kris (Eds.), *Psychoanalytic study of the child* (Vol. 13, pp. 255–278). New York: International Universities Press.

Freud, S. (1959). The predisposition to obsessional neurosis. In *Collected papers* (Vol. 2, pp. 122–131). New York: Basic Books. (Original work published 1913)

Freud, S. (1962). *The ego and the id.* New York: W. W. Norton. (Original work published 1923)

Goldstein, K. (1939). *The organism.* New York: American Book Company.

Greenspan, S. I. (1979). *Intelligence and adaptation.* New York: International Universities Press.

Greenwald, A. G. (1982). Ego task analysis: An integration of research on ego-involvement and self-awareness. In A. H. Hastorf & A. M. Isen (Eds.), *Cognitive social psychology* (pp. 109–147). New York: Elsevier.

Grolnick, W., Frodi, A., & Bridges, L. (1984). Maternal control styles and the mastery motivation of one-year-olds. *Infant Mental Health Journal, 5,* 72–82.

Grolnick, W. S., & Ryan, R. M. (1987). Autonomy in children's learning: An experimental and individual difference investigation. *Journal of Personality and Social Psychology, 52,* 890–898.

Grolnick, W. S., & Ryan, R. M. (1989). Parent styles associated with children's self-regulation and competence in school. *Journal of Educational Psychology, 81,* 143–154.

Grolnick, W. S., Ryan, R. M., & Deci, E. L. (1991). The inner resources for school achievement: Motivational mediators of children's perceptions of their parents. *Journal of Educational Psychology, 83*, 508–517.

Harackiewicz, J. (1979). The effects of reward contingency and performance feedback on intrinsic motivation. *Journal of Personality and Social Psychology, 37*, 1352–1363.

Harlow, H. F. (1958). The nature of love. *American Psychologist, 13*, 673–685.

Harter, S. (1988). The construction and conservation of the Self: James and Cooley revisited. In D. K. Lapsley & F. C. Power (Eds.), *Self, ego, and identity: Integrative approaches* (pp. 43–70). New York: Springer-Verlag.

Heider, F. (1958). *The psychology of interpersonal relations.* New York: John Wiley.

Henley, N. M. (1977). *Body politics: Power, sex, and nonverbal communication.* New York: Simon and Schuster.

Hilgard, E. R. (1977). *Divided consciousness.* New York: John Wiley.

Horney, K. (1950). *Neurosis and human growth.* New York: W. W. Norton.

Jacob, F. (1973). *The logic of life: A history of heredity.* New York: Random House.

James, W. (1890). *The principles of psychology.* New York: Holt.

Jung, C. G. (1959). Aion. In *Collected works* (Vol. 9, 2). New York: Pantheon Books. (Original work published 1951)

Kaplan, B. (1983). Genetic-dramatism: Old wine in new bottles. In S. Wapner & B. Kaplan (Eds.), *Toward a holistic developmental psychology.* Hillsdale, NJ: Lawrence Erlbaum.

Kierkegaard, S. (1954). *Concept of dread.* Princeton, NJ: Princeton University Press. (Original work published 1849)

Kierkegaard, S. (1968). *The sickness unto death.* Princeton, NJ: Princeton University Press. (Original work published 1849)

Koestner, R., & McClelland, D. C. (1990). Perspectives on competence motivation. In L. A. Pervin (Ed.), *Handbook of personality: Theory and research* (pp. 527–548). New York: Guilford Press.

Koestner, R., Ryan, R. M., Bernieri, F., & Holt, K. (1984). Setting limits on children's behavior: The differential effects of controlling versus informational styles on intrinsic motivation and creativity. *Journal of Personality, 52*, 233–248.

Koestner, R., Zuckerman, M., & Koestner, J. (1987). Praise, involvement, and intrinsic motivation. *Journal of Personality and Social Psychology, 53*, 383–390.

Lasch, C. (1978). *The culture of narcissism: American life in an age of diminishing expectations.* New York: W. W. Norton.

Lazlo, E. (1987). *Evolution: The grand synthesis.* Boston: New Science Library.

Lepper, M. R., Greene, D., & Nisbett, R. E. (1973). Undermining children's intrinsic interest with extrinsic rewards: A test of the "overjustification" hypothesis. *Journal of Personality and Social Psychology, 28*, 129–137.

Lerner, H. G. (1988). *Women in therapy.* New York: Harper and Row.

Locke, E. A., & Latham, G. P. (1990). *A theory of goal setting and task performance.* Englewood Cliffs, NJ: Prentice-Hall.

Loevinger, J. (1976). *Ego development.* San Francisco: Jossey-Bass.

Loevinger, J., & Blasi, A. (1991). Development of the self as subject. In J. Strauss & G. R. Goethals (Eds.), *The self: Interdisciplinary approaches* (pp. 150–167). New York: Springer-Verlag.

Maccoby, E. E., & Martin, J. A. (1983). Socialization in the context of the family: Parent-child interaction. In E. M. Hetherington (Ed.), *Handbook of child psychology: Vol. 4. Socialization, personality, and social development* (4th ed., pp. 1–102). New York: John Wiley.

Maslach, C., Stapp, J., & Santee, R. T. (1985). Individuation: Conceptual analysis and assessment. *Journal of Personality and Social Psychology, 49,* 729–738.

Mayr, E. (1982). *The growth of biological thought: Diversity, evolution, and inheritance.* Cambridge: Harvard University Press.

Meissner, W. W. (1981). *Internalization in psychoanalysis.* New York: International Universities Press.

Meissner, W. W. (1988). *Treatment of patients in the borderline spectrum.* Northvale, NJ: Jason Aronson.

Memmi, A. (1984). *Dependence.* Boston: Beacon Press.

Minsky, M. (1982). Why people think computers can't. *The AI Magazine,* Fall, 3–15.

Nicholls, J. G. (1984). Achievement motivation: Conceptions of ability, subjective experience, task choice, and performance. *Psychological Review, 91,* 328–346.

Nicolis, G., & Prigogine, I. (1977). *Self-organization in nonequilibrium systems: From dissipative structures to order through fluctuation.* New York: John Wiley.

O'Connor, B. P., & Vallerand, R. J. (1990). Religious motivation in the elderly: A French-Canadian replication and an extension. *Journal of Social Psychology, 130,* 53–59.

Papousek, H., & Papousek, M. (1987). Intuitive parenting: A dialectic counterpart to the infant's integrative competence. In J. D. Osofsky (Ed.), *Handbook of infant development.* New York: John Wiley.

Parpal, M., & Maccoby, E. E. (1985). Maternal responsiveness and subsequent child compliance. *Child Development, 56,* 1326–1334.

Parsons, T. (1952). The superego and the theory of social systems. *Psychiatry, 15,* 15–25.

Pelletier, L. G., Vallerand, J. R., Blais, M. R., & Briere, N. M. (1990, June). *Leisure motivation and mental health: A motivational analysis of self-determination and self-regulation in leisure.* Paper presented at the Canadian Psychological Association meetings, Ottawa.

Pfander, A. (1967). *Phenomenology of willing and motivation* (H. Spiegelberg, Trans.). Evanston, IL: Northwestern University Press. (Original work published 1908)

Piaget, J. (1952). *The origins of intelligence in children.* New York: International Universities Press.

Piaget, J. (1967). *Six psychological studies* (D. Elkind, Ed.). New York: Vintage.

Piaget, J. (1971). *Biology and knowledge.* Chicago: University of Chicago Press.

Plant, R. W. (1990). *Motivation, expectation, and psychiatric severity in predicting early dropout from outpatient alcoholism treatment.* Unpublished doctoral dissertation, University of Rochester.

Plant, R., & Ryan, R. M. (1985). Intrinsic motivation and the effects of self-consciousness, self-awareness, and ego-involvement: An investigation of internally controlling styles. *Journal of Personality, 53,* 435–449.

Polanyi, M. (1958). *Personal knowledge.* Chicago: University of Chicago Press.

Popper, K. R., & Eccles, J. C. (1977). *The self and its brain.* London: Routledge and Kegan Paul.

Rempel, J. K., Holmes, J. G., & Zanna, M. P. (1985). Trust in close relationships. *Journal of Personality and Social Psychology, 49,* 95–112.

Ricoeur, P. (1966). *Freedom and nature: The voluntary and the involuntary* (E. V. Kohak, Trans.). Evanston, IL: Northwestern University Press.

Rogers, C. (1963). The actualizing tendency in relation to "motives" and to consciousness. In M. R. Jones (Ed.), *Nebraska symposium on motivation, 1962* (pp. 1–24). Lincoln: University of Nebraska Press.

Rosenberg, A. (1985). *The structure of biological science.* New York: Cambridge University Press.

Ryan, R. M. (1982). Control and information in the intrapersonal sphere: An extension of cognitive evaluation theory. *Journal of Personality and Social Psychology, 43,* 450–461.

Ryan, R. M. (1989). The relevance of social ontology to psychological theory. *New Ideas in Psychology, 7,* 115–124.

Ryan, R. M. (1991). The nature of the self in autonomy and relatedness. In J. Strauss & G. R. Goethals (Eds.), *The self: Interdisciplinary approaches* (pp. 208–238). New York: Springer-Verlag.

Ryan, R. M., & Connell, J. P. (1989). Perceived locus of causality and internalization: Examining reasons for acting in two domains. *Journal of Personality and Social Psychology, 57,* 749–761.

Ryan, R. M., Connell, J. P., & Deci, E. L. (1985). A motivational analysis of self-determination and self-regulation in education. In C. Ames & R. E. Ames (Eds.), *Research on motivation in education: The classroom milieu* (pp. 13–51). New York: Academic Press.

Ryan, R. M., Connell, J. P., & Grolnick, W. S. (1992). When achievement is *not* intrinsically motivated: A theory of self-regulation in school. In A. K. Boggiano & T. S. Pittman (Eds.), *Achievement and motivation: A social-developmental perspective* (pp. 167–188). New York: Cambridge University Press.

Ryan, R. M., & Deci, E. L. (1989). Bridging the research traditions of task/ego involvement and intrinsic/extrinsic motivation: A commentary on Butler (1987). *Journal of Educational Psychology, 81,* 265–268.

Ryan, R. M., & Grolnick, W. S. (1986). Origins and pawns in the classroom:

Self-report and projective assessments of individual differences in children's perceptions. *Journal of Personality and Social Psychology, 50*, 550–558.

Ryan, R. M., Koestner, R., & Deci, E. L. (1991). Ego-involved persistence: When free-choice behavior is not intrinsically motivated. *Motivation and Emotion, 15*, 185–205.

Ryan, R. M., & Kuczkowski, R. (in press). The imaginary audience, self-consciousness, and public individuation in adolescence. *Journal of Personality.*

Ryan, R. M., & Lynch, J. (1989). Emotional autonomy versus detachment: Revisiting the vicissitudes of adolescence and young adulthood. *Child Development, 60*, 340–356.

Ryan, R. M., Mims, V., & Koestner, R. (1983). Relation of reward contingency and interpersonal context to intrinsic motivation: A review and test using cognitive evaluation theory. *Journal of Personality and Social Psychology, 45*, 736–750.

Ryan, R. M., Rigby, S., & King, K. (1992). *Two types of religious internalization and their relations to religious orientations and mental health.* Unpublished manuscript, University of Rochester.

Ryan, R. M., & Stiller, J. (1991). The social contexts of internalization: Parent and teacher influences on autonomy, motivation and learning. In P. R. Pintrich & M. L. Maehr (Eds.), *Advances in motivation and achievement: Vol. 7. Goals and self-regulatory processes* (pp. 115–149). Greenwich, CT: JAI Press.

Ryan, R. M., Stiller, J., & Lynch, J. H. (1992). *Representations of relationships to teachers, parents, and friends as predictors of academic motivation and self-esteem.* Unpublished manuscript, University of Rochester.

Schafer, R. (1968). *Aspects of internalization.* New York: International Universities Press.

Sherif, M., & Cantril, H. (1947). *The psychology of ego involvements, social attitudes and identifications.* New York: John Wiley.

Skinner, B. F. (1971). *Beyond freedom and dignity.* New York: Alfred Knopf.

Spiegelberg, H. (1972). *Phenomenology in psychology and psychiatry.* Evanston, IL: Northwestern University Press.

Sroufe, L. A. (1990). An organizational perspective on the self. In D. Cicchetti & M. Beeghly (Eds.), *The self in transition: Infancy to childhood.* Chicago: University of Chicago Press.

Sroufe, L. A. & Waters, E. (1977). Attachment as an organizational construct. *Child Development, 48*, 1184–1199.

Steinberg, L., & Silverberg, S. (1986). The vicissitudes of autonomy in adolescence. *Child Development, 57*, 841–851.

Stern, D. N. (1985). *The interpersonal world of the infant.* New York: Basic Books.

Vallerand, R. J., & Bissonnette, R. (1992). Intrinsic, extrinsic, and amotivational styles as predictors of behavior: A prospective study. *Journal of Personality, 60*, 599–620.

Vandenberg, B. (1991). Is epistemology enough? An existential consideration of development. *American Psychologist, 46*, 1278–1286.

Varela, F. J. (1979). *Principles of biological autonomy.* New York: Elsevier–North Holland.

Varela, F. J., Maturana, H. R., & Uribe, R. (1974). Autopoiesis: The organization of living systems, its characterization and model. *BioSystems, 5,* 187–196.

von Bertalanffy, L. (1968). *General systems theory.* New York: George Braziller.

Wapner, S., Ciottone, R. A., Hornstein, G. A., McNeil, O. V., & Pacheco, A. M. (1983). An examination of studies of critical transitions through the life cycle. In S. Wapner & B. Kaplan (Eds.), *Toward a holistic developmental psychology.* Hillsdale, NJ: Lawrence Erlbaum..

Webster, M., Jr., & Sobieszek, B. (1974). *Sources of self-evaluation: A formal theory of significant others and social influence.* New York: John Wiley.

Werner, H. (1948). *Comparative psychology of mental development.* New York: International Universities Press.

Westen, D. (1985). *Self and society: Narcissism, collectivism, and the development of morals.* Cambridge: Cambridge University Press.

White, R. W. (1959). Motivation reconsidered: The concept of competence. *Psychological Review, 66,* 297–333.

White, R. W. (1963). *Ego and reality in psychoanalytic theory.* New York: International Universities Press.

Wild, J. (1965). Authentic existence: A new approach to "value theory." In J. M. Edie (Ed.), *An invitation to phenomenology: Studies in the philosophy of experience* (pp. 59–78). Chicago: Quadrangle Books.

Winnicott, D. W. (1965). *The maturational process and the facilitating environment.* New York: International Universities Press.

Zuckerman, M., Porac, J., Lathin, D., Smith, R., & Deci, E. L. (1978). On the importance of self-determination for intrinsically motivated behavior. *Personality and Social Psychology Bulletin, 4,* 443–446.

The Measurement of Flow in Everyday Life: Toward a Theory of Emergent Motivation

Mihalyi Csikszentmihalyi
University of Chicago

Kevin Rathunde
University of Utah

The concept of intrinsic motivation explored in this chapter focuses on rewards emergent from the interaction of a person with his or her environment. Our approach differs from theories that look to the past for the key to motivation (those that stress the importance of drives, needs, learning, or other responses programmed in the individual) and also from theories that look to the future (those that stress the importance of goals in directing action). Instead, we are interested in what propels people to initiate or to continue an activity *because they enjoy its performance in the present.*

Theories of motivation generally neglect the phenomenology of the person to whom motivation is being attributed. They explain the reason for action in functional terms, that is, by considering outcomes rather than processes. How the person feels while acting tends to be ignored. Yet people constantly monitor and evaluate the quality of experience in the stream of consciousness, and we often decide whether to continue or terminate a given behavior sequence in terms of such evaluations. If the experience meets certain criteria and the action is rewarding in itself, we are likely to keep going, and we say that we "want to do" whatever we are doing. This is the class of behaviors we call intrinsically motivated. If the experience is not rewarding we stop the activity, or else we go on because we "have to do it," in which case the behavior is said to be extrinsically motivated.

There is a further distinction to be made within the class of intrinsically motivated actions. Some of them are rewarding because they involve sensations that our nervous system has been programmed to seek out. *Pleasure* includes positive responses to food, sex, relaxation, and the stimulation of certain chemical substances (Tiger, 1992). The other category of intrinsically motivated behavior includes emergent rewards (Csikszentmihalyi, 1985a). These are positive sensations arising from the experience of holistic involvement that follows upon concentration and skilled performance. This kind of reward we call *enjoyment,* and it is the one we shall examine further in the present chapter.

Pleasure and enjoyment, and indeed intrinsic and extrinsic motivation, are not mutually exclusive, and they can be present in consciousness at the same time. For example, a chef creating a gourmet dinner may be extrinsically rewarded because he is getting paid and admired for it. At the same time, he may get pleasure from preparing and tasting delicious food. Finally, he could enjoy the challenge of developing a new dish in a way never before prepared. Even though these three kinds of rewards are often present at the same time, and under the right conditions can reinforce each other, for the sake of clarity it is useful to consider them separately.

Flow and Emergent Motivation

Why do people perform time-consuming, difficult, and often dangerous activities for which they receive no discernible extrinsic rewards? This was the question that originally prompted one of us into a program of research that involved extensive interviews with hundreds of rock climbers, chess players, athletes, and artists (Csikszentmihalyi, 1975). The basic conclusion was that in all the various groups studied, the respondents reported a very similar subjective experience that they enjoyed so much that they were willing to go to great lengths to experience it again. This we eventually called the *flow* experience, because in describing how it felt when the activity was going well, several used the metaphor of a current that carried them along.

Since those early studies, a great number of replications have found the same basic set of experiential dimensions in samples as diverse as Japanese motorcycle riders, Australian sailors, Korean farmers, and Thais, as well as various European and North American groups (e.g., Csikszentmihalyi, 1990; Csikszentmihalyi & Csikszentmihalyi, 1988; Massimini & Inghilleri, 1986). In just one research center, at the Medical School of the University of Milan, over 7,000 flow interviews from around the world have been collected and analyzed. Respondents as young as 7 and as old as 87 years report their most enjoyable experiences in very much the same terms. Men and women, people high and low in socioeconomic class describe the same phenomenological state. What people do to enter the flow state varies by culture, gender, age, class, and personal inclination, but the structure of the experience appears to be remarkably similar (see Table 1).

Flow is a subjective state that people report when they are completely involved in something to the point of forgetting time, fatigue, and everything else but the activity itself. It is what we feel when we read a well-crafted novel, or play a good game of squash, or take part in a stimulating conversation. The depth of involvement is something we find enjoyable and intrinsically rewarding. This flow experience is relatively rare in everyday life, but almost everything—play and work, study and religious ritual—is able to produce it provided the conditions are conducive to deep concentration.

But what makes the optimal experience of flow possible? In the first place, a deeply involving flow experience usually happens when there are clear goals a person tries to reach, and when we get immediate and unambiguous feedback as to how well we are doing. Clear goals and feedback are readily available in most games and sports and in many artistic and religious performances, which is the reason such activities provide flow readily and are intrinsically motivating. In everyday life, and all too often on the job or in classrooms, people do not really know the purpose of their activities, and it takes them a long time to find out how well they are doing.

A second condition that makes flow experiences possible is balance between the opportunities for action in a given situation and one's ability to act. When challenges and skills are relatively high and well matched, as in a close game of tennis or a satisfying musical performance, all one's attention needs to be focused on the task at hand.

Table 1

Characteristic Dimensions of the Flow Experience

When people enjoy what they are doing, they typically report most of the following:

Clear goals: it is clear what should be done; *immediate feedback:* one knows how well one is doing.

The opportunities for action are relatively high, and they are met by one's perceived ability to act; *challenges = skills.*

Action and awareness merge; one-pointedness of mind.

Concentration on the task at hand; irrelevant stimuli disappear from consciousness, worries and concerns are temporarily eliminated.

A sense of potential *control.*

Loss of self-consciousness, transcendence of ego boundaries, a sense of growth and of being part of some greater entity.

Sense of time altered; usually time seems to pass faster.

Experience becomes autotelic—if several of the previous conditions are present, what one does becomes autotelic, or worth doing for its own sake.

Acting within doable parameters, people report a sense that, at least in principle, they are in control of the situation. This introduces another element of the flow experience: the merging of action and awareness. One becomes so concentrated and involved that the usual dualism between actor and action disappears; one feels as if on automatic pilot, doing what needs to be done without conscious effort.

This in turn results in a focusing on the present, so that thoughts and worries that in everyday life are a drain on psychic energy tend to disappear. People report forgetting their troubles because the intensity of the experience precludes ruminating on the past or the future. This further leads to a loss of self-consciousness, so that we no longer worry about how we look, or whether others like us; in fact, people often mention a feeling of self-transcendence, as when musicians listening to a particularly beautiful melody feel at one with the order of the cosmos, or dancers feel their bodies moving to the same rhythm as others. Similarly, a distortion of the sense of time is often reported, so that hours seem to pass by in minutes.

When most of these dimensions are present in consciousness, the activity tends to become autotelic—worth doing for its own sake. This is because the experience is so enjoyable that we want to repeat whatever helped to make it happen. If one experiences flow in scuba diving, one will want to dive again so as to have a similar experience. If one gets into the flow state by solving a mathematical problem, one will seek out more problems to solve.

Why Is the Flow Experience Rewarding?

Of course, we must still explain why people prefer to experience flow in different activities. One popular explanation has been that the enjoyment derived from apparently self-rewarding activities really occurs because they are a disguised release for repressed desires. For example, people play chess as a substitute for expressing aggressive impulses, especially of an Oedipal nature (Fine, 1967; Jones, 1931). Another explanation holds that those who engage in dangerous sports like hang gliding or rock climbing have peculiar personality traits that drive them to seek sensation (Zuckerman, 1979). Such accounts that offer "deep" reasons in the personality makeup of the actor are often on the mark in explaining why a person chooses one activity rather than another to experience flow, but they tend to miss the forest for the trees in that they fail to recognize the common subjective state that underlies the various activities and accounts for why they are rewarding.

Another explanation of why some individuals are drawn to rock climbing and others to chess is provided by the concept of interest. Although this concept has a long history in psychology (e.g., Dewey, 1913; James, 1890/1950), its link to motivation has been rediscovered only recently (Renninger, Hidi, & Krapp, in press; Rathunde, in press a,b; Schiefele, 1991). A person is predisposed to become involved in an activity either because of previous positive feelings associated with it or because value has been attributed to it—both of these constituting *individual interest* (Schiefele, 1992); or the person may be predisposed by *situational interest*, if the activity produces enjoyable stimulation (Hidi, 1990).

Whatever the original motivation for playing chess, or playing the stock market, or going out with a friend, such activities will not continue unless they are enjoyable—or unless they are motivated by extrinsic rewards. Castration anxieties, the need for taking risks and seeking sensation, interest, and other similar constructs could be the distal causes for intrinsically motivated behavior. But flow seems to be the proximal cause, and its reality is amply confirmed by subjective experience.

More recent explanations for why people keep engaging in activities for their own sake refer to the addiction that results when certain activities— such as jogging, or gambling, or playing music—release endorphins that stimulate the pleasure centers of the brain. According to this perspective, intrinsic motivation can be reduced to a chemical dependence connected to certain stimuli. This argument, however, begs the question in that it fails to explain why these particular activities resulted in the release of endorphins in the first place. It is rather clear by now that endocrine secretion and other physiological changes affecting the nervous system are not always—or even usually—the causes of mental processes. They are just as often the consequences. That intrinsic rewards must be mediated by neurophysiological processes is beyond question; this, however, does not mean that intrinsic motivation can be explained by resorting to neurophysiological accounts.

Almost every activity seems to be able to produce flow. Some, such as games, sports, artistic performances, and religious rituals, are created expressly to promote the experience. But in everyday life flow experiences are reported more frequently in the context of work, family interaction, and driving a car than in leisure activities (Csikszentmihalyi & LeFevre, 1989), provided that work, family life, and so on provide the necessary conditions, such as a balance of challenges and skills.

The phenomenology of flow further suggests that we enjoy a particular activity not because this has been previously *programmed* in our nervous system, but because of something *discovered* through interaction. It is commonly reported, for instance, that a person is at first indifferent or bored by a certain activity, such as listening to classical music or using a computer. Then, when the opportunities for action become clearer or the individual's skills improve, the activity begins to be interesting and finally enjoyable. It is in this sense that the rewards of these types of intrinsically motivating activities are "emergent" or open ended. This is an important conclusion, because it suggests that the rewards available to motivate human behavior are not finite and zero-sum. On the contrary, a very broad range of activities could become intrinsically rewarding if the proper conditions were present.

The dimensions of experience reported when an activity is enjoyable suggest why flow is intrinsically rewarding. The sensation of being fully involved, performing at the limits of our potential, is apparently highly desirable. This is especially true in contrast with much of everyday life, where we cannot act with total involvement because the opportunities for action are too few or too many, unclear, confusing, or contradictory. Many jobs, for instance, consist of repetitive actions that require little concentration; therefore the worker's attention begins to wander. In this state of split attention a person begins to wish for more desirable things to do or begins to ruminate on unpleasant thoughts. In either case the present situation is devalued, and we experience boredom or frustration. In comparison with this all-too-frequent condition of everyday life, the total involvement of flow is experienced as enjoyable.

In fact, our studies over the years suggest that when attention is not focused on a goal, the mind typically begins to be filled by disjointed and depressing ideation. The normal condition of the mind is chaos. Only when involved in goal-directed activity does it acquire order and positive moods. It is not accidental that one of the worst forms of punishment is to place a person in solitary confinement. Only those who can discipline their attention without recourse to external structures can survive such a situation. The rest of us need either an involving activity or a prestructured package of stimuli such as a book or a television program to keep our minds from unraveling (Kubey & Csikszentmihalyi, 1990).

But why should full immersion in a challenging activity be so enjoyable? The answer requires a distal explanation that must remain tentative and speculative. The same holds true for explaining why the much better understood rewards of eating and sexuality are experienced as pleasurable. For these rewards the proximal mechanisms are known, but the distal ones also remain speculative. The best distal explanation of why food and sex are pleasurable is that animal species that find pleasure in activities necessary for survival have a better chance surviving (Burhoe, 1982; Cabanac, 1971; Tiger, 1992). Presumably hominids for whom eating and sex were not such a big deal produced relatively fewer offspring and were eventually replaced by humans on whose chromosomes these behaviors had been accidentally connected with pleasurable sensations.

In a similar vein, it is plausible to assume that humans who experience a positive state of consciousness when they use their skills to the utmost in meeting an environmental challenge will have a decided selective advantage. The connection between flow and enjoyment may have been a fortuitous genetic accident, but once it occurred, it would make the individuals who had it much more likely to be curious, to explore, to take on new tasks and develop new skills. And this proactive approach, motivated by the enjoyment in facing challenges, might have had such a positive survival value that with time it spread to most of the human population.

Conversely, the negative feelings of boredom and frustration we experience when not totally involved seem to function like the thermostat that triggers the furnace to function. Boredom directs us to seek new challenges, and anxiety suggests we develop new skills; the net result is that the organism is forced by these negative feelings to grow in complexity. Or to put the same idea in more positive terms, the flow experience acts as an attractor that motivates people to take on greater challenges and improve their skills so as to avoid the less desirable phenomenological states of boredom and anxiety. This situation might be genetically determined: "The motivational portions of the brain, particularly the hypothalamus, have functional characteristics relevant to the apparent chronicity of human dissatisfaction. Animal experiments on the lateral hypothalamus suggest . . . that the organism's chronic internal state will be a vague mixture of anxiety and desire—best described perhaps by the phrase 'I want,' spoken with or without an object for the verb" (Konner, 1991, p. 119). It is because it provides an alternative to this chronic state of internal dissatisfaction that flow is experienced as such a positive state. And its long-term effects are also positive in that evolution is likely to favor organisms motivated to escape anxiety and desire.

However, it is time to abandon these speculative reflections about why flow is enjoyable and return to the safer ground of phenomenology, where the data are. At this level it seems clear that when the conditions of flow are present, people tend to report an optimal state that they desire to experience again. Aristotle already realized that enjoyment was the result of achieving excellence in an activity (MacIntyre, 1984). Dante expressed it well over six hundred years ago: "In every action . . . the main intention of the agent is to express his own image; thus it is that every doer, whenever he does, enjoys the doing; because everything that is desires to be, and in doing the doer unfolds his being, enjoyment naturally follows" (Dante Alighieri, 1317/1921, bk. I, chap. 13; translated by M. C.).

In terms of the work of contemporary scholars, flow has many similarities to Maslow's concept of self-actualization (1968), White's notion of competence (1959), deCharms's concept of personal causation (1968), Bandura's effectance motivation (1977), Deci and Ryan's autonomy (1985), Amabile's findings on intrinsic motivation (1983), and the influential concept of optimal arousal formulated by Hebb (1955) and further developed by many others (e.g., Apter, 1989; Berlyne, 1960; Fiske & Maddi, 1986). Our contribution differs mainly in that it focuses more on what happens in the ongoing stream of consciousness and less on the subjective or objective outcomes the experience might serve.

The Measurement of Flow

Many profound and interesting ideas in psychology end up making little difference in the development of the domain because they cannot be measured. Many others fall by the wayside beause the measuring instrument ends up distorting or trivializing the underlying idea. Therefore it became very important to find a way to operationalize flow so as to make it amenable to measurement without robbing the concept of its complexity and richness.

Originally we obtained accounts of the flow experience through interviews in which respondents were asked to describe how they felt when their favorite activity (e.g., chess for dedicated chess players, basketball for outstanding basketball players) was going well. The answers were then content analyzed and coded. This open-ended qualitative approach is still the best at the start of any new investigation, because a good interview gives a contextualized, holistic, integrated account of the flow experience and its place in a person's life.

Interviews are time consuming, however, and yield data that are difficult to code and compare. So the next step in our investigations was to develop a more focused Flow Questionnaire. This instrument consists of a series of quotations taken from earlier interviews describing the flow experience; for example: "My mind isn't wandering. I am not thinking of something else. I am totally involved in what I am doing." Respondents are asked if they have ever felt like that. If they say yes, they are asked how often, and asked to describe the activity that would produce such an experience. In this way readily quantifiable data about flow can be easily collected. Some examples of research using the Flow Questionnaire are reported in Csikszentmihalyi and Csikszentmihalyi (1988) and in Csikszentmihalyi, Rathunde, and Whalen (1993).

Even more quantifiable data can be obtained by using a variation of the Flow Scales first used in a doctoral dissertation by Pat Mayers (1978). These scales use ten or more items derived from the flow model and ask respondents to rate a target activity in terms of these scales. For example, to find out how close to a flow experience studying math is for a given student, we can ask the person to rate "studying mathematics" along ten scales such as "I am involved" or "I know how well I am doing," with possible answers running from 1 (not at all true) to 10 (very true). Again, the usefulness of these scales can be assessed from studies reported in Csikszentmihalyi and Csikszentmihalyi (1988) and in Csikszentmihalyi, et al. (1993).

These ways of measuring flow can be applied to many important research questions, and their results can be very illuminating. In order to get more precise indications of the intensity and frequency of flow experiences in everyday life, however, a more finely calibrated method for obtaining data was necessary. It is for this reason that over the years we developed what came to be known as the experience sampling method, or ESM.

The ESM is a method for obtaining repeated self-reports from normal, everyday life. It consists in providing respondents with an electronic pager and a booklet of self-report forms (ESFs) and asking them to fill out a page of responses whenever the pager signals. Typically eight signals will be sent each day for a week, yielding up to 56 records for each respondent. Each ESF contains information about time, location, activity, content of thought, and companionship. It also contains semantic differential and Likert scales describing the quality and intensity of various moods, motivations, cognitive effort, self-esteem, and so forth. Information about the validity and reliability of the ESM can be found in Csikszentmihalyi, Larson, and Prescott (1977); Csikszentmihalyi and Larson (1987); Hormuth (1986); Wheeler and Reis (1991); and Larson and Csikszentmihalyi (1983), as well as in monographs based on the method (e.g., Csikszentmihalyi & Csikszentmihalyi, 1988; Csikszentmihalyi & Larson 1986; Csikszentmihalyi et al., in press; Kubey & Csikszentmihalyi, 1990).

Many variations on the basic method are possible. For instance, internally programmed watches or pocket computers can be used to generate the signals. The items in the ESFs can be changed according to the goals of the study. Instead of intensive signaling for one week, it is possible to signal less frequently for longer periods. In one case followed by Fausto Massimini and his group in Milan, a respondent (who is a well-known poet) has been filling out ESFs for one week every two months for over two years. The same group has administered the ESM to seven members of a climbing expedition a month before the expedition started, for three weeks in the Himalayas during the climb itself, and then again one month after the party returned from India. This one study generated over 8,000 completed ESF self-reports, each one containing over 40 variables.

The experience sampling method was originally developed to study the frequency, intensity, and context of flowlike experiences in everyday life. It turned out to be a powerful method for gathering important data about a great number of social and psychological issues. Because the responses are given at random times during the day, the ESM is able to give accurate estimates of behaviors, thoughts, and subjective states as they occur in normal, everyday life. For instance, a single study of 107 working adults who gave over 6,000 responses, conducted in 1976, yielded publications about the experience of freedom in everyday life (Csikszentmihalyi & Graef, 1980), the experience of television viewing (Csikszentmihalyi & Kubey, 1981; Kubey & Csikszentmihalyi, 1990), the experience of leisure (Graef, Csikszentmihalyi, & McManama Gianinno, 1983), the relation between energy consumption and well-being (Graef, McManama Gianinno, & Csikszentmihalyi, 1981), the experience of self-awareness (Csikszentmihalyi & Figurski, 1982), and the flowlike characteristics of work versus leisure (Csikszentmihalyi & LeFevre, 1989). The extreme versatility of the ESM makes it an exceptionally economical research tool: although the collection and the analysis of the data are very time consuming, the yield of any study that uses the ESM is potentially enormous. In this context, however, we are going to focus exclusively on how the ESM can be used to study flow in everyday life.

Flow Activities in Adolescence

To illustrate the relative frequency of flow in various everyday activities, we shall report some data from a soon to be published longitudinal study of talented teenagers (Csikszentmihalyi et al., 1993). The question this study addressed was, Why do some talented teenagers keep developing their talents whereas others give up the effort? Do teenagers who experience flowlike states when working in their talent areas keep developing their talents further? We followed 210 high-school freshmen for four years, and in the first year of the study they all responded to the ESM for one week. The question to be addressed here is, In what activities of daily life do these teenagers most frequently find flow? Because these adolescents were nominated by their teachers as having unusual talent in math, science, art, and music, it would be inappropriate to generalize to all adolescents from this study. We are presenting these data primarily as an indication of how flow can be operationalized with the ESM and what sorts of findings one can look for with this method.

The first issue to be decided is which ESM responses should be used to represent flow. The convention we have adopted over the years is to use two items included in every pager response—challenges of the activity and skills in the activity—scored on a 10-point scale. As we saw earlier, high challenge matched by skills is one of the most often mentioned conditions for flow to occur. Therefore *a flow response can be operationalized as one in which a person scores both of these scales above his or her personal average for the week* (Massimini & Carli, 1988; Csikszentmihalyi & LeFevre, 1989), or *when he or she scores both of these scales above the group's average* (Csikszentmihalyi et al., 1993). Both ways of measuring flow lead to similar results.

Of course this convention is a very liberal one. It is possible to define flow much more narrowly, for example, as a response that is at least one standard deviation above the mean on both variables, or as one where the standardized challenge and skill scores are exactly the same or within a few decimal places of each other. Figure 1 shows one often-used model for determining flow, based on eight "channels" instead of four quadrants. Naturally if one operationalizes flow in terms of eight channels instead of four quadrants, fewer instances of flow will be found. Just as we can change the magnification of a microscope to see smaller details instead of more organic

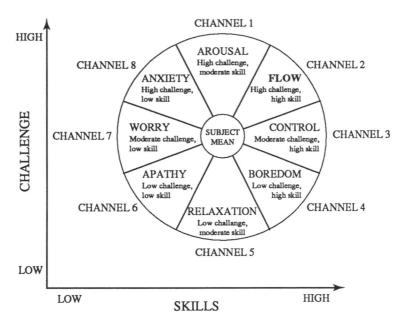

FIGURE 1: A model for the analysis of experience. Perceived challenge is on the ordinate, perceived skill is on the abscissa.

connections, so we can change the definition of flow depending on whether we want to study the more intense and rare forms of it or its less intense but more frequent manifestations in everyday life.

When the "above average on skill and challenge" definition of flow is adopted, ESM responses can be divided into four groups: (1) those in which both challenges and skills are above the person's weekly average (Flow); (2) those where skills, but not challenges, are above the group average (Boredom); (3) those in which challenges, but not skills, are above average (Anxiety); (4) those in which both challenges and skills are below average (Apathy). Table 2 shows how often teenagers report being in one of these four quadrants while engaged in the most frequent daily activities.

Looking at the first column, we see that the highest proportion of flow is reported in extracurricular school activities (such as band, theater, and athletic events). Exactly half of these 146 responses were in the flow quadrant. Very close are leisure activities involving sports and games; almost half of these 80 events were in the flow

DEVELOPMENTAL PERSPECTIVES ON MOTIVATION

Table 2

Adolescents' Percentages in Flow, Boredom, Anxiety,
and Apathy Quadrants While Doing Various Activities

Type of Activity	High Skill, High Challenge	High Skill, Low Challenge	Low Skill, High Challenge	Low Skill, Low Challenge
	Flow	Boredom	Anxiety	Apathy
Productive				
Classwork	30.5	13.7	40.9	14.9
Homework	39.8	9.1	43.1	7.9
Studying for exam	33.3	4.4	52.2	10.0
Extracurricular	50.7	8.9	31.5	8.9
Job	38.4	26.3	20.2	15.2
Leisure				
Socializing	18.7	33.9	17.5	29.9
Sports and games	48.8	2.5	41.3	7.5
Watching television	7.7	50.6	3.6	38.0
Listening to music	11.8	44.1	8.8	35.3
Reading (nonschool)	21.2	42.9	8.7	27.3
Thinking	21.8	35.1	17.6	25.6
Hobbies	41.9	16.3	28.5	13.4
Other leisure	13.0	44.4	13.0	29.6
Maintenance				
Eating	9.3	49.7	8.2	32.7
Personal care	13.9	41.2	12.0	32.9
Transportation	9.2	49.1	7.4	34.4
Chores and errands	12.2	42.8	17.1	27.9
Resting	4.7	53.4	8.2	33.6
Looking for something	10.9	29.7	20.3	35.2
Other maintenance	12.3	37.4	15.1	35.2

Note: Approximate number of ESM signals in each activity: classwork = 1,729; homework = 758; studying for exam = 90; extracurricular = 146; job = 99; socializing = 1,105; sports and games = 80; watching television = 686; listening to music = 102; reading (nonschool) = 231; thinking = 262; hobbies = 172; other leisure = 54; eating = 364; personal care = 517; transportation = 393; chores and errands = 222; resting = 232; looking for something = 128; other maintenance = 179.

quadrant. It is interesting, however, that nearly 40% of the 758 episodes of homework were also in flow, as were almost one-third of the 1,729 times these students were involved in classwork at school. By contrast, fewer than 8% of the 686 episodes of watching television were in flow by this definition.

Boredom characterized about half of the responses given when the adolescents were resting, watching television, eating, or traveling. On the other hand, only 2% of sports, 4% of studying for exams, and 9% of homework and of extracurricular activities fell into that category. Students tended to rate themselves in the anxiety quadrant in scholastic activities and in sports and games, but not when using media (television, music, reading), resting, and using transportation. Apathy, like boredom, was typical of media use and maintenance activities like resting, transportation, eating, and personal care. It seems clear that daily life alternates between activities characterized by boredom and apathy and those that are potentially anxiety inducing. Occasionally teenagers can do things that have the attributes of intrinsically rewarding pursuits—such as sports and games, hobbies, and extracurricular activities.

Flow and the Quality of Experience

But is the experience when a person is in a flow situation—when challenges and skills are both high—really intrinsically rewarding? Does the quality of experience differ in the four quadrants of the model? Table 3 gives one example: it shows how teenagers rate themselves in terms of happiness in the twenty most frequent daily activities, depending on which of the flow quadrants they happen to be in at the moment of response. In 11 of the 20 activities, whether or not a person is in flow (by our very liberal definition) makes a significant difference. In seven of these 11 cases, the most positive mood is reported in the flow quadrant. In three activities, the happiest experience is reported in the boredom quadrant—when doing homework and preparing for exams, students are happier with a surfeit of skills rather than just enough to balance challenges. Apparently, in activities that are usually anxiety producing, boredom is preferable to flow. There is one activity in which students report being happiest in the anxiety quadrant, and that is reading. Perhaps reading is seen as basically such a safe activity that teenagers prefer it when the challenges outdistance their skills. When an activity is generally boring, anxiety may be preferable to flow. Happiness is never highest in the apathy quadrant.

The *overall* quality of experience is always highest in the flow

DEVELOPMENTAL PERSPECTIVES ON MOTIVATION

Table 3

Adolescents' Percentage of Happiness by Flow Quadrant

Type of Activity	High Skill, High Challenge	High Skill, High Challenge	Low Skill, Low Challenge	Low Skill, Low Challenge	F
Productive					
Classwork	5.0	4.9	4.6	4.6	12.2**
Homework	4.7	4.9	4.4	4.5	5.0**
Studying for exam	5.1	5.3	4.1	4.3	5.5**
Extracurricular	5.4	5.2	5.0	4.8	1.6
Job	5.4	4.9	4.4	4.4	3.6*
Leisure					
Socializing	5.5	5.4	5.1	5.0	8.4**
Sports and games	5.8	6.0	5.1	5.0	1.9
Watching television	5.2	4.8	4.6	4.6	3.9**
Listening to music	5.1	4.9	3.9	4.7	1.1
Reading (nonschool)	4.5	4.7	5.3	5.0	2.8*
Thinking	4.9	4.7	4.4	4.2	2.3
Hobbies	5.3	4.7	4.9	4.7	1.9
Other leisure	6.1	5.0	4.3	5.1	1.9
Maintenance					
Eating	5.0	5.1	4.8	5.1	0.5
Personal care	5.2	4.8	5.0	4.8	2.2
Transportation	5.1	4.9	4.7	4.5	4.0**
Chores and errands	5.3	4.9	4.7	4.6	2.8*
Resting	4.4	4.6	4.4	4.1	2.5
Looking for something	5.6	4.8	4.4	4.9	2.7*
Other maintenance	5.3	5.4	4.8	4.7	3.2*

Note: Approximate number of ESM signals in each activity: classwork = 1,729; homework = 758; studying for exam = 90; extracurricular = 146; job = 99; socializing = 1,105; sports and games = 80; watching television = 686; listening to music = 102; reading (nonschool) = 231; thinking = 262; hobbies = 172; other leisure = 54; eating = 364; personal care = 517; transportation = 393; chores and errands = 222; resting = 232; looking for something = 128; other maintenance = 179.

*$p < .05$. ** $p < .01$.

quadrant, or in the flow channel if an eight-channel model is used to operationalize flow. This is true for adolescents from different cultures (Carli, Massimini, & Delle Fave, 1988; Csikszentmihalyi & Wong, 1991); as well as working adults (Csikszentmihalyi & Le-Fevre, 1989) and working mothers (Wells, 1988a, 1988b). Figure 2 shows the average level of three dimensions of self-esteem fitted into an eight-channel model (see Figure 1). Two of the three dimensions of self-esteem are highest in the flow channel. The third, "How satisfied I am with how well I am doing," peaks in the boredom channel—apparently, satisfaction with one's performance is highest when skills are greater than challenges. But "How good I feel about myself" and "How well I am living up to others' expectations" are significantly greater when high skills are matched with challenges.

Not every dimension of experience is most positive in the flow channel. Some— for instance, the level of concentration, creativity, and involvement—are highest in the arousal channel (1); others, like satisfaction, strength, and control, are highest in the control channel (3). But experience in the flow channel is consistently optimal in the sense that it combines the best consequences of using skills and confronting challenges. The quality of experience in channel 2 is never significantly less than that in channels 1 and 3, whereas channel 3 is significantly lower than channel 1 in concentration, creativity, and involvement, and channel 1 is significantly lower than channel 3 in satisfaction, strength, and control.

The Flow Experience and Growth of the Self

These findings confirm the theoretical expectation: flow is rewarding because it offers the most complete expression of one's potential—a personal peak performance. Any activity can become intrinsically rewarding when a person begins to recognize opportunities for action in it, challenges that will stretch the ability to respond. Intrinsic motivation follows from the realization that one is growing in complexity as a result of matching one's skills to difficult challenges.

Although during the flow experience people typically forget themselves and are oblivious to the usual demands of the ego, paradoxically the self tends to emerge stronger and more confident afterward. For example, a violinist playing a solo at her personal best cannot afford to think about how well she is doing, about the audience's reaction, or about how her hair looks. Any distraction would result in split attention, cause a momentary decrease in the level of her effective skills, and thus eventuate in a musical mistake. But after the performance is concluded, when complete concentration is

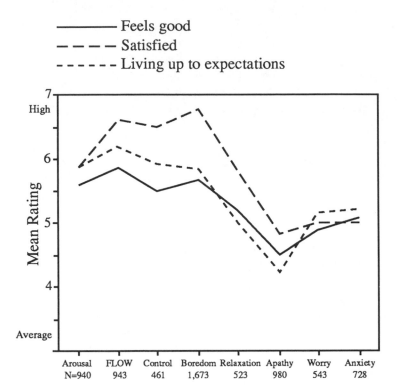

FIGURE 2: Components of self-esteem in the challenge/skill channels. "Feeling good about self," "Satisfied with how well I am doing," and "Living up to others' expectations." Sample of 210 talented adolescents, total of 6,791 self-reports.

no longer necessary, self-awareness will reappear in consciousness. Reflecting on her successful performance, the violinist will realize that her skills have met a new challenge. This in turn will result in a more *complex* self-concept, one that includes greater skills and the mastery of a higher level of challenges than the self before the performance.

Figure 3 shows the consequences of flow over time in making possible the growth of the self. Let us suppose that a man decides to start playing tennis for the first time. In the beginning he is likely to enjoy just hitting the ball with the racket any which way; in terms of the diagram in Figure 3, he would be in the position designated A1. But this level of enjoyment is very unstable; it cannot be experienced

The Measurement of Flow in Everyday Life

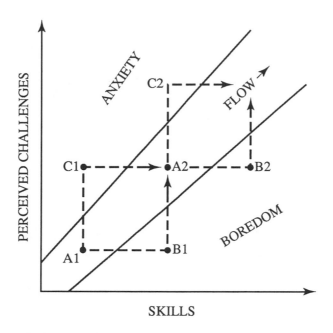

FIGURE 3: The dynamics of flow.

for long. Our man may be confronted by a better player, in which case his challenges would suddenly increase, and he would find himself outside the flow channel in C1. Or his skills would slowly increase through practice, in which case just hitting the ball at random would no longer be enjoyable; in that case he would leave the flow channel and find himself in boredom, at B1.

Now, neither C1 nor B1 is enjoyable. The would-be tennis player would like to enjoy himself again and return to the flow channel. But he can no longer return to A1 and have fun. Once outside the flow channel, the only way to return to it is by increasing complexity. The way back from C1 involves acquiring greater skills; the way back from B1 requires higher challenges. The new point of balance, A2, is more complex than the earlier one at A1. It includes higher skills and higher challenges. In fact, after reaching A2, playing at the level of A1 would no longer be flow, but an experience of apathy. However, A2 is not a permanent destination either. Sooner or later a new challenge presents itself, and our tennis player will either experience anxiety in C2 or will improve and start getting bored with the accustomed competition in B2. At that point the only way to recapture enjoyment is to move up even higher in the diagonal of flow.

Intrinsic motivation acts like a ratchet on the development of personal capacities. A person who has experienced flow will want to experience it again. But the only way to do so is by taking on new or greater challenges or by developing more skills. In a sense, a person is forced to become more complex in order to avoid anxiety and boredom. Or, to put it another way, the attraction of the intrinsic rewards of flow pulls us forward into development.

Studies with adults (Wells, 1988a, 1988b; Wells & Csikszentmihalyi, in preparation) and adolescents (Csikszentmihalyi et al., 1993) have shown that the amount of time people spend in the flow quadrant is positively related to the strength of their self-concepts. For instance, mothers who spent more time in flow were very significantly more likely to rate their parental competence higher, and they had higher self-esteem on the Rosenberg scale (Wells, 1988a, p. 335).

Of course, such association does not tell us anything about causation. It is possible that more competent, more self-assured individuals have more numerous flow experiences, and that it is self-esteem that causes flow rather than the other way around. Probably both causes are in effect at the same time, in a mutually reinforcing feedback loop. The kind of within-person fluctuations in self-esteem illustrated in Figure 2 do show that whenever a person is in flow, the level of self-esteem increases; over time, it makes sense to assume that frequent flow will result in a higher overall level of self-esteem. But only longitudinal studies will be able to confirm the exact process of causation.

The Consequences of Flow

THE DEVELOPMENT OF TALENT

The one longitudinal study in which it is possible to see causal relations involves the research with talented teenagers. These 210 young people were given the ESM when they were at the beginning of their high school career. Four years later we measured how far they were still committed to pursuing their talent. For this analysis

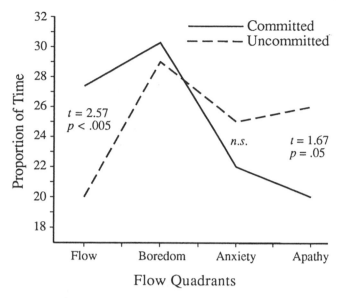

FIGURE 4. Time spent in flow quadrants for the entire week by students who four years later were and were not committed to their talent.

we shall call "committed" those teenagers who at the end of high school were clearly intending to practice their talent in college and beyond; who were spending more time on developing their talent than they did at the beginning of high school; and whose teachers felt they had lived up to their expectations. Only 46 students met these stringent criteria; the remaining were classified as "uncommitted." Figure 4 shows how much time these two groups of students had spent in the four flow quadrants four years earlier, when they completed the ESM at the beginning of high school.

As Figure 4 shows, students who at 17 years of age were still committed to developing their talent had been spending significantly more time in flow at age 13 and less time in apathy. These figures apply to their entire week's experience. But does it matter in what activities flow was experienced? Figures 5 and 6 answer that question. Figure 5 shows that in watching television the quality of experience for both the committed and the uncommitted students was almost identical. Neither group was in flow more than 5 percent of the time when watching television, and both were equally often in the regions of boredom and apathy. However, in school-related

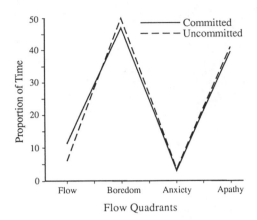

FIGURE 5. Time spent in flow quadrants while watching television by students who four years later were and were not committed to their talent.

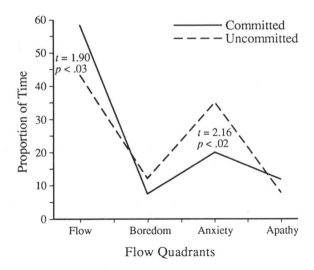

FIGURE 6. Time spent in flow quadrants while working in talent areas by students who four years later were and were not committed to their talent.

activities like classwork and homework, significant differences appear (Figure 6). Students who were still committed four years later spent significantly more time in flow while doing schoolwork and significantly less time in the region of anxiety. Interviews also confirmed that in each talent area, students who reported enjoying talent-related activities were very much more likely to keep developing their talents. For instance, students who found doing math more flowlike were significantly more committed to becoming mathematicians than those who did not, after controlling for mathematical abilities and other potentially confounding variables (Csikszentmihalyi et al., 1993). It seems that intrinsic rewards are indeed strong motivators for developing difficult personal skills. It is also important to note that the ESM can pinpoint with precision the activities in which intrinsic rewards matter (e.g., studying vs. television viewing).

CLINICAL APPLICATIONS OF FLOW

One important potential application of the ESM and the flow model involves therapeutic applications. The most developed strategy is the one used at the medical school of the University of Milan. Essentially, the ESM is administered to patients at the beginning of therapy and used as a diagnostic instrument. What activities, what situations of everyday life are associated with the most flow for this person? With the most anxiety? Based on the patient's profile, a therapeutic intervention strategy can then be custom designed. If the patient is almost always alone but enjoys the rare occasions when other people are around, the therapist may try to find out what prevents the patient from socializing more and at the same time may try to find ways to increase the patient's exposure to people in unthreatening settings—for instance, by suggesting joining a voluntary organization or special interest group.

Finally, the ESM is used as an evaluative tool, to monitor patients' progress. One week on the ESM every two months provides specific information about changes in the patients' life-style and subjective well-being. Successful therapy typically shows decrease in time alone spent in passive pursuits, increasing involvement in a variety of new activities, a steady increase in the frequency of flowlike experiences (high in challenges and skills), and improvement in self-concept and in the quality of experience (Delle Fave & Massimini, 1992; Massimini, Csikszentmihalyi, & Carli, 1987).

The variety of diagnostic and therapeutic uses of the ESM in conjunction with the flow model of optimal experience is suggested in the current volume edited by DeVries (1992), titled *The Experience of Psychopathology.* Marten DeVries, who heads a community psychiatric hospital in the Netherlands, has succesfully rehabilitated even chronic schizophrenics by finding out their most enjoyable activities, then trying to increase their frequency and intensity. For instance, a woman hospitalized for over a decade as a chronic schizophrenic reported being somewhat happy only twice during the week of the ESM: both times she was cutting her fingernails. This information provided a clue to her therapist, who had her trained as a manicurist. The patient took eagerly to the training, was released in the community under supervision, hung a shingle on her door, and went on manicuring in reasonable content.

A more generalized application of these principles is included in the new model for occupational therapy advanced by Johnson and Yerxa (1989). Their point is that a physically and psychologically healthy life must include a meaningful occupation, that is, a rule-bound, goal-directed activity over which a person has control—in short, a flow activity.

These clinical applications are nothing but common sense, based on the assumption that if we know more precisely what is intrinsically rewarding to a person and find ways to broaden the scope of intrinsic rewards in everyday life, then that person's subjective reality is going to improve. It may be useful to remember Karl Popper's definition of science as "common sense writ large" (Popper, 1959, p. 22). The power of the ESM consists in magnifying objective and subjective details of everyday life that would otherwise remain invisible. And the flow model makes it possible to order these details into meaningful patterns that make positive interventions possible.

Social Context and Personality Development

To this point we have emphasized the importance of motivation that emerges from activities enjoyed in the present. This focus on momentary experience, however, does not exclude more traditional questions about individual differences and social influences. On the contrary, focusing on the stream of consciousness provides new perspectives on how individual differences may affect motivation and how socialization may influence the quality of experience.

Although it does not require a drastic change in thinking to move from other theories focused on, for instance, the past learning of motives to a perspective that weights heavily the importance of momentary experience, a subtle yet consistent shift in emphasis is necessary. Where it might be asked, "What type of environment leads children to internalize goals and to see themselves as self-directed rather than other-directed?" a more experience-centered question would ask, "What type of experiences must an environment provide for children to pursue their goals with full involvement?"

An example of how questions can change when focusing on emergent processes is illustrated by the following anecdote from an undergraduate class on parent-child relationships. The class was discussing why fathers, despite recent trends encouraging more paternal involvement, were still relatively unmotivated to engage in child care. The first answers volunteered by the students conformed to typical nature versus nurture explanations: fathers are not biologically prepared to respond to infant signals; and fathers are not socialized to internalize child care as a goal. In motivational terms, such reasoning parallels theories that explain motives in terms of programmed biological drives or learned goals that direct future action.

Such perspectives, it was agreed, helped to explain fathers' lack of involvement, but they did not tell the whole story for one puzzled student. "Despite gender differences and social expectations for men," she commented, "fathers seldom get the opportunity to find out whether they like taking care of an infant." She went on to tell about a friend, hospitalized for complications resulting from childbirth, and her husband, who was burdened with the challenge of taking care of the baby. To his surprise he came to enjoy the job and still takes an active role in child care (along with his wife, who is fully recovered). From this student's perspective, biology and social expectations were not the deciding factors. What seemed important were the opportunity for action afforded by the particular circumstances of the family (the mother's ill health and the encouragement she gave her husband) and the fact that this particular man seemed to thrive on challenge in many aspects of his professional and private life.

This story illustrates how new questions about the influence of social and personality processes can arise when focusing on emergent motivation. Whether socialization predisposes a person to be motivated by particular goals is less important than whether actual conditions in the social context both provide and support an opportunity for action. The genotype of a person (or a particular trait) that predisposes a specific range of behaviors is less important than the person's flexibility in engaging unforeseen challenges with full involvement.

The first step toward this change of perspective involves realizing the developmental importance of autotelic experiences such as flow. After this step, a number of provocative questions follow. Exploring such questions prompted Rathunde to initiate research aimed at identifying characteristics of an "autotelic context" (a social context that promotes intrinsically motivated behavior) and understanding how such contexts may prepare an individual to find intrinsic motivation when unforeseen challenges arise (Rathunde, 1989a, 1989b).

Autotelic contexts were investigated in our longitudinal study of talented teenagers. Given the assumption that flow experiences lead to the growth of talent (a hypothesis that has now received some support), we asked, How do families create contexts that promote flow and intrinsic motivation in teenagers? Since we posed that question, progress has been made toward understanding how families foster and develop children's intrinsic motivation.

Interpersonal Processes and the Dynamics of Intrinsic Motivation

It is seldom asked how families support intrinsic motivation, yet a number of developmental perspectives suggest this might be a theoretically meaningful question. Since intrinsic motivation is likely to occur along with many other positive outcomes in the course of a child's development (e.g., it may be correlated with competence, ego development, or self-esteem), theories that provide some insight on families and on healthy child development in general are likely to add important information about the optimal context for intrinsic motivation as well. Thus, before summarizing our own work in this area, we will first present a link between previous theories and the dynamics of intrinsic motivation.

The flow model simplifies the dynamics of intrinsic motivation: the experience of boredom makes the decision to increase challenges more likely, and feelings of anxiety signal the need to increase skills. This view is consistent with models of optimal arousal that emphasize increasing or decreasing stimulation in order to find a physiological optimum (Apter, 1989; Berlyne, 1960; Fiske & Maddi, 1961). Common to both these lines of research, then, is an underlying dialectical logic suggesting that both comfort and stimulation are sometimes desirable and that the oscillation between these states is essential for motivation. Too much of one or the other overwhelms the dialectical tension, leading to negative experiential consequences and an impasse in the growth of the self.

The first conceptual bridge between theories of intrinsic motivation and family influences on child development is made possible, we believe, by identifying dialectical themes comparable to the one just discussed. In other words, perspectives that suggest families must negotiate some ongoing balance between poles related to comfort and stimulation are likely to be helpful in thinking about the social context of intrinsic motivation.

Freud (1933) articulated the first modern developmental perspective that implied a need for balance. In his theory of the id, ego, and superego he suggested that parents' poor timing in indulging or restricting children could damage their ability (or the ego's ability) to negotiate between the impulsive id and the demanding superego. Inappropriate indulgence (e.g., at the oral stage) or inappropriate restrictiveness (e.g., at the anal stage) could result in uninhibited gratification (the id's dominance over the superego) or repressed feelings (the superego's dominance over the id). Although the analogy to optimal arousal dynamics is not to be taken literally, the implication of Freud's theory is that parenting can affect children's ability to regulate their own arousal.

A more specific connection can be made between optimal arousal theories and attachment theories (Rathunde & Csikszentmihalyi, 1991a). Influenced in large part by Bowlby (1969), researchers have investigated the interactive behaviors between mothers and infants on a microanalytic level. Field (1985) suggests that the attachment between a mother and an infant, or between any two individuals, is based on both stimulation (e.g., the possibility of novelty, play, or exploration), and comfort (e.g., the possibility for soothing, understanding, or support). Overstimulating or understimulating mothers can disrupt the formation of secure attachments (Isabella & Belsky, 1991). Thus if a caretaker cannot successfully negotiate a balance of comfort and stimulation, an infant's over- or underarousal can lead to psychic disorganization and problems with later self-regulation of arousal.

Just as a young child needs security and support in order to enjoy exploration and play (Ainsworth, Bell, & Stayton, 1971), so do teenagers (Rathunde & Csikszentmihalyi, 1991a). Trust allows infants, as well as teenagers, to leave security behind and go off to explore their environment. This is a perspective that is receiving growing support from researchers on adolescent development: paradoxically, "dependence" allows independence to be expressed (see, for instance, Grotevant & Cooper, 1983).

One final theory relevant to optimal experience is Baumrind's (1989) notion of authoritative parenting. Authoritative parents are both responsive and demanding; they avoid the extremes of being permissive (responsive but not demanding) and authoritarian (demanding but unresponsive). The balance created in authoritative homes seems to provide an optimal environment for the growth of children's competence. From an experiential perspective, one might surmise that parents who are always accommodating their children, providing security without asking anything of them, would create a relatively bland environment in terms of stimulation and arousal; on the other hand, parents who are full of demands and expectations, without much understanding and empathy, are more likely to create aversive, anxiety-producing environments.

In sum, several influential developmental theories that are relevant for thinking about healthy child development are likewise relevant for thinking about creating optimal contexts for emergent motivation and flow. The connection is the common dialectical theme emphasizing the tension between complementary "opposites." In other words, the interplay between the family dimensions of indulgence and restriction, responsiveness and demandingness, and so on, is presumably related to the interplay of states of boredom and anxiety. Each theory suggests that the experiential effects of "imbalance" in the home can seriously impair children's later ability to self-regulate arousal.

Despite these apparent similarities, it is impossible to know for certain whether these theories are relevant for explaining variations in the quality of children's experience. They were not constructed to answer experience-centered questions because they did not consider momentary experience important, nor did they assign central importance to emergent processes. To know whether family interaction affects quality of experience requires a reorientation of perspective and a method (such as the ESM) that can systematically reveal changes in the relevant dimensions of subjective experience. The study of talented adolescents provided the opportunity to ask new questions within an experiential framework, and to test them with experience sampling. We turn next to the specifics of the study.

COMPLEX FAMILIES AND OPTIMAL EXPERIENCE

With the assumption that flow promotes healthy development and the growth of talent, we asked two questions: How do families create contexts that encourage flow and intrinsic motivation in teenagers? Do such contexts prepare them to find intrinsic motivation in new situations? To begin answering these questions we constructed a questionnaire to assess what "opportunities" families must provide so that teens can experience flow more often.

It is clear that flow marks an experience characterized by a combination of experiential states that usually are mutually exclusive: enjoyment and intense concentration. Others have studied intrinsically rewarding experiences under different names, such as interest, and have identified the same "unlikely" occurrence in consciousness. For instance, Dewey (1933, p. 286) defines this "ideal mental condition" of interest as being "playful and serious at the same time," thus avoiding the extremes of fooling (just playfulness) and drudgery (just seriousness) (see also Rathunde, 1992). Schiefele (1991) similarly characterizes interest in terms of an emotion-cognition combination, such that interested people have positive feelings that accompany involvement with objects of value to their goals. Clearly, then, to create a context for interest or flow a family must provide teenagers with opportunities to experience playfulness, enjoyment, and positive feelings, along with concentration, seriousness, and goal-directedness (Rathunde, 1991; Rathunde & Csikszentmihalyi, 1991b).

The Complex Family Questionnaire (CFQ) was designed to measure two orthogonal dimensions in families—referred to as *integration* and *differentiation*, reflecting a systems theory orientation—that were presumably relevant for generating the unlikely combination of experiences. Questions such as, "If you are feeling depressed, or having a problem, do others notice even though you may not say anything about it?" and "Does your family have traditional ways of celebrating birthdays and holidays that enhance a feeling of family togetherness?" highlighted teenagers' opportunities for integration and support from other family members. Differentiation in the family, or the existence of opportunities for teenagers to pursue their "own" unique goals, was assessed with such questions as, "Is it hard to find privacy at home and escape into your 'own world' when you need to?" and "Are family members serious and intense when engaged with things that are important to them?"

This combination of opportunities to integrate and differentiate within the family was expected to provide the widest range of flexibility in regard to arousal regulation. Family integration provides teenagers with opportunities to find comfort and support. Hypothetically, teens who could count on these things at home would experience "better" moods, would be happier and more energetic, than those who often waste energy in divisive conflicts with parents. Family differentiation, on the other hand, creates a more demanding, stimulating, and challenging environment. Teenagers would have more occasion to define themselves in relation to parents and other family members who have their own strong interests, opinions, and goals (e.g., through observation, opportunities for action, or perhaps dialogue).

The combination of both dimensions offers the widest range of opportunities to cope with feelings of boredom and anxiety. Families that are able to provide this combination are complex in the sense of affording an environment where usually polarized experiences are both present. For instance, a child who is anxious about too many challenges in school will get support and reassurance, whereas a child lulled by the monotony of boring classes will get stimulation and challenge.

To see whether family complexity had any effect on children's quality of experience, talented students were first divided into four family types based on the CFQ (complex, integrated, differentiated, and simple), and then their responses were tabulated into two clusters. To measure the "playful" dimension of experience, which was expected to correlate with family integration, responses to the mood items happy, cheerful, alert, and excited were selected. To measure the "serious" dimension expected to correlate with family differentiation, the following variables were chosen: living up to own expectations, living up to others' expectations, importance of the activity to oneself, and importance of the activity to one's overall goals.

Table 4 reports standardized scores while teenagers were at home ("0" represents the group's average score on the given variable when the respondent was at home). The findings confirmed that teenagers from complex families reported the highest momentary experiences as well as the highest involvement with long-term goals. Compared with those whose families were neither integrated nor differentiated, teens from complex families reported significantly higher affect, potency, expectations, and involvement with important goals ($p < .001$ in each case).

Follow-up analyses confirmed the expected effects of integration and differentiation. Teens from integrated (but not differentiated) families reported better momentary experience but no greater sense of involvement with long-term goals. The opposite was true for teenagers from families that were only differentiated. Only teenagers from families that had both dimensions reported experiences that were both playful and serious.

Even stronger differences betweeen teens from these four family types emerged when they were at school doing productive work. Those from integrated families tended to be relatively happier, those from differentiated families were more concentrated and involved, and those from complex families were both happy and involved when doing scholastic work.

Looking at the week of paging in its entirety, adolescents from complex families also reported flow experiences more frequently than those from any other family type. When contrasting the percentage of time teenagers spent in the various flow quadrants for the week of paging, those from complex families reported a significantly higher amount of flow ($p < .01$: complex 28.8 percent; integrated 16.5 percent; differentiated 22.5 percent; simple 20.8 percent), as well as less apathy ($p < .05$: complex 17.8 percent; integrated 28.7 percent; differentiated 21.7 percent; simple 26.9 percent). Since each percent-

DEVELOPMENTAL PERSPECTIVES ON MOTIVATION

Table 4

Adolescents' Quality of Experience at Home (%)
(Average "Z" Scores)

ESM Variables	Complex (N = 689)[a]	Integrated (N = 559)	Differentiated (N = 392)	Simple (N = 765)	ANOVA F	t-value[b]
Affect and activation						
Happy/cheerful	.28	.10	−.30	−.08	10.2****	3.9***
Alert/excited	.37	−.03	−.44	−.05	20.1****	4.7***
Expectations and goals						
Living up to own/						
others' expectations	.56	−.18	−.02	−.10	21.2****	6.7***
Importance to self						
and overall goals	.33	−.32	−.14	−.04	15.0****	4.0***

Note: All results reported in the table are also significant ($p < .05$) when first aggregating by individual student and then comparing family means. Follow-up ANOVAs (high/low integration by high/low differentiation) on affect and activation showed main effects for family integration (not differentiation), and further analyses of expectations and goals showed main effects for differentiation (not integration). [a]Number of ESM signals. [b]Contrast between complex and simple family groups. *** $p < .001$. **** $p < .0001$.

age point for a week of paging corresponds to approximately one hour of time, a rough estimate suggests that teens from complex families spend about 9 hours more each week in high skill, high challenge conditions conducive to flow; in addition, they spend approximately 8 1/2 hours less per week in circumstances more likely to produce apathy.

THE GROWTH OF AUTOTELIC PERSONALITY

An autotelic person is one who finds intrinsic motivation and flow in everyday life (Csikszentmihalyi, 1990; Logan, 1988), who finds enjoyment in activities that would make others bored or anxious. Like the father discussed earlier who learned to like child care, the autotelic person is more complex in the sense of being less predictable and more able to recognize and take on new challenges. This may involve an ability to regulate one's own arousal levels—to calm oneself and boost one's confidence when overchallenged and underskilled and to open up to new stimulations and take risks when underchallenged and overskilled.

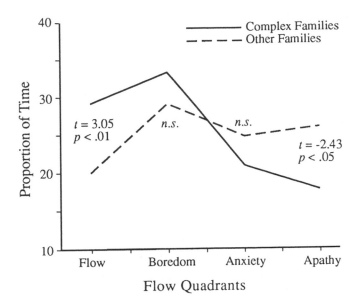

FIGURE 7. Time spent in flow quadrants for the entire week by students from complex families versus other family types.

Are adolescents from complex families more likely to become autotelic persons? That teens from complex families experienced more flow and optimal experience even away from home (at school) does suggest the association of family background and autotelic traits, but the association does not prove a causal connection. Another piece of correlational evidence comes from the use of the Jackson's (1984) Personality Research Form (PRF) in the talent study. Two superordinate factors from this questionnaire (which contains 20 personality scales in total) captured our notion of the characteristics of autotelic persons: "orientation toward work" (the sum of the scales Achievement and Endurance) and "orientation toward aesthetic/intellectual stimulation" (the combination of the scales Sentience and Understanding). High scorers on the "work" factor perceive themselves as active, capable, persistent, and industrious; high scorers on the "stimulation" factor see themselves as receptive to many forms of experience, observant, curious, and seeking understanding in many areas of knowledge.

The combination of both dimensions would depict someone

with autotelic qualities: qualities of being energetic and capable along with an orientation toward remaining open to new stimulation and challenge. Not surprisingly, these two factors distinguished our talented sample from "normal" teenagers. In other words, both males and females in the talented sample scored significantly higher on achievement, endurance, sentience, and understanding than did their peers in a normative comparison group (Csikszentmihalyi et al., 1993).

Scores on the work and stimulation factors were split at their respective medians to create high and low "active" teenagers, and high and low "receptive" teens. These two groups were then compared on how they perceived their family environments (Rathunde, 1988). Results showed that high active teens reported more integration ($p < .05$) but not more family differentiation; and high receptive ones reported more differentiation ($p < .05$) but not more family integration. Furthermore, a chi-square analysis showed that a greater percentage of the complex family group manifested the high active, high receptive profile that distinguished the talented group from normal adolescents, and more teens with below-average scores on both personality dimensions were from families with low integration and low differentiation.

Teenagers with relatively more autotelic personalities (those high on both the active and the receptive dimensions) reported more flow during the week than teens with any other profile ($p < .01$); in addition, they reported approximately 9 hours less a week in the apathy condition ($p < .01$).

In sum, though it is impossible to answer with certainty whether complex families "socialize" a more autotelic personality, teens from such families do report more optimal experience in contexts outside their homes, and their personality profiles suggest they may be more flexibile in modulating their arousal (they seem able to work with confident persistence and are also able to seek new challenges and stimulation). A plausible causal argument would be that a child's habitual ways of paying attention to the self and to the environment are "constructed" within the family context (Reiss, 1981). In other words, years of repeated opportunities for integration within the family (leading to repeated experiences of feeling happy and energetic, etc.) and numerous opportunities for differentiation (and thus experiences of being focused on challenging goals) would eventually develop corresponding "structures of attention" (or personality orientations) in children. These orientations would then positively affect their ability to regulate arousal and to optimize experience in new settings.

Is Flow Always a Good Thing?

Up to now we have emphasized the positive contributions of flow to human development and well-being. It is important to note, however, that though flow is an optimal state of consciousness and might well lead to personal growth and to the evolution of the species, it does not necessarily have positive ethical or social consequences. There are two dangers inherent in flow: one is that the enjoyment can become addictive, the other that it can be experienced in antisocial contexts. When lacking other opportunities for action, or if deprived of sufficient skills, people will seek flow in destructive activities like violence, gambling, excessive risks, or drugs (Csikszentmihalyi & Larson, 1978). Many people derive intrinsic rewards from crime or warfare; that they enjoy it does not justify their actions. It is for this reason that Aristotle, who recognized that excellence of action is the highest form of happiness, believed that nevertheless it was not the highest human good—given that it was possible to excel in actions that were harmful to the self and to the community (MacIntyre, 1984, p. 160).

Flow is a form of energy that spurs people to action. Like other forms of energy, from fire to nuclear fission, it can be used for both positive and destructive ends. As Plato noted long ago, the main task of education is to teach young people to "find pleasure in the right things." Of course we may be less certain than Plato what these "right things" are, but at least it is easier to agree on what things are undesirable—random violence, unwanted pregnancy, excessive use of drugs—and these will be chosen by default if no better alternatives are available. If there are not enough pro-social activities to enjoy, young people will be driven to find flow wherever they can, which usually means in antisocial contexts.

Taking a broader view, one might ask if the constant spur of desire for novelty and challenge might not have turned from an asset into a liability for the human species. Unless we are more discriminating in the kind of challenges we choose, we might needlessly endanger our survival. For example, Robert Oppenheimer, one of the physicists who developed the atomic bomb, frequently referred to the work on nuclear fission as his "sweet problem" (Csikszentmihalyi, 1985b). As Thomas Kuhn described it in *The Structure of Scientific Revolutions* (1970), every scientific problem is sweet to the scientist who works on it, regardless of its consequences. It would be indeed ironic, or perhaps a case of cosmic poetic justice, if the human race was destroyed by the same mechanism that made it so powerful: the enjoyment of meeting a new challenge.

Conclusions

Human behavior can be explained in terms of a variety of motivations. Some of these are based on rewards built into the nervous system by stimulus-response connections established during the long evolutionary past. Instincts, drives, and needs denote the organism's readiness to experience pleasure when stimulation conducive to its survival, comfort, and selective fitness is available. In contrast, *emergent motivation* refers to the rewards the organism experiences when it is involved in an activity that is intrinsically enjoyable because it helps develop potential not already programmed into its repertoire of responses.

The flow experience describes the phenomenology of emergent motivation. Whenever people are able to match their abilities to opportunities in the pursuit of a clear goal, receive immediate feedback, be able to concentrate and eliminate distractions, the feeling they experience is so rewarding that they will seek to repeat it again and again. Innate skills, temperament, interests, and dispositions help determine which pursuits are likely to provide this sort of experience; however, almost any activity can become intrinsically rewarding if performed under such conditions.

One of the main tasks of an applied psychology of motivation is to find ways to generate flow in socially desirable areas such as learning, work, family interaction, community involvment, and helping each other—especially in comparison with destructive ones such as drugs, violence, or warfare, which some turn to when life becomes too boring or frustrating. In addition to improving the structure of desirable activities, people must also be helped to get in touch with their genuine experiences, instead of being swayed by public opinion and commercial messages. Currently we tend to assume that enjoyment comes only from expensive leisure, consumption, and entertainment. Work and family life are seen as consisting of drudgery, to be avoided if possible. Few people realize that the most intensely enjoyable experiences come from the least expected sources—from a job well done, from a stimulating conversation. By better understanding the dynamics of emergent motivation, psychologists could make a substantial contribution to improving the quality of life.

REFERENCES

Ainsworth, M. D. S., Bell, S. M., & Stayton, D. J. (1971). Individual differences in strange-situation behavior of one-year-olds. In H. R. Schaffer (Ed.), *The origins of human social relations.* London: Academic Press.

Amabile, T. M. (1983). *The social psychology of creativity.* New York: Springer.

Apter, M. J. (1989). *Reversal theory: Motivation, emotion, and personality.* London: Routledge.

Bandura, A. (1977). Self-efficacy: Toward a unifying theory of behavioral change. *Psychological Review, 84,* 191–215.

Baumrind, D. (1989). Rearing competent children. In W. Damon (Ed.), *Child development today and tomorrow.* San Francisco: Jossey-Bass.

Berlyne, D. E. (1960). *Conflict, arousal, and curiosity.* New York: McGraw-Hill.

Bowlby, J. (1969). *Attachment and loss: Vol. 1. Attachment.* London: Howarth.

Burhoe, R. W. (1982). Pleasure and reason as adaptations to nature's requirements. *Zygon, 17,* 113–131.

Cabanac, M. (1971). Physiological role of pleasure. *Science, 173,* 1103–1107.

Carli, M., Massimini, F., & Delle Fave, A. (1988). The quality of experience in the flow channels: Comparison of Italian and US students. In M. Csikszentmihalyi & I. Csikszentmihalyi (Eds.), *Optimal experience: Psychological studies of flow in consciousness.* New York: Cambridge University Press.

Csikszentmihalyi, M. (1975). *Beyond boredom and anxiety.* San Francisco: Jossey-Bass.

Csikszentmihalyi, M. (1985a). Emergent motivation and the evolution of the self. In D. Kleiber and M. H. Maehr (Eds.), *Motivation in adulthood* (93–119). Greenwich, CT: JAI Press.

Csikszentmihalyi, M. (1985b). Reflections on enjoyment. *Perspectives in Biology and Medicine, 28,* 469–497.

94

Csikszentmihalyi, M. (1990). *Flow: The psychology of optimal experience*. New York: Harper/Collins.

Csikszentmihalyi, M., & Csikszentmihalyi, I. (Eds.). (1988). *Optimal experience: Psychological studies of flow in consciousness*. New York: Cambridge University Press.

Csikszentmihalyi, M., & Figurski, T. (1982). Self-awareness and aversive experience in everyday life. *Journal of Personality, 50*, 15–28.

Csikszentmihalyi, M., & Graef, R. (1980). The experience of freedom in daily life. *American Journal of Community Psychology, 8*, 401–414.

Csikszentmihalyi, M., & Kubey, R. (1981). Television and the rest of life. *Public Opinion Quarterly, 45*, 317–328.

Csikszentmihalyi, M., & Larson, R. (1978). Intrinsic rewards in school crime. *Crime and Delinquency, 24*, 322–335.

Csikszentmihalyi, M., & Larson, R. (1986). *Being adolescent: Conflict and growth in the teenage years*. New York: Basic Books.

Csikszentmihalyi, M., & Larson, R. (1987). Validity and reliability of the experience-sampling method. *Journal of Nervous and Mental Disease, 175*, 526–536.

Csikszentmihalyi, M., Larson, R., & Prescott, S. (1977). The ecology of adolescent activity and experience. *Journal of Youth and Adolescence, 6*, 281–294.

Csikszentmihalyi, M., & LeFevre, J. (1989). Optimal experience in work and leisure. *Journal of Personality and Social Psychology, 56*, 815–822.

Csikszentmihalyi, M., Rathunde, K., & Whalen, S. (1993). *Talented teenagers: A longitudinal study of their development*. New York: Cambridge University Press.

Csikszentmihalyi, M., & Wong, M. (1991). The situational and personal correlates of happiness: A cross-national comparison. In F. Strack, M. Argyle, & N. Schwartz (Eds.), *The social psychology of subjective well-being* (193–212). London: Pergamon Press.

Dante Alighieri (1921). *De monarchia*. Florence: Rostagno. (Originally published 1317)

deCharms, R. (1968). *Personal causation: The internal affective determinants of behavior*. New York: Academic Press.

Deci, E. L., & Ryan, R. M. (1985). *Intrinsic motivation and self-determination in human behavior*. New York: Plenum Press.

Delle Fave, A., & Massimini, F. (1992). The ESM and the measurement of clinical change: A case of anxiety disorder. In M. De Vries (Ed.), *The experience of psychotherapy* (280–289). Cambridge: Cambridge University Press.

De Vries, M. (Ed.). (1992). *The experience of psychopathology: Investigating mental disorders in natural settings*. Cambridge: Cambridge University Press.

Dewey, J. (1913). *Interest and effort in education*. Boston: Riverside.

Dewey, J. (1933). *How we think*. Boston: D. C. Heath.

Field, T. (1985). Attachment as psychobiological attunement: Being on the same wavelength. In M. Reite & T. Field (Eds.), *The psychobiology of attachment and separation*. New York: Academic Press.

Fine, R. (1967). *The psychology of the chess player.* New York: Dover.

Fiske, D. W., & Maddi, S. R. (1961). *Functions of varied experience.* Homewood, IL: Dorsey Press.

Freud, S. (1933). *New introductory lectures on psychoanalysis.* New York: W. W. Norton.

Graef, R., Csikszentmihalyi, M., & McManama Gianinno, S. (1983). Measuring intrinsic motivation in everyday life. *Leisure Studies, 2,* 155–168.

Graef, R., McManama Gianinno, S., & Csikszentmihalyi, M. (1981). Energy consumption in leisure and perceived happiness. In J. D. Claxton et al. (Eds.), *Consumers and energy conservation* (47–55). New York: Praeger.

Grotevant, H. D., & Cooper, C. R. (Eds.). (1983). *Adolescent development in the family.* San Francisco: Jossey-Bass.

Hebb, D. O. (1955). Drives and the C.N.S. *Psychological Review, 62,* 243–254.

Hidi, S. (1990). Interest and its contribution as a mental resource for learning. *Review of Educational Research, 60,* 549–571.

Hormuth, S. (1986). The sampling of experiences in situ. *Journal of Personality, 54,* 262–293.

Isabella, R. A., & Belsky, J. (1991). Interactional synchrony and the origins of infant-mother attachment: A replication study. *Child Development, 62,* 373–384.

Jackson, D. (1984). *Personality research form manual.* Port Huron, MI: Research Psychologists Press.

James, W. (1950). *The principles of psychology.* New York: Dover (Originally published 1890)

Johnson, J. A., & Yerxa, E. J. (Eds.). (1989). *Occupational science: The foundation for new models of practice.* New York: Haworth Press.

Jones, E. (1931). The problem of Paul Morphy. *International Journal of Psychoanalysis, 12,* 1–23.

Konner, M. (1991). Human nature and culture: Biology and the residue of uniqueness. In J. J. Sheehan & M. Sosna (Eds.), *The boundaries of humanity* (103–124). Berkeley and Los Angeles: University of California Press.

Kubey, R., & Csikszentmihalyi, M. (1990). *Television and the quality of life.* Hillsdale, NJ: Lawrence Erlbaum.

Kuhn, T. S. (1970). *The structure of scientific revolutions.* Chicago: University of Chicago Press.

Larson, R., & Csikszentmihalyi, M. (1983). The experience sampling method. In H. T. Reis (Ed.), *Naturalistic approaches to studying social interaction.* San Francisco: Jossey-Bass.

Logan, R. D. (1988). Flow in solitary ordeals. In M. Csikszentmihalyi & I. Csikszentmihalyi (Eds.), *Optimal experience: Psychological studies of flow in consciousness* (172–183). New York: Cambridge University Press.

MacIntyre, A. (1984). *After virtue.* Notre Dame, IN: University of Notre Dame Press.

Maslow, A. (1968). *Towards a psychology of being.* New York: Van Nostrand.

Massimini, F., & Carli, M. (1988). The systematic assessment of flow in daily experience. In M. Csikszentmihalyi & I. Csikszentmihalyi (Eds.), *Opti-*

mal experience: Psychological studies of flow in consciousness (266–287). New York: Cambridge University Press.

Massimini, F., Csikszentmihalyi, M., & Carli, M. (1987). The monitoring of optimal experience: A tool for psychiatric rehabilitation. *Journal of Nervous and Mental Disease, 175,* 545–549.

Massimini, F., & Inghilleri, P. (Eds.). (1986). *L'esperienza quotidiana: Teoria e metodi d'analisi.* Milan: Franco Angeli Editore.

Mayers, P. (1978). *Flow in adolescence and its relation to the school experience.* Unpublished doctoral dissertation, University of Chicago.

Popper, K. (1959). *The logic of scientific discovery.* New York: Harper Torchbooks.

Rathunde, K. (1988). Family context and optimal experience. In M. Csikszentmihalyi and I. Csikszentmihalyi (Eds.), *Optimal experience: Psychological studies of flow in consciousness.* New York: Cambridge University Press.

Rathunde, K. (1989a). The context of optimal experience: An exploratory model of the family. *New Ideas in Psychology, 7,* 91–97.

Rathunde, K. (1989b). *Family context and optimal experience in the development of talent.* Unpublished doctoral dissertation, University of Chicago.

Rathunde, K. (1991, April). *Family influences on student interest and talent development.* Paper presented at the American Educational Research Association annual meeting (Motivation in Education Program), Chicago.

Rathunde, K. (1992). Playful and serious interest: Two faces of talent development in adolescence. In N. Colangelo, S. G. Assouline, & D. L. Ambroson (Eds.), *Talent development: Proceedings from the 1991 Henry B. & Jocelyn Wallace National Research Symposium on Talent Development.* Unionville, NY: Trillium Press.

Rathunde, K. (in press a). The role of interest in the development of talent. In A. Krapp & M. Prentzel (Eds.), *Interesse, Lernen und Leistung: Neuere Ansätze einer pädagogisch-psychologischen Interessenforschung.* Münster: Aschendorff.

Rathunde, K. (in press b). The experience of interest: A theoretical and empirical look at its role in adolescent talent development. In P. Pintrich & M. Maehr (Eds.), *Advances in motivation and achievement* (Vol. 8). Greenwich, CT: JAI Press.

Rathunde, K., & Csikszentmihalyi, M. (1991a). Adolescent happiness and family interaction. In K. Pillemer & K. McCartney (Eds.), *Parent-child relations throughout life.* Hillsdale, NJ: Lawrence Erlbaum.

Rathunde, K., & Csikszentmihalyi, M. (1991b). *Interest and talent development: A longitudinal study of talented teenagers and their families.* Manuscript submitted for publication.

Reiss, D. (1981). *The family's construction of reality.* Cambridge: Harvard University Press.

Renninger, K. A., Hidi, S., & Krapp, A. (Eds.). (1992). *The role of interest in learning and development.* Hillsdale, NJ: Lawrence Erlbaum.

Schiefele, U. (1991). Interest, learning, and motivation. *Educational Psychologist, 26*, 299–323.

Schiefele, U. (1992). Topic interest and levels of text comprehension. In K. A. Renninger, S. Hidi, & A. Krapp (Eds.), *The role of interest in learning and development*. Hillsdale, NJ: Lawrence Erlbaum.

Tiger, L. (1992). *The pursuit of pleasure.* Boston: Little, Brown.

Wells, A. J. (1988a). Self-esteem and optimal experience. In M. Csikszentmihalyi & I. Csikszentmihalyi (Eds.), *Optimal experience: Psychological studies of flow in consciousness* (327–341). New York: Cambridge University Press.

Wells, A. J. (1988b). Variations in mothers' self-esteem in daily life. *Journal of Personality and Social Psychology, 55*, 661–668.

Wells, A. J., & Csikszentmihalyi, M. (in preparation). *Relationship between women's variation in self-esteem and optimal experience (flow).*

Wheeler, L., & Reis, H. T. (1991). Self-recording of everyday life events: Origins, types, and uses. *Journal of Personality, 59*, 339–354.

White, R. (1959). Motivation reconsidered: The concept of competence. *Psychological Review, 66*, 297–333.

Zuckerman, M. (1979). *Sensation seeking.* Hillsdale, NJ: Lawrence Erlbaum.

NOTE: The research reported in this chapter was funded through grants from the Spenser Foundation.

Visions of Self: Beyond the Me in the Mirror

Susan Harter
University of Denver

Introduction: The Distinction Between the I-Self and the Me-Self

Imagine, for a moment, that you are gazing into a mirror and you make the following observation: I see myself, *I* see *Me*. There are two distinct aspects of self in this rather mundane experience. There is the *I*, the active *observer*, and there is the *Me* in the mirror, the Me as *observed*. Yet this distinction is hardly mundane.

Most scholars who have devoted thoughtful attention to the self, beginning with William James (1892) and George Herbert Mead (1934), have come to the conclusion that two conceptually distinct, but experientially intertwined, aspects of self can be meaningfully identified, the I-self and the Me-self. The I-self is the active *observer*, the *knower*, the information processor, as it were, the self that is the architect and *constructor* of knowledge. One such construction is the Me-self. That is, the Me-self is the self that is *known*, *observed*, the self that is *constructed*—in short the *self*-concept, our self-image, including our sense of self-esteem.

Within our Western philosophical tradition, scholars have studied how the I-self constructs, packages, protects, and enhances the Me-self, the self-concept. In this literature the self is treated as a cognitive construction whose architecture, by evolutionary design, is extremely *functional* (see Allport, 1961; Bartlett, 1932; Brim, 1976; Damon & Hart, 1988; Epstein, 1973, 1981, 1991; Greenwald, 1980;

Harter, 1983; Kelly, 1955; Lecky, 1945; Lynch, 1981; Markus, 1980; Piaget, 1965; Rogers, 1951; Sarbin, 1962). One such widely touted function is to maintain high *self-esteem*. Considerable evidence now exists that most people do exhibit a modest self-enhancing bias (Taylor & Brown, 1988).

Our own research represents an outgrowth of this Western tradition. For over fifteen years I and my colleagues have studied how the Me-self—one's self-concept—is constructed, packaged, protected, and enhanced (Harter, 1986, 1987, 1990a).

By way of an overview, I will first share that theoretical and empirical portrait with you by presenting our framework and supportive findings. But then I will ask a more searching question: What's wrong with this picture? What is wrong with this approach to the self? How, in packaging the Me-self as a marketable commodity, might we be selling ourselves short?

We need to bear in mind that from a Western perspective the I-self is typecast as a conspirator in this intrapsychic plot, since it has been commissioned not only to create the self-concept, but in many instances to *conceal* the true Me-self. But is this really the best use of the I-self's time and energy? In exploring these themes, I will conclude with the suggestion that an Eastern, Buddhist perspective might enlarge our vision of self and give the I-self its rightful due.

Mirror Images of Self

The mirror metaphor of self that I began with is not merely an analogy. Infant studies (see Bertenthal & Fischer, 1978; Harter, 1983; Lewis & Brooks-Gunn, 1979) have demonstrated that the mirror provides the developing infant with critical information about the emerging capacities and characteristics of both the I-self and the Me-self. In fact, Western entrepreneurs have capitalized on this research, touting mirrors as the experiential path to self-development for infants! A recent advertisement in a magazine for parents claims that their crib or playpen "Mirror-Mate" will accelerate a baby's development, provoking a positive sense of self.

Older children as well turn their gaze toward reflective surfaces as sources of information about the self. Adolescents seem magnetically drawn to the Me-self in the mirror, as the I-self spends hours preparing the Me-self for its entrance onto the stage where one confronts either a real or an imagined audience of peers (see Harter, 1990b). Adults are also preoccupied with evaluating the Me-self in the mirror—their self-image—primping and practicing the posture they will present to the world (see Hatfield & Sprechner, 1986). Given the creation of these self-images, we next need to inquire into the bases on which these portraits of the self are created.

On What Bases Do We Evaluate the Me-Self and Construct Our Self-Esteem?

What are the evaluative dimensions along which the Me-self is judged? What features of our self-image do we focus on? What constitutes the bases on which our self-esteem is actually formed? By self-esteem I mean the level of global regard one has for the self as a person (Harter, 1985, 1986), a definition that has much in common with Rosenberg's (1979, 1986). In developing our original model of self-esteem, we turned to two historical scholars of the self, James (1982) and Cooley (1902), for theoretical guidance. However, these two scholars put forth very different determinants of one's global sense of worth as a person.

JAMES'S FORMULATION

William James (1892), writing at the turn of the century, offered the following provocative suggestion. According to James, we do not scrutinize our every action or attribute. Rather, we focus primarily on our abilities in domains of *importance;* we attend to our performance in those domains where we aspire to success. James formalized this observation by postulating that our overall sense of self-esteem represents the *ratio* of our *successes* to our *pretensions.*

Thus, for James our metaphorical gaze into the mirror provokes us to evaluate how successful we are in domains where we have pretensions or, in less arcane language, in those areas of our lives where we aspire to be successful. If we are rewarded by a vision of ourselves as competent in domains where we want to excel, we will have high self-esteem. Conversely, if we fall short of our ideals, if we regard ourselves as unsuccessful in domains where we aspire to be competent, low self-esteem will result.

It is critical to appreciate that from a Jamesian perspective, lack of competence in domains deemed *unimportant* to the self will *not* adversely affect self-esteem. For example, you may consider yourself unathletic; but if athletic prowess is not one of your aspirations, your self-esteem will not be negatively affected. That is, you can *discount* the importance of athletics or any other domain in which success is not personally valued.

COOLEY'S FORMULATION

Charles Horton Cooley (1902), a contemporary of William James, took the mirror metaphor very seriously in his concept of the "looking-glass self." For Cooley, the self was a social construction, created by casting one's gaze into the social mirror to ascertain the opinions of significant others toward the self. As Cooley poetically observed:

> Each to each a looking glass
> Reflects the other that doth pass.

Thus others become the mirrors we gaze into for information about the self, and these opinions, the reflected appraisals of others, are incorporated as the self. From this perspective, if others hold one's self in high regard, one's own sense of self-esteem will be high. Conversely, if others have little regard for one's self, one will incorporate these opinions in the form of low self-esteem.

To summarize, in the theorizing of these two scholars, James and Cooley, we have two rather different origins of the regard in which one holds the Me-self—one's level of self-esteem. For James, self-esteem was the product of one's own evaluation of one's competence in domains that the I-self judges to be important. In Cooley's formulation of the looking-glass self, self-esteem mirrored the opinions that others held toward the self.

Our Own Research Documenting James's and Cooley's Contentions

How have we researched these formulations? How have we empirically put them to a test in the lives of children, adolescents, and adults? We embarked on this journey by first deciding to test James's formulation on the antecedents of self-esteem. However, we first needed to delineate the possible dimensions along which the Me-self is evaluated, the domains in which one perceives the self to be a success or a failure.

THE ASSESSMENT OF DOMAINS
RELEVANT TO CHILDREN'S SELF-CONCEPT

We initiated our inquiry with older children and young adolescents, aged 8 to 13, selecting five specific domains that seemed salient during this age period: Scholastic Competence, Athletic Competence, Likability by Peers, Physical Appearance, and Behavioral Conduct. One goal was to understand how adequacy in these domains affected global self-esteem, defined as the extent to which, overall, one likes oneself as a person. To address these issues, we developed an instrument titled the Self-Perception Profile for Children (Harter, 1985a).

We began by designing a new questionnaire format that would allow us to tap older children's perceptions of their competence or adequacy in each of the five specific domains, as well as their sense of global self-esteem. In Figure 1 three sample items are presented to demonstrate precisely how these evaluative judgments are obtained. The first sample item is from the Scholastic Competence domain, the second sample item is from the domain of Physical Appearance, and the third item is prototypical of our Global Self-Esteem subscale.

The questionnaire is titled "What I Am Like." The child's task is to read through an entire item—for example, "Some kids have trouble figuring out the answers in school BUT Other kids almost always can figure out the answers"—and first decide whether he or she is more like the children described in the first part of the statement or those described in the second half. After selecting which half of the statement is more like the self, the child indicates whether that description is "Sort of True for Me" or "Really True for Me." The scores in the boxes (they are not on the form the child fills out) indicate the score assigned to each choice, ranging from 4, for the most competent or adequate evaluation of the self, to a low of 1, representing

Sample Items

Really True for Me	Sort of True for Me				Sort of True for Me	Really True for Me
1	2	Some kids have *trouble* figuring out the answers in school	**BUT**	Other kids almost *always* can figure out the answers.	3	4
1	2	Some kids wish their physical appearance was *different*	**BUT**	Other kids *like* their physical appearance the way it is.	3	4
4	3	Some kids *like* the kind of *person* they are	**BUT**	Other kids often wish they were someone else.	2	1

FIGURE 1: Sample items from the Self-Perception Profile.

the least adequate evaluation. Each of the six subscales, five for the specific domains and one for global self-worth, contains several items. Scores for each subscale are averaged, resulting in a *profile* of scores across the specific domains, with a separate score for global self-esteem. It is critical to appreciate that self-esteem is *not* the sum of the specific domains. Rather, self-esteem is tapped by its own set of items that directly inquire about how much the individual likes the self as a person, overall.

A PROFILE APPROACH TO THE SELF-CONCEPT

The type of instrument we have constructed allows us to obtain a *profile* of self-concept scores across the specific domains we have tapped, as well as a separate index of the child's sense of *global self-esteem*. After examining thousands of profiles, several conclusions are apparent. The vast majority of children do *not* feel equally competent or adequate across the various domains of their lives. Most have "sawtooth" profiles in which they feel very good about themselves in some areas and less adequate in others. Moreover, two children whose profiles look very different across the specific domains can have equally high global self-esteem. For example, Child A may feel very good about his or her scholastic competence, and very poorly about athletic competence, yet have high self-esteem. A second child, Child B, may have the opposite pattern—self-perceptions of low scholastic competence but high athletic competence—and also have high self-esteem. Initially we puzzled over how such children were able to maintain high self-esteem in the face of perceptions of inadequacy in one or more domains.

Even more puzzling, however, were the profiles of children whose scores across the five specific domains were virtually identical, yet whose global self-esteem scores were very different. The profiles of Child C and Child D, depicted in Figure 2, provide such a contrast. Both children have relatively poor evaluations of their scholastic performance; they feel totally inadequate with regard to their athletic competence; however, in the other three domains, social acceptance or likability, behavioral conduct, and physical appearance, they both feel far better about themselves. Yet the global self-esteem of Child C is quite *high,* whereas the global self-esteem of Child D is very *poor.* How were these self-esteem differences to be explained, given that the domain-specific profiles of these two children looked so similar?

A TEST OF JAMES'S FORMULATION

Here is where William James came to the conceptual rescue. For James, one's sense of adequacy in a specific domain will have an impact only if success in that domain is deemed important. Applying this reasoning, one might therefore infer that Child C *does not* value scholastic or athletic competence, and therefore inadequacy in these areas does not take its toll on self-esteem. In contrast, one might infer that Child D *does* value scholastic and athletic competence, and therefore perceived inadequacy in these domains lowers the sense of global self-esteem.

To examine these inferences empirically, however, it was necessary to directly assess the importance individuals attached to success in the various domains we had tapped. Thus, the next step in our research program was to devise items to obtain *importance judgments* for each domain. Statements were written in the same format as our original items designed to tap competence or adequacy (see Figure 1). For example, in the scholastic domain an item reads: "Some kids think it is important to do well at schoolwork in order to feel good about themselves as a person BUT Other kids don't think

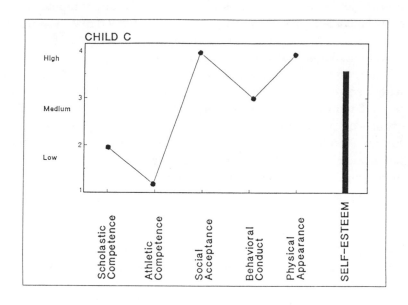

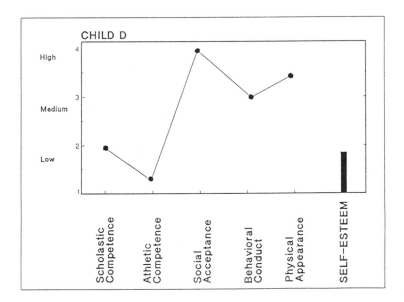

FIGURE 2: Competence/adequacy scores of two children with similar domain-specific profiles but very different levels of global self-esteem.

that how well they do at schoolwork is that important to how they feel about themselves." Children first selected the type of child that was most like them and then endorsed that statement as either Sort of True for Me or Really True for Me.

Our findings revealed precisely what James predicted. As can be seen in Figure 3, where we have superimposed each child's importance ratings on his or her judgments of competence/adequacy, Child C judged scholastic and athletic competence to be relatively unimportant. That is, Child C can *discount* the areas in which he or she is less than adequate while touting the importance of those areas in which he or she is doing well. Conversely, Child D is unable to discount the importance of scholastics and athletics, leading to a vast *discrepancy* between very high importance judgments in these two domains and relatively low competence evaluations. It is this discrepancy, then, that takes its toll on self-esteem.

The sample children were selected to illustrate the potential of James's contentions. However, we have examined this formulation more systematically among *groups* of older children and young adolescents. Numerous studies have now revealed that the findings are robust (see Harter, 1986, 1990a). The pattern is presented in Figure 4. Here we first grouped individuals into one of five categories depending on their self-reported competence in only those domains they rated as important. Thus the first group on the bottom left reported low competence in domains that they themselves judged important, with scores of from 1.0 to 1.9 (on our four-point scale). From left to right, the groups increased in perceived competence for the domains they judged important, such that the group on the far right felt the *most* competent (scores from 3.5 to 4.0) in the domains where they had aspirations for success.

The bar graph presents the average *self-esteem* for each of the five groups. Here we can clearly see that there is a very dramatic and systematic relation between one's competence in domains judged important and one's self-esteem. Those with the lowest competence levels profess to have self-esteem scores below the midpoint of the scale. Self-esteem scores increase as a function of rising competence levels, such that those who report the highest levels of competence in domains of importance report extremely high levels of self-esteem.

Converging correlational approaches reveal that the relation be-

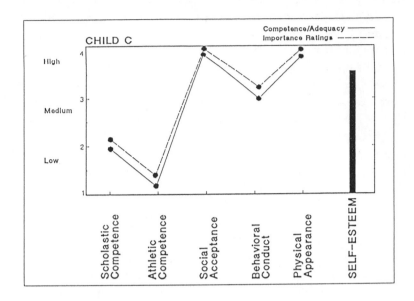

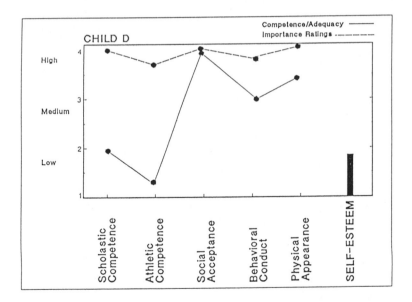

FIGURE 3: How the discrepancy between importance ratings and competence/adequacy judgments predicts self-esteem.

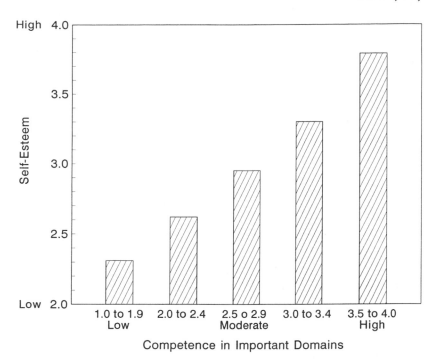

FIGURE 4: General relationship between competence in domains of importance and self-esteem.

tween competence in important domains and self-esteem ($r = .70$) far exceeds the correlation between competence in *un*important domains and self-esteem ($r = .30$). This pattern is by no means restricted to older children and young adolescents in regular classroom settings. It has been documented for both gifted and learning-disabled children, as well as among normative samples of older adolescents, college students, and adults in the world of work and family (see Harter, 1990a). Moreover, this pattern of findings is not unique to our own data but converges with other literature that has focused on the discrepancy between one's ideal and one's real self (see Glick & Zigler, 1985; Higgins, 1987, 1991; Markus & Nurius, 1986; Rosenberg, 1979; Tesser, 1988; Tesser & Campbell, 1983). As will become evident in a subsequent section, such discrepancies are predictive not only of self-esteem, but of associated affects such as depression and anxiety (Higgins, 1987, 1989).

A TEST OF COOLEY'S FORMULATION

During this testimonial to James, Cooley has been patiently waiting in the conceptual wings. Recall that his looking-glass self formulation postulates that the positive regard from significant others is the critical determinant of self-esteem. That is, the regard or esteem of others—these reflected appraisals—becomes incorporated into one's own esteem for the self.

To examine this issue directly, we first had to devise instruments through which we could assess the regard or support, particularly the approval, that one receives from significant others in one's life. For children and adolescents, the range of significant others has included parents, teachers, classmates, and close friends. Among college students we have added peers in campus organizations, and for adults in the world of work and family, we have added co-workers as well as spouses and children, if relevant.

We have written items in the same format to tap the level of approval or regard that individuals feel they are receiving from these various sources of support. A sample item designed to assess classmate support among students reads: Some kids have classmates that like the kind of person they are BUT Other kids have classmates who do not like the kind of person they are (see Social Support Scale for Children and Adolescents, Harter, 1985b). In creating such items, we can then directly examine the link between perceived regard from others and perceived regard or esteem for the self.

Summarizing across numerous studies among all the groups we have examined, spanning ages 8 to 50, we consistently obtain the pattern presented in Figure 5. Here we have grouped individuals into those reporting low levels of support, medium support, and high support from significant others and have examined their self-esteem. As predicted, those with the lowest levels of support report the lowest self-esteem, those with moderate support have moderate levels of self-esteem, and those receiving the most support hold the self in high regard. Thus, Cooley's looking-glass self model on the origins of self-esteem also appears to be clearly documented by our findings.

Moreover, our findings reveal that, taken together, James's and Cooley's formulations provide a powerful explanation for the level of self-esteem displayed by older children and adolescents (Harter, 1987). As can be seen in Figure 6, the effects of these two determi-

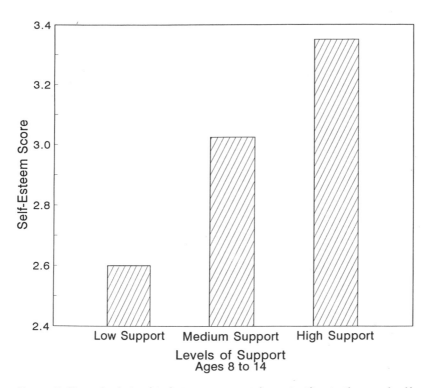

FIGURE 5: General relationship between support from significant others and self-esteem.

nants are additive. At each level of social support (representing the average of classmate and parent approval), greater competence in domains of importance leads to higher self-esteem. Similarly, at each level of competence in domains of importance, the more support one garners from classmates and parents, the higher one's self-esteem. Those individuals with the lowest self-esteem therefore are those who report both incompetence in domains of importance and the absence of supportive approval from others.

Why Should We Care about Self-Esteem?

In the past three decades considerable attention has been devoted to an analysis of the determinants of self-esteem in the lives of children and adolescents (see Coopersmith, 1963; Harter, 1986, 1987, 1990a;

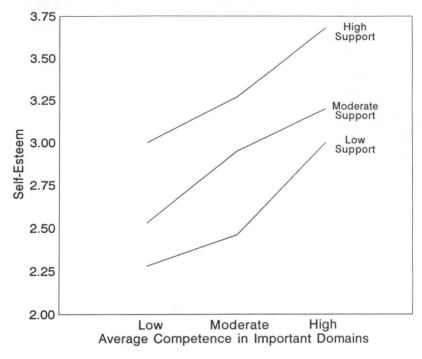

FIGURE 6: Additive model demonstrating effects of both competence in domains of importance and support from significant others.

Rosenberg, 1979, 1986; Wylie, 1979). Yet why should we be concerned about self-esteem unless we can demonstrate that it plays a role in individuals' lives—unless we can demonstrate that it performs some critical, motivational function? What are some likely candidates? What of any significance might self-esteem influence? A major candidate is one's *mood*, along the dimension of cheerful to depressed. Recent theory and research have placed increasing emphasis on cognitions that give rise to, or accompany, depression. Cognitions involving the *self* have found particular favor. There is clear historical precedent for including negative self-evaluations as one of a constellation of symptoms experienced in depression, beginning with Freud's (1968) observations of the low self-esteem displayed by adults suffering from depressive disorders. Those within the psychoanalytic tradition have continued to afford low self-esteem a central role in depression (Bibring, 1953; Blatt, 1974).

More recently a number of theorists who have addressed the

manifestations of depression in children and adolescents as well as in adults have focused heavily on cognitive components involving the self. For example, attention has been drawn to the role of self-deprecatory ideation and hopelessness in depression (Abramson, Metalsky, & Alloy, 1989; Baumeister, 1990; Beck, 1975; Hammen & Goodman-Brown, 1990; Kovacs & Beck, 1977, 1978, 1986), to attributional style (Abramson, Seligman, & Teasedale, 1986; Nolen-Hoeksema, Girgus, & Seligman, 1986; Seligman, 1975; Seligman & Peterson, 1986), and to cognitive and sociocognitive influences and self-discrepancies (Baumeister, 1990; Higgins, 1987, 1989; Kaslow, Rehm, & Siegel, 1984; McCauley, Mitchell, Burke, & Moss, 1988). Higgins's work is particularly relevant, since he finds that discrepancies between what one would *like* to be and what one *perceives* oneself to be produce dejection-related emotions such as depression.

In our own studies we consistently find that among older children and adolescents, self-esteem is highly related to affect, along a continuum of cheerful to depressed (with correlations ranging from .72 to .80). These findings are consistent with those of other investigators (Battle, 1987; Beck, 1975; Kaslow et al., 1984). Moreover, the relationship exists at all points along the continuum. Of particular interest are findings that among normative populations those older children and adolescents reporting low self-esteem consistently report depressed affect (Renouf & Harter, 1990). In clinical samples of adolescents with psychiatric diagnoses of depression, the vast majority also report low self-esteem (Harter and Marold, in press.) Thus the two causal constructs in our model—competence in domains of importance and social support—not only influence one's level of self-esteem but provoke a powerful emotional reaction that, for the child or adolescent with low self-esteem, results in a chronic mood state of depression.

The mental health implications of these findings are profound. Donna Marold and I, in collaboration with Nancy Whitesell, have embarked on a major program of research examining the implications of low self-esteem and depressed mood among adolescents in our middle and high schools (Harter & Marold, 1991, 1992). A major outcome variable is suicidal thinking. Suicidal behaviors have increased threefold over the past decade (Carlson & Cantwell, 1982; Cantor, 1987; Hawton, 1986; Pfeffer, 1988; Shaffer, 1974, 1985; Shaffer & Fisher, 1981).

Thus we have been challenged by several related questions. What provokes many youths to even consider terminating their lives? What cognitive and emotional factors conspire to convince an adolescent that life is not worth living? What role does the self-concept play in this conspiracy, this intrapsychic plot that has such a potentially tragic outcome? What features of adolescents' social support system cause them to question their worth as persons and the value of their lives?

A MODEL OF RISK FACTORS LEADING TO DEPRESSION AND SUICIDAL THINKING

In addressing these questions we have developed a model of risk factors that predispose adolescents to depression and suicidal thinking, a model that builds upon our earlier findings documenting the causes of self-esteem, based on the formulations of James and Cooley. In broad outline, Figure 7 summarizes the *sequence* of events that results in depressive reactions, including, for many, thoughts of suicide (cf. Baumeister, 1990).

Building upon James's contribution, we now know that competence in domains where success is important to the individual, as well as in domains perceived to be important to the *parents* of adolescents, is a powerful risk factor at the beginning of the chain of potential events. Equally powerful is support, in the form of approval, from two sources—parents and peers—as derived from Cooley's looking-glass self formulation. Of particular interest is the discovery by my collaborator Donna Marold that not only is level of support critical, but so is the extent to which support is *conditional* upon adolescents' meeting extremely high standards set by parents or peers.

Thus, if adolescents feel incompetent in domains important to them, as well as to their parents, and feel lack of support from peers and parents, or conditional support, the response will be hopelessness that can potentially be associated with each of these causes. These reactions in turn lead to a constellation of factors that we have labeled the "depression composite," which includes low self-esteem, depressed mood, and general hopelessness, in that the future looks bleak. This constellation of depressive symptoms is highly likely to lead adolescents to thoughts of suicide.

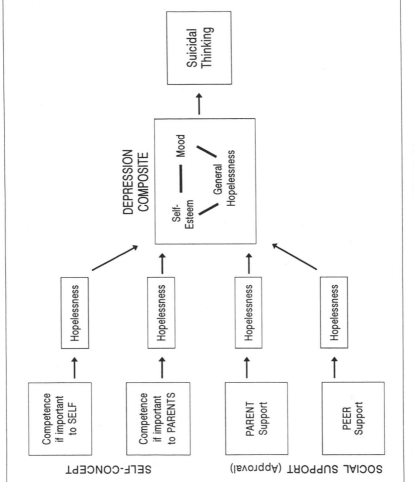

FIGURE 7: A model of risk factors predicting depression and suicidal thinking.

In several studies (see Harter & Marold, 1991) we have statistically documented these relationships, providing strong support for such a model. I would like to humanize this pattern, however, by sharing the insights of one adolescent whose poignant self-disclosure provides a cameo of the model that has evolved in our research:

> I look in the *mirror* and most days I don't like what I see. I don't like how I look, I don't like myself as a person. So I get depressed, bummed out. Plus, my family has rejected me and that makes me feel pretty lousy about myself. My mother is really on my case because I'm not living up to what she wants me to be. If I get A's in school, she's nice, and is proud of me. But if I don't, she doesn't approve of me, you could say that how she treats me is *conditional* on how I do. Mostly she tells me I am a failure, and I'm beginning to believe it. Doing well in school has always been important to me, but now I feel like I'll never amount to anything. There's no way I'll ever be able to please her; it's pretty hopeless. I can't expect anything from my family; they have totally rejected me. I don't get much support from other kids either. I probably never will because I'm an introvert so I don't even try to make friends. So a lot of the time I get depressed, really bummed out. I feel so depressed that I often think about just killing myself. Life is worthless. But so is death. So what's the use?

The pattern we have documented appears compelling. We have identified critical precursors of self-esteem and related outcomes such as depression and suicidal ideation. Moreover, there are powerful implications for *prevention* as well as *intervention*. For example, our findings suggest that intervening at the front end of the model, by influencing self-concept and social support, will have the biggest impact, since it is here that the chain of causal influences appears to begin. Thus we can intervene to improve self-esteem by helping individuals to become more competent in areas where they have aspirations, or by helping them discount the importance of domains in which high levels of success are unlikely. Self-esteem can also be improved by intervening to provide more opportunities for support and approval from significant others. Such interventions should not only enhance individuals' self-esteem, but prevent the more insidious cycles that involve hopelessness, depression, and associated suicidal thoughts and gestures that may serve as the ultimate path of escape.

What's Wrong with This Picture, with This Approach to the Self?

Many of the implications of the portrait we have painted in broad brushstrokes seem very promising. In all honesty, however, after considerable reflection, I find myself compelled to raise the following questions: What's wrong with this picture? What is wrong with this approach to the self? At this juncture it is critical to share some troubling findings that we have encountered along our empirical journey, findings we would rather have left in the dust.

IS SELF-ESTEEM ONLY SKIN DEEP? THE INEXTRICABLE LINK BETWEEN APPEARANCE AND SELF-ESTEEM

In study after study, at any developmental level we have examined, including older children, adolescents, college students, and adults in the world of work and family (Harter, 1990a), we have repeatedly discovered that self-evaluations in the domain of physical appearance are inextricably linked to global self-esteem. The correlations between perceived appearance and self-esteem are staggeringly high and robust across the life span, typically between .70 and .80. Moreover, we find this relationship to be just as high in special populations such as the intellectually gifted (Zumpf & Harter, 1991) and the learning disabled (Renick & Harter, 1991), where one might anticipate that scholastic performance would bear a stronger relation to self-esteem. The correlation between appearance and self-esteem is equally high among adolescents identified as behaviorally disruptive (Junkin, Harter, & Whitesell, 1991), exceeding the correlation between conduct and self-esteem. Among all these groups, the evaluation of looks takes precedence over every other domain as the number one predictor of self-esteem, causing us to question whether self-esteem is only skin deep. That is, the Me-self appears to be, quite literally, one's image in the mirror.

Why should one's *outer*, physical self be so closely tied to one's *inner*, psychological self? One possibility is that the domain of physical appearance is qualitatively different from the other arenas we have tapped, in that it is an omnipresent feature of the self, always on display for others or for the self to observe. In contrast, one's adequacy in such domains as scholastic or athletic competence, peer social acceptance, conduct, or morality is not constantly open to evaluation, but rather is more context specific. Moreover, one has more control over whether, when, and how such characteristics will be revealed.

Studies reveal that others begin to react to the ever-present display of the physical self when a person is an infant and toddler (Langlois, 1981; Maccoby & Martin, 1983). Those who are attractive by societal standards are responded to with more positive attention than those who are judged less physically attractive. Thus, from a very early age the physical or outer self appears to be a highly salient dimension that provokes evaluative psychological reactions that may well be incorporated into the emerging sense of one's inner self.

Clearly, a critical contributing factor is the emphasis contemporary society places on appearance at every age (see Elkind, 1979; Hatfield & Sprechner, 1986). Movies, television, magazines, rock videos, advertising, all tout the importance of physical attractiveness for males and females, glamorizing the popular role models one should emulate. An examination of women's magazines such as *Family Circle*, *Woman's Day*, and *First for Women* reveals that for women the standards are paradoxical and punishing. All of these magazines relentlessly insist that women attend fiercely to their appearance (hair, face, and particularly weight) while they simultaneously cook a vast array of fattening foods for themselves and their families! Moreover, articles and advertisements specifically preach that altering one's looks, often by invasive cosmetic overhaul, to approximate rather narrowly defined cultural stereotypes of beauty will enhance one's self-esteem.

In one issue of *Woman's Day* the feature articles depicted on the cover demand that women "walk away weight twice as fast" as well as bake "our best old-fashioned cookies," pictured in all their mouth-watering glory. In the companion issue of *Family Circle*, the feature articles include one-dish meals (with exceedingly fattening ingredients), beauty guides, and how to take off 10 pounds by Christmas! Even more appalling is a relative newcomer to the scene of women's magazines, titled *First for Women*. The feature articles listed on the cover instruct women to "take years off your face," cook "comforting one-pot meals" (for which they get "eight free recipe cards"), and "get thin doing housework." This last article includes a series of photographs in which a woman, grinning from ear to ear in sheer ecstasy, is ironing, dusting, sweeping, laundering, and vacuuming her way to fitness, beauty, and high self-esteem! It is a sad commentary on the societal nonevolution of women.

What do we know about the women, primarily homemakers, who purchase these magazines and in all likelihood feel they should religiously follow these directives? In our own research, we have learned that their self-concepts are not necessarily enhanced. We compared those wives and mothers who are full-time homemakers (with no employment outside the home) and those who are employed full time in paying jobs outside the home (Harter & Messer, 1992). We discovered that the two groups of women felt equally nurturant toward those in their care, but the differences between their self-concepts were striking. Full-time homemakers felt markedly and significantly less intelligent and less adequate in the realm of intimate relationships than did the full-time working women. Ironically, despite the advice they are getting from women's magazines to simultaneously attend to their appearance and cook gourmet meals for their families, or perhaps *because* of this barrage of idealized advice, the full-time homemakers also felt considerably worse about their physical appearance and their skills at household management than did the full-time working wives and mothers. Thus the self-concept of full-time homemakers suffers in numerous domains, including those most glorified by society.

Although the media are also increasingly emphasizing the importance of appearance for men, it appears that there is more latitude in the standards of attractiveness for men. Moreover, there is not the singular focus on looks as the pathway to acceptance and esteem that one finds for women. For men, intelligence, job competence, athletic ability, wealth, and power are all routes to positive evaluation in the eyes of others as well as the self.

The difficulty females have in meeting the cultural stereotypes

DEVELOPMENTAL PERSPECTIVES ON MOTIVATION

for appearance appears to be brought home over the course of development, the closer girls come to adopting their role as women in this society. Our own data (see Figure 8) reveal that, for females, perceptions of physical attractiveness systematically decline with grade level, whereas there is no such drop for males. In middle childhood girls and boys feel equally good about their appearance, but by the end of high school females' scores are dramatically lower than males'.

Gender differences in self-esteem also increase with development, paralleling the trajectories for physical appearance. Beginning in junior high school and continuing into high school, self-esteem is consistently lower for females than for males. As other investigators have also noted, self-perceptions of attractiveness appear to be implicated (Allgood-Merton, Lewinsohn, & Hops, 1990; Nolen-Hoeksema, 1987; Simmons & Blyth, 1987). In our own data, however, females' self-esteem does not decline as dramatically with age as does perceived physical appearance. Rather, there is another mediating factor—the perceived *direction* of the link between appearance and self-esteem.

THE DIRECTION OF THE LINK
BETWEEN APPEARANCE AND SELF-ESTEEM

The robust relationship between perceived appearance and self-esteem raised an intriguing question for us: Which comes first? Does appearance influence one's self-esteem? Does the evaluation of one's appearance precede—that is, determine—one's sense of worth as a person? Or conversely, does one's self-esteem influence the evaluation of one's appearance, such that if one feels worthy as a person, one will favorably evaluate one's looks?

We have begun to research this issue by putting the question—this choice—directly to young adolescents (Zumpf & Harter, 1989). That is, we have asked them to select which of these two options best describes the nature of the link between their appearance and their self-esteem. Our findings reveal that one group of adolescents acknowledges that their evaluation of appearance precedes or determines their sense of self-esteem, whereas an equal number endorse the opposite orientation, reporting that their sense of self-esteem determines how much they like the way they look. Converging evi-

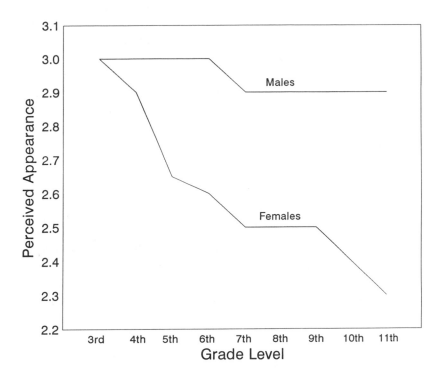

FIGURE 8: Gender differences in perceived appearance as a function of grade level.

dence indicates that those in the first group, whose appearance determines their self-esteem, also report that appearance is more important, that they are more preoccupied with appearance, and that they worry more about how they look than the group whose self-esteem precedes judgments of appearance (Harter & Waters, 1991).

Moreover, there is a particularly distressing pattern for the first group, who are basing their self-esteem on their appearance, a pattern that is more pronounced for girls. Adolescent females reporting that appearance determines their sense of personal worth feel worse about their appearance, have lower self-esteem, and also report feeling more affectively depressed than females for whom self-esteem precedes judgments of appearance (Harter & Waters, 1991; Zumpf & Harter, 1989). Thus those adolescent females espousing the Jamesian model, in which self-evaluations in domains of importance determine one's self-esteem, are more at risk for low self-esteem and associated maladaptive outcomes. Sadly, this is the orientation that is underscored by our society and by the media. The irony therefore is that endorsement of a Jamesian perspective with regard to the domain of physical appearance is a psychological liability for females in particular, undermining their evaluation of both the outer and the inner self. As we shall see next, there are dangers in tying one's Me-self closely not only to one's image in the physical mirror, but to one's image in the *social* mirror as well.

THE LIABILITIES OF THE LOOKING-GLASS SELF

We have seen how the creation of the Me-self, from a Jamesian perspective, leads many to devalue the self, given the salience of physical appearance. Our studies have also revealed that there are liabilities resulting from the construction of the looking-glass self— forming a Me-self by incorporating the opinions of significant others.

In thinking about the process through which other's opinions come to influence the self, according to Cooley's looking-glass self formulation, we were driven to ask:

Mirror, mirror on the wall,
Whose opinion is most critical of all?

Here we discovered an unsettling finding that has been replicated at every age level we have examined: older children, adolescents, college students, and adults in the world of work and family. Positive regard, in the form of approval from *peers in the more public domain*— for example, classmates, those in organizations or groups one belongs to, co-workers, and so on—is far more critical to self-esteem than is the support of close friends and family members, who presumably know one best (Harter, 1990a). To document this claim most convincingly, we have identified two groups of adolescents: those with *high classmate* support but *low close-friend* support and those displaying the opposite pattern, *low classmate* support accompanied by *high close-friend* support.

Self-esteem is extremely high (3.6 on a four-point scale) for the first group that is receiving high *public* support from classmates, even when close-friend support is low. However, self-esteem is relatively low (2.6) for those with low public support from classmates even when close-friend support is high. Thus, support for the self one presents to the world, support for one's public image, has a major impact on self-esteem. Support from close friends, as well as family members, for what is presumably one's more authentic self, however, does not have a major impact on self-esteem.

THE EFFECT OF PREOCCUPATION
WITH THE LOOKING-GLASS SELF

Although one can demonstrate a statistical relation between approval for one's public self and self-esteem, a more interesting question is whether people are psychologically aware of the link between approval and their self-esteem. More specifically, are there individuals who blatantly endorse a looking-glass model of self-esteem, who consciously acknowledge that the approval of others is critical to their own approval of self? Conversely, are there individuals who feel that approval of the *self* comes first, and that it is a prerequisite to garnering the favor of others?

In our earlier model we had postulated that approval from others preceded or determined self-esteem. However, there is reason to be cautious about inferring that the direction of the effects postulated reflects individuals' phenomenological experience of the order of these components. That is, statistical modeling procedures, applied to group data collected at any given point in time, do not necessarily simulate the psychological processes underlying the sequence in which perceptions about the self and others unfold.

Thus we addressed this question in a study with adolescents ranging in age from 12 to 18 (Harter, Stocker, & Robinson, 1992). We first asked each subject to choose between these two orientations:

If others like or approve of me (first) then I will like and approve of myself.
If I (first) like and approve of myself, then others will like and approve of me.

We found that approximately half of the adolescents endorsed the first option; that is, they acknowledged that they were operating according to the looking-glass self model in which the approval of others directly influences their approval of themselves. The remaining half opted for the second orientation, in which self-approval precedes, or will result in, approval from others.

How compelling is this pattern of choices? How do we know, given the 50–50 split in choices, that subjects are not merely responding randomly? Since subjects had to provide a description or example of how the orientation they selected was personally relevant for them, we next examined these responses, finding that most were convincing. Adolescents endorsing the looking-glass self model gave the following types of examples: "When I find that new people approve of me, I look at myself and say 'I'm not so bad,' and it makes me feel good about myself." "Usually, if other people like me as a person, then that shows that I must be a pretty good person; I care what people say about me." "Let's say I get a new haircut or new clothes; I need to have other people like it first, and then I'll like it too."

Those adolescents reporting that self-approval precedes the approval of others justified their choice by the following kinds of descriptions: "When I first came to this school, I liked myself and was confident, so that probably made other people respect me." "If you can't like the person you are first, then how do you expect other people to like you?" "I really think I must feel good about myself as a person first. Others must know that you appreciate yourself as a person. If you wait for other people to make you feel good, then you'll be waiting for a long time!"

We were next intrigued with whether these two groups differed in self-esteem, and if so, which orientation would result in greater regard for the self (see Robinson & Harter, 1991). We discovered that those who endorsed the looking-glass model, the first group who felt that approval from others preceded self-esteem, had considerably lower self-esteem (See Figure 9). Thus our findings reveal that those preoccupied with the social mirror will invariably have lower self-esteem as a result of this psychological posture. A preoccupation with the looking-glass self therefore appears not to be self-enhancing.

More recently, we broadened the range of correlates of these two orientations (Harter et al., 1992). Our findings revealed additional liabilities of the looking-glass self orientation. Those adoles-

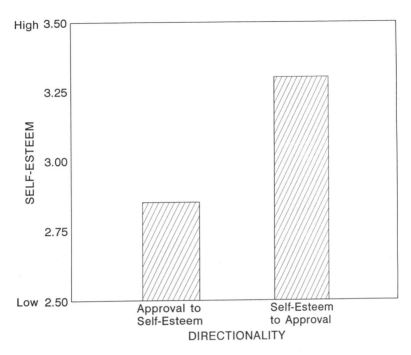

FIGURE 9: Level of self-esteem for those who report that approval from others influences self-esteem and those who report that self-esteem influences approval.

cents who acknowledged that they were basing their self-esteem on peer approval or disapproval provided descriptive accounts that focused on *negative* peer evaluations, whereas those reporting that approval of the self preceded approval of others provided very *positive* descriptions. Moreover, looking-glass self subjects reported greater preoccupation and concern with the link between approval and self-esteem than did those for whom self-esteem preceded the reactions of others. Moreover, both level of peer support and self-esteem were lower for the looking-glass self subjects.

Of futher interest was support for the prediction that looking-glass self subjects should report more *fluctuating* peer support and, relatedly, more fluctuating self-esteem. Although adolescence as a general developmental period tends to usher in volatility in the self-concept (Rosenberg, 1986; Harter, 1986; Harter & Monsour, in press), there appears to be predictable individual difference in the extent to which one's self-esteem fluctuates. Looking-glass self sub-

126

jects, who by definition are basing their self-esteem on peer approval, are particularly vulnerable because, as our findings reveal, they perceive peer approval to be fluctuating more than do subjects for whom self-esteem comes first. Whether fluctuations in peer approval are real or imagined is unclear in these findings and therefore is a topic for further study. The Approval to Self-Worth group is clearly more sensitive to peer approval, as revealed by our measures of preoccupation and concern, and may therefore be more likely to interpret peer opinions of them as changing.

Finally, the liabilities of a looking-glass self orientation extend beyond mere perceptions, in that teachers observed behavioral ramifications in the classroom. Students basing their self-esteem on peer approval were rated by teachers as significantly more likely to conform to classmates' opinions rather than to defend their own point of view. Of even greater interest are the implications for students' ability to function academically. Teachers' ratings revealed that looking-glass self students were more socially distracted from their scholastic activities, given their preoccupation with and worry over peer approval. Their inability to concentrate on the academic demands in the classroom may also have predictable consequences in terms of poorer school performance, a hypothesis we plan to examine in future research.

SPECULATION ON TWO BROADER PATTERNS

I have shared two sets of findings in which we asked people "Which comes first." In the first set, we asked subjects to think about the order of their perceptions of *appearance* and their self-esteem. In the second set, we addressed the directionality of *social support* and self-esteem. I will now suggest that there may be two broader patterns that build upon whether appearance and approval precede or follow self-esteem.

In the first pattern, domains of adequacy, such as appearance or competence, *precede* self-esteem; that is, self-esteem is currently based on judgments of adequacy. The approval of significant others, particularly those in the more public arena, also precedes self-esteem. In pattern 1 (Figure 10), self-esteem is written in upper- and lowercase letters to reflect that subjects in this group typically have

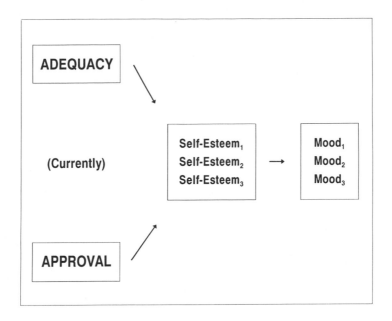

FIGURE 10: Overall pattern for those who currently base their self-esteem on adequacy—for example, appearance—and approval.

lower self-esteem, as our findings reveal. Several levels of self-esteem are depicted in pattern 1, to convey that the self-esteem of such individuals is more likely to *fluctuate*, that it is less stable over time. We are conjecturing that one source of fluctuation in level of self-esteem may stem from the assumption that *social comparison* figures fluctuate. On a given day one may compare oneself with a friend, another day with a classmate who is relatively average, and on yet another day with whomever is perceived as the most attractive or brightest in one's reference group.

Based on our findings about the liabilities of the looking-glass self, fluctuations should also be expected to the extent that the approval of significant others fluctuates. The feedback from different significant others will invariably differ; additionally, even the very same people—for example, classmates or parents—will have different opinions at different points in time (see Rosenberg, 1986). Moreover, given the extremely powerful link between self-esteem and mood, along the dimension of cheerful to depressed, mood should

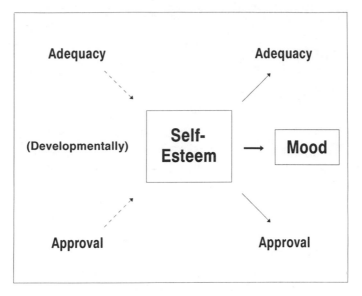

FIGURE 11: Overall pattern for those who no longer base their self-esteem on adequacy—for example, appearance and approval. Self-esteem precedes adequacy and approval.

be lower among those in pattern 1 and should fluctuate in tandem with changes in self-esteem (a hypothesis we are currently testing).

For individuals defined by pattern 2 (Figure 11), we hypothesize that adequacy and approval *did* precede self-esteem developmentally—that is, in the past. They have since been incorporated or internalized, however, and thus the individual is not nearly as dependent on these external sources to sustain a sense of self-esteem. (The dotted line means that currently the influences on self-esteem are less powerful.) For these individuals, the paths leading from self-esteem to adequacy (e.g., appearance) and approval are more salient—adequacy and approval are perceived to be *consequences* of self-esteem. Thus, if one likes oneself as a person, one will like the way one looks and will feel supported by others.

Individuals exhibiting this second pattern of directionality report higher self-esteem as well as more *stable* self-esteem. Finally, given the strong relationship between self-esteem and mood, mood should be higher in this group as well as more stable (a prediction currently under study).

The Conflict of the Multiple Mes

Until now the discussion has implied that there is a single Me-self. However, the picture is quite a bit more complicated given that, beginning in adolescence, one is forced to construct *multiple selves,* multiple Mes. That is, the I-self creates different Me-selves to correspond to the different social roles one must play, such as self with friends, in school or on the job, with family members, with romantic partners, and so on. What liabilities might be lurking as the result of the need to construct multiple Mes? William James pointed quite clearly to one possible outcome that he labeled the "conflict of the different Mes." Our various Me-selves do not always speak with a single voice. In support of this contention, let me share another set of troublesome findings on the conflict of the multiple Mes.

A series of several studies (see Harter & Bresnick, 1992; Harter & Monsour, 1992) has revealed that internal conflict over the different selves one must construct becomes rampant in middle adolescence, about age 15. What do we mean here by conflict? In this research, we first asked adolescents to describe themselves, to produce a list of attributes reflecting what they were like in several roles—for example, with friends, with parents, with romantic others, and at school, as students.

We then asked them to identify those attributes in their self-portrait that appear to be contradictory—to clash or to be in conflict. For example, one may be easygoing with friends but uptight on a date. One may be well behaved in school but rowdy with friends. One may be understanding with one's friends but moody with one's parents. The following quotation describes the last conflict in more detail: "I really think of myself as an understanding person, and I usually am with my friends, but then it really bugs me—I mean, how can I be so moody and difficult with my parents when I think I am really an understanding person who is easy to get along with? It doesn't make sense! I contemplate on this a lot, but I can't really resolve it."

Our studies on the conflict between these multiple Mes have revealed a general pattern that involves both age and gender differences. Conflict over seemingly opposed self-attributes is relatively low in early adolescence but increases in middle adolescence, for males as well as females. At every age, however, females report

DEVELOPMENTAL PERSPECTIVES ON MOTIVATION

FIGURE 12: Conflict between multiple selves for women.

more conflict. This gender difference is particularly pronounced in late adolescence, when conflict increases for females but abates for males. Thus, throughout adolescence females are far more concerned because they are different selves in different contexts than are males, who seem to be able to move more facilely between their different selves. We speculate that this gender difference continues into adulthood, a topic we plan to pursue in further research. Figure 12 portrays the very crowded psychological stage for women, where the seemingly contradictory roles played by multiple characters result in considerable intrapsychic conflict.

Females also spontaneously agonize more over which of these selves is the "real Me." In the context of our interviews of conflict, we recorded a number of such comments: "I hate the fact that I get so nervous on a date. I wish I wasn't so inhibited. The *real* Me is talkative; I just want to be natural." Another female adolescent remarked: "I really think of myself as a happy person, but then I get depressed with my family and it bugs me because I don't know which is the real me." Another confessed: "I think of myself as friendly, but then I act like an introvert, and then I get confused because I don't know which is my true self. I wish I could just become immune to myself!"

It is of interest that a female self-theorist, Mary Caulkins, writing at the turn of the century, seemed particularly attuned to this psychological dilemma. She poetically punctuated both the conflict and the search for the true self by drawing on the following verse:

Within my earthly temple there's a crowd
There's one of us that's humble, and one that's proud
There's one in eager search for earthly wealth
And one who loves her neighbor as herself
There's one who's broken-hearted for her sins
And one who, unrepentant, sits and grins
From much corroding care I should be free
If just once I could determine which is me.

In our research on the conflict of the multiple Mes we serendipitously stumbled across these clues to the search for the true self. In retrospect one can well appreciate why the creation of multiple selves ushers in doubt about which is the real Me and leads to the suspicion that certain selves, or certain behaviors in the various roles one must play, may be *false*. Thus these observations and insights lead to the final set of findings I will describe on the emergence of the false self.

The Emergence of the False Self

In a recent program of research designed to pursue these issues, we asked adolescents directly whether they felt they were being their true self or their false self in the different social roles they must play. We have discovered that it is not until early adolescence (age 11 or 12) that the concept of a false self emerges (Harter & Lee, 1989). At that point in development many begin to describe the false self as "acting

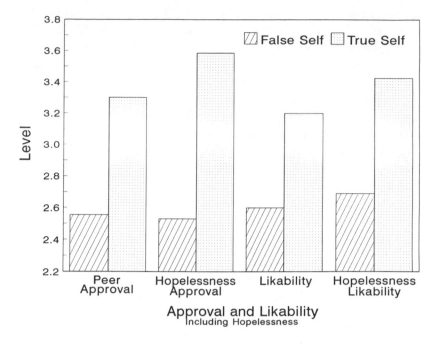

FIGURE 13: Approval and likability scores for those engaging in high levels of true- and false-self behaviors.

like someone you are not," "being phony," "not expressing your true feelings," "not being who you really are inside, as a person."

Adolescents also develop insights into the motivation to engage in false-self behavior. One powerful cluster of motives involves the desire to gain the acceptance or approval of others, to impress peers, and to improve social relationships. Other adolescents cite, as a reason to engage in false-self behavior, their perception that others may not like or understand them or that they themselves may not like or be sure of their true self.

If these are the primary motives, we can ask whether false-self behavior works toward its intended effects. In addressing this question, Gabby Cobbs and I have compared two groups of adolescents: those acknowledging high levels of *false*-self behavior with peers, who report that they are trying to obtain support by acting, dressing, and thinking like those whose acceptance they desire, and those reporting high levels of *true*-self behavior, who do not feel they need to conform to specific peer standards in order to gain approval.

Comparison of these two groups suggests that the false-self strategy backfires. Those engaging in high levels of false-self behavior report less classmate approval, have greater hopelessness about ever attaining it, feel less liked by peers, and are more hopeless about ever becoming likable than are those engaging in high levels of true-self behavior. Moreover, the false-self adolescents also report lower self-esteem and typically admit that they do not even know their true self. Thus, engaging in false-self behavior does not seem to yield the desired or intended effect.

We have also begun to examine adolescent false-self behavior with parents, finding that the more one presents a false self to one's mother and father, the lower one's self-esteem. Thus, with both peers and parents there is a relation between false-self behavior and low self-esteem. These patterns have raised another intriguing set of questions involving the *direction* of these effects. The ordering of one's perceptions of false-self behavior and self-esteem can be cast in the form of another pair of possible options. Is it that when I become my false self I don't like myself as a person? Such a stance might be psychologically commendable. Or, alternatively, is it that *because* I don't like myself as a person, I become my false self? Although we do not yet have the answer, the second option, in which one becomes a false self because one does not like one's true self, appears to be a more troubling outcome.

IMPLICATIONS FOR WOMEN

This issue appears to be of particular concern for women in our society. Contemporary feminists such as Carol Gilligan (1982) and those at the Stone Center in Boston—for example, Jean Baker Miller and Judith Jordan (see Miller, 1986)—have pointed out that many features of a woman's true self are not valued in this society, making it difficult for a woman to value herself. These features include the importance of close, interpersonal relationships, of intimacy and connectedness with others; the expression of one's own emotions; and the value of caring and cooperation rather than competition.

What are some likely outcomes for women if these characteristics are devalued by society? Drawing on feminist literature, several seem apparent. The devaluation of these characteristics by society will cause women to devalue themselves as people—to develop lower self-esteem. Our own research (Harter & Messer, 1992) reveals that women, particularly traditional women primarily in the role of homemaker, invariably report lower self-esteem than men do. A woman may feel compelled to twist or distort the self into a person she is not—to develop a false or inauthentic self that is requested or required by others. As a result, she will become more compliant, submissive, docile, or dependent than her true nature would normally dictate.

We may develop an emotional false self by trying to match our feelings to others', such that when others are happy we try to be happy and when others are sad we try to be sad. We may suppress our true self by suppressing or silencing our voice, saying nothing when we truly have something to say. Perhaps the ultimate outcome of being one's false self is that eventually one becomes so alienated from one's own experience that one may not even *know* one's true self. One may wear different masks with such constancy that one has lost touch with one's true, inner identity. Our own recent findings on what we have termed "overly connected" women reveals just such a pattern (Harter, Waters, & Pettitt, 1992).

I emphasize *women* because women's voices have not been sufficiently heard. The story of women's development either has not been told or has not been listened to. The problem is not limited to women, however. Men are socialized into their own forms of false-self behavior, becoming alienated from their true feelings. Often they are hiding an inner core that is very tender and vulnerable. During the recent Gulf War, thousands of soldiers in Saudi Arabia acted big, bold, brave, and bellicose when secretly they felt very small and very scared.

What are the implications for self-esteem of *not knowing* one's true self? We have begun to address this question for female as well as male adolescents. A very systematic relationship has emerged, revealing that those who acknowledge that they do not know who their real self is report much lower self-esteem than those who say they *do* know their true self (see Figure 14). Thus, inaccessibility to one's true self seems to represent a double liability.

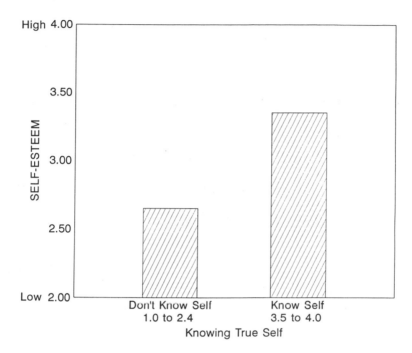

FIGURE 14: Self-esteem among those who do not know and those who do know their true self.

SUMMARY OF TROUBLESOME FINDINGS

To summarize, there are several causes for consternation, several reasons for asking, "What's wrong with this picture?" For many individuals the I-self, in devoting its energies to packaging the Me-self, appears busily at work primping and preening in front of the mirror to ensure that the Me-self looks good, since appearance is so critical to self-esteem. The I-self devotes considerable attention to the social mirror as well, seeking the approval of significant others in the public domain. The I-self is also frantically trying to juggle the many different Mes in the mirror, the different personas it has come to adopt. In the process, the I-self often loses sight of which, if any, is the real Me. Paradoxically, as our findings have demonstrated, each of these strategies for packaging the Me-self appears to backfire, since each ultimately undermines the very self-esteem it was designed to enhance.

Is It Really Worth the Energy?

Is this really how the I-self should be spending its time, devoted to the protection, enhancement, and distortion of the Me-self? Should this be the I-self's primary job description? Aren't there better things for the I-self to be doing? Appreciating art? Enjoying nature? Practicing the game of inner tennis? Openly experiencing other people? Honestly expressing feelings? Those espousing a more Eastern perspective think so, and I tend to agree.

The perspective I have developed thus far represents a very Western view of the self. Westerners appear to be preoccupied with the self. Witness the large number of professional publications on the topic, not to mention the vast array of books and articles in the popular press that are devoted to enhancing one's self-concept. A judicious selection from this menu is viewed as the contemporary regimen for psychological health. This is by no means a universal window on self-processes, however. In fact, it departs dramatically from those perspectives that have grown out of an Eastern, Buddhist, tradition.

An Eastern, Buddhist Perspective

Consider the following observation from a Buddhist scholar (Tarthang Tulku) who appears to *begin* with a looking-glass self perspective, although the implications take a decidedly different turn: "Each of us has a self-image that is based on who we think we are and how we think others see us. When we look in a mirror, we know that what we see there is only a reflection. Even though our self-image has the same illusory quality, we often believe it to be real. Our belief in this image draws us away from the true qualities of our nature. Because the self-image is based on how we wish we were, on what we fear we are, or how we would like the world to see us, it prevents us from seeing ourselves clearly."

Another Buddhist scholar (Trungpa) describes how we attempt to create the illusion that self and other are solid, continuous, and consistent. He writes: "We build up an idea, a preconception, that self and other are solid and continuous, and once we have this idea, we manipulate our thoughts to confirm it, and are afraid of any contrary evidence."

From this particular Buddhist perspective, the preoccupation with the self, watching oneself as an external object, is a form of ignorance, labeled self-observing ignorance. Trungpa notes that self-observation can be very dangerous; it can involve watching yourself like a hungry cat watching mice. According to Trungpa, we create a *watcher* that is actually a very complicated bureaucracy set up seemingly to protect and enhance the self. In our own parlance, the watcher represents the rather frenetic, and at times desperate, I-self preoccupied with strategies for managing the impression that the Me-self is making on the world. From a Buddhist perspective, however, we must go beyond this form of self-observation, we must remove the watcher and the complicated bureaucracy it creates to preserve the permanence of the self. As Trungpa observes, once we take away the watcher, there is a tremendous amount of space, since the watcher and the bureaucracy take up so much room. If we eliminate the role of watcher, the space becomes sharp, precise, and intelligent. In fact, we do not really need the watcher or observer of the self at all.

One can see in this brief comparative analysis rather divergent views of how the I-self should be occupying its time. From the perspective of Western psychology, the I-self should be gainfully employed in observing and protecting the Me-self, packaging it as a valued commodity in the psychological marketplace. From an Eastern, Buddhist perspective, however, far more benefits will accrue if the I-self averts this myopic gaze, since it represents a distorted lens that obscures one's true nature. Rather, the I-self should direct its energies outward, exercising its capabilities and enjoying life experiences, rather than turning inward in its preoccupation with the construction of a Me-self that it considers acceptable to society at large.

On Me-People and I-People

Having contrasted the Western and Eastern perspectives, it becomes apparent that the I-self does have a variety of potential job definitions. This insight suggested to me, and to Sam Rose, a recent graduate of our program, that people's lives may differ with regard to which particular path they have opted, or been compelled, to pursue. Metaphorically speaking, we can recognize Me-people and I-people in the world around us.

Me-people are very much like one of the patterns presented earlier, in Figure 10. They are preoccupied with their image, are very concerned about the approval of others, and cannot put the mirror down. Yet they see through a glass darkly because their stance leads to lowered self-esteem, to fluctuating self-esteem, and to depressed affect. They are more likely to don the mantle of a false self and to adopt a judgmental attitude toward others as well as the self.

I-people share characteristics with the second pattern presented, in Figure 11. They are not preoccupied with their image in either the physical or the social mirror. Although they do appreciate themselves, they cast their gaze toward the outside world, toward enjoying others, toward experiencing and living life. They are attuned to what it feels like to appreciate a rainbow, or a sunset, or the fragrance of the flowers after a spring rain, or the gentle touch of a caring friend. I-people are more likely to know, and to be, their true self.

Sam Rose and I have conducted some pilot studies in which we have identified certain features of Me-people and I-people, although here I will merely present illustrative, if not exaggerated, examples of each stance. We all know the fictional prototype of the Me-person: Narcissus! A recent cartoon depicts Narcissus preoccupied with his reflection in a pool. At his side is a woman who plaintively queries, "Narcissus, is there someone else?"

As a fictional prototype of the I-person, I suggest Alice in *Through the Looking Glass*. In this story and its illustrations, Alice literally moves through the mirror, emerging on the other side in search of adventure. To further explore the distinction between possible I-people and Me-people, allow me to briefly indulge in a light-hearted excursion into several contrasts. Playing opposite Alice as an I-person might be Miss Piggy as a Me-person. Historically, in the real world of artists, consider Mozart as an I-person versus Salieri as a Me-person. Or Gauguin as an I-person versus van Gogh, obsessed with self-portraits, as a Me-person. In the legendary world, we encounter King Arthur as an I-person versus Sir Lancelot (C'est moi, c'est moi!) as a Me-person. In the world of drama, Katharine Hepburn as an I-person versus Madonna as a Me-person. Or Paul Newman versus Woody Allen!

In the world of the young at heart, consider E.T. as an I-alien versus Charlie Brown as a Me-character. Or Superman as an I-figure versus Clark Kent as his Me-counterpart! In the world of politics, Golda Meir as an I-person versus Evita as a Me-person. On the more contemporary scene, we have Desmond Tutu as an I-prototype versus Saddam Hussein as a Me-personality to contend with. Finally, at the corporate level, Nike, with the slogan "Just do it!" versus Lady Clairol hair coloring and Grecian Formula Number Nine.

Conclusion

These contrasts may cause us to sense the stirrings of our own I-selves as well as recognize how far we perhaps indulge our Me-selves, since we seem drawn to both the physical and social mirrors more often than we care to admit. However, I submit that we can and must allow our I-selves a bit more breathing room, feeling room, room to let us be our true selves. Perhaps each of us needs to let our Me-self step out of the mirror, move beyond it and make friends with our I-self, and in the process discover the truth about both.

Let me make my point in one final form. How many times in the past month have you had an experience in the company of another person that caused you to comment or observe, with some combination of surprise, joy, and relief: "I really felt like myself!" Once, twice, three times? For most people it is relatively rare. But if one so rarely has such an experience, if each of us so rarely feels like our *true* self, the real me, then who *are* we the vast majority of the time? I rest my case!

REFERENCES

Abramson, L. Y., Metalsky, G. I., & Alloy, L. B. (1989). Hopelessness depression: A theory-based subtype of depression. *Psychological Review, 96,* 358–372.
Abramson, L. Y., Seligman, M. E. P., & Teasedale, J. D. (1986). Learned helplessness in humans: Critique and reformulation. In J. C. Coyne (Ed.), *Essential papers on depression.* New York: New York University Press.

Allgood-Merten, B., Lewinsohn, P. M., & Hops, K. (1990). Sex differences and adolescent depression. *Journal of Abnormal Psychology, 99*, 55–63.

Allport, G. W. (1961). *Pattern and growth in personality*. New York: Holt, Rinehart and Winston.

Bartlett, F. C. (1932). *Remembering*. Cambridge: Cambridge University Press.

Battle, J. (1987). Relationship between self-esteem and depression among children. *Psychological Reports, 60*, 1187–1190.

Baumeister, R. F. (1990). Suicide as escape from self. *Psychological Review, 97*, 90–113.

Beck, A. T. (1975). *Depression: Causes and treatments*. Philadelphia: University of Pennsylvania Press.

Bertenthal, B. I., & Fischer, K. W. (1978). Development of self-recognition in the infant. *Developmental Psychology, 14*, 44–50.

Bibring, E. (1953). The mechanism of depression. In P. Greenacre (Ed.), *Affective disorders: Psychoanalytic contribution to their study*. New York: International Universities Press.

Blatt, S. J. (1974). Levels of object representation in anaclitic and introjective depression. *Psychoanalytic Study of the Child, 29*, 107–157.

Brim, O. G. (1976). Life span development of the theory of oneself: Implications for child development. In H. W. Reese (Ed.), *Advances in child development and behavior* (Vol. 11). New York: Academic Press.

Cantor, P. (1987). *Young people in crisis: How you can help*. A film presentation of the National Committee on Youth Suicide Prevention and American Association of Suicidology, in consultation with Harvard Medical School, Department of Psychiatry, Cambridge Hospital.

Carlson, G. A., & Cantwell, D. P. (1982). Suicidal behavior and depression in children and adolescents. *Journal of the American Academy of Child Psychiatry, 21*, 361–368.

Cooley, C. H. (1902). *Human nature and the social order*. New York: Charles Scribner's Sons.

Coopersmith, S. (1967). *The antecedents of self-esteem*. San Francisco: W. H. Freeman.

Damon, W., & Hart, D. (1988). *Self understanding in childhood and adolescence*. New York: Cambridge University Press.

Elkind, D. (1979). Growing up faster. *Psychology Today, 12*, 38–45.

Epstein, S. (1973). The self-concept revisited or a theory of a theory. *American Psychologist, 28*, 405–416.

Epstein, S. (1981). The unity principle versus the reality and pleasure principles, or the tale of the scorpion and the frog. In M. D. Lynch, A. A. Norem-Hebeisen, & K. Gergen (Eds.), *Self concept: Advances in theory and research*. Cambridge, MA: Ballinger.

Epstein, S. (1991). Cognitive-experiential self theory: Implications for developmental psychology. In M. R. Gunnar & L. A. Sroufe (Eds.), *Self processes and development: The Minnesota symposium on child development* (Vol. 23). Hillsdale, NJ: Lawrence Erlbaum.

Freud, S. (1968). Mourning and melancholia. In J. Strachey (Ed.), *The stan-

dard edition of the complete psychological works (Vol. 14). London: Hogarth Press. (Originally published 1917)

Gilligan, C. (1982). *In a different voice.* Cambridge: Harvard University Press.

Glick, M., & Zigler, E. (1985). Self-image: A cognitive-developmental approach. In R. Leahy (Ed.), *The development of the self.* New York: Academic Press.

Greenwald, A. G. (1980). The totalitarian ego: Fabrication and revision of personal history. *American Psychologist, 7,* 603–618.

Hammen, C., & Goodman-Brown, T. (1990). Self-schemas and vulnerability to specific life stress in children at risk for depression. *Cognitive Therapy and Research, 14,* 215-227.

Harter, S. (1983). Developmental perspectives on the self-system. In E. M. Hetherington (Ed.), *Handbook of child psychology: Vol. 4. Socialization, personality, and social development* (pp. 275–386). New York: John Wiley.

Harter, S. (1985a). *The Self-Perception Profile for Children.* Manual, University of Denver.

Harter, S. (1985b). *The Social Support Scale for Children and Adolescents.* Unpublished Manual, University of Denver.

Harter, S. (1986). Processes underlying the construction, maintenance, and enhancement of the self-concept in children. In J. Suls & A. G. Greenwald (Eds.), *Psychological perspectives on the self* (Vol. 3, pp. 137–181). Hillsdale, NJ: Lawrence Erlbaum.

Harter, S. (1987). The determinants and mediational role of global self-worth in children. In N. Eisenberg (Ed.), *Contemporary issues in developmental psychology* (pp. 219–242). New York: John Wiley.

Harter, S. (1990a). Causes, correlates and the functional role of global self-worth: A life-span perspective. In J. Kolligan & R. Sternberg (Eds.), *Perceptions of competence and incompetence across the life span* (pp. 43–70). New York: Springer-Verlag.

Harter, S. (1990b). Adolescent self and identity development. In S. S. Feldman & G. R. Elliot (Eds.), *At the threshold: The developing adolescent* (pp. 352–387). Cambridge: Harvard University Press.

Harter, S., & Bresnick, S. (1992). *Developmental and gender differences in the conflict caused by opposing attributes within the adolescent self.* Unpublished manuscript, University of Denver.

Harter, S., & Lee, L. (1987). *Manifestations of true and not true selves in adolescents.* Paper presented at the Society for Research in Child Development, Kansas City, MO.

Harter, S., & Marold, D. B. (1991). A model of the determinants and mediational role of self-worth: Implications for adolescent depression and suicidal ideation. In G. Goethals & J. Strauss (Eds.), *The self: An interdisciplinary approach.* New York: Springer-Verlag.

Harter, S., & Marold, D. B. (1992). *The directionality of the link between self-esteem and affect: Beyond causal modeling.* Unpublished manuscript, University of Denver.

Harter, S., & Marold, D. B. (in press). Psychosocial risk factors contributing to adolescent suicidal ideation. In G. Noam & S. Borst (Eds.), *Child and adolescent suicide: Clinical-developmental perspectives.* New Directions Series: Child Development. San Francisco: Jossey-Bass.

Harter, S., & Messer, B. (1992). *Gender differences in the self-concept of adult men and women.* Unpublished manuscript, University of Denver.

Harter, S., & Monsour, A. (1992). Developmental analysis of opposing self-attributes in the adolescent self-portrait. *Developmental Psychology, 28,* 251–260.

Harter, S., Stocker, C., & Robinson, N. (1992). *The perceived directionality of the link between approval and self-worth: The liabilities of a looking glass self orientation among young adolescents.* Unpublished manuscript, University of Denver.

Harter, S., & Waters, P. (1991). *Correlates of the directionality of perceived physical appearance and global self-worth.* Unpublished manuscript, University of Denver.

Harter, S., Waters, P., & Pettitt, L. (1992). *Orientations involving autonomy and connectedness among adult men and women.* Unpublished manuscript, University of Denver.

Hatfield, E., & Sprechner, S. (1986). *Mirror, mirror: The importance of looks in everyday life.* Albany: State University of New York Press.

Hawton, K. (1986). *Suicide and attempted suicide among children and adolescents.* Beverly Hills, CA: Sage.

Higgins, E. T. (1987). Self-discrepancy: Theory relating self and affect. *Psychological Review, 94,* 319–340.

Higgins, E. T. (1989). Self-discrepancy theory: What patterns of self-beliefs cause people to suffer? In L. Berkowitz (Ed.), *Advances in experimental social psychology* (Vol. 22). New York: Academic Press.

Higgins, E. T. (1991). Development of self-regulatory and self-evaluative processes: Costs, benefits, and trade-offs. In M. R. Gunnar & L. A. Sroufe (Eds.), *Self processes in development.* Twenty-third Minnesota Symposium on Child Psychology. Hillsdale, NJ: Lawrence Erlbaum.

James, W. (1892). *Psychology: The briefer course.* New York: Henry Holt.

Junkin, L., Harter, S., & Whitesell, N. R. (1991). *Correlates of global self-worth among normally achieving, learning disabled, and behaviorally disordered adolescents.* Unpublished manuscript, University of Denver.

Kaslow, N. J., Rehm, L. P., & Siegel, A. W. (1984). Social-cognitive and cognitive correlates of depression in children. *Journal of Abnormal Child Psychology, 12,* 605-620.

Kelly, G. A. (1955). *The psychology of personal constructs.* New York: W. W. Norton.

Kovacs, M., & Beck, A. T. (1977). An empirical-clinical approach towards a definition of childhood depression. In J. G. Schulterbrandt & A. Raskin (Eds.), *Depression in childhood: Diagnosis, treatment, and conceptual models.* New York: Raven Press.

Kovacs, M., & Beck, A. T. (1978). Maladaptive cognitive structures in depression. *American Journal of Psychiatry, 135,* 525–533.

Kovacs, M., & Beck, A. T. (1986). Maladaptive cognitive structures in depression. In J. C. Coyne (Ed.), *Essential papers on depression*. New York: New York University Press.

Langlois, J. H. (1981). Beauty and the beast: The role of physical attractiveness in the development of peer relations and social behavior. In S. S. Brehm, S. M. Kassin, & F. X. Gibbons (Eds.), *Developmental social psychology: Theory and research*. New York: Oxford University Press.

Lecky, P. (1945). *Self-consistency: A theory of personality*. New York: Island Press.

Lewis, M., & Brooks-Gunn, J. (1979). *Social cognition and the acquisition of self*. New York: Plenum Press.

Lynch, M. D. (1981). Self-concept development in childhood. In M. D. Lynch, A. A. Norem-Hebeisen, & K. Gergen (Eds.), *Self concept: Advances in theory and research*. Cambridge, MA: Ballinger.

Maccoby, E., & Martin, J. (1983). Socialization in the context of the family: Parent-child interaction. In E. M. Heatherington (Ed.), *Handbook of child psychology: Vol. 4. Socialization, personality and social development*. New York: John Wiley.

Markus, H. (1980). The self in thought and memory. In D. M. Wegner & R. R. Vallacher (Eds.), *The self in social psychology*. New York: Oxford University Press.

McCauley, E., Mitchell, J. R., Burke, P., & Moss, S. (1988). Cognitive attributes of depression in children and adolescents. *Journal of Consulting and Clinical Psychology, 56*, 903–908.

Mead, G. H. (1934). *Mind, self, and society*. Chicago: University of Chicago Press.

Miller, J. B. (1986). *Toward a new psychology of women*. Boston: Beacon Press.

Nolen-Hoeksema, S. (1987). Sex differences in unipolar depression: Evidence and theory. *Psychological Bulletin, 101*, 259–282.

Nolen-Hoeksema, S., Girgus, J. S., & Seligman, M. E. P. (1986). Learned helplessness in children: A longitudinal study of depression, achievement, and explanatory style. *Journal of Personality and Social Psychology, 51*, 435–442.

Pfeffer, C. R. (1988). Risk factors associated with youth suicide: A clinical perspective. *Psychiatric Annals, 18*, 652–656.

Piaget, J. (1965). *The child's conception of the world*. Paterson, NJ: Littlefield, Adams.

Renick, M. J., & Harter, S. (1989). Impact of social comparisons on the developing self-perceptions of learning disabled students. *Journal of Educational Psychology, 81*, 631–638.

Renick, M. J., & Harter, S. (1991). *A model of the determinants of self-worth in learning disabled children*. Paper presented at the Society for Research in Child Development Conference, Kansas City, MO.

Renouf, A. G., & Harter, S. (1990). Low self-worth and anger as components of the depressive experience in young adolescents. *Development and Psychopathology, 2*, 293–310.

Robinson, N., & Harter, S. (1991). *Which comes first from the adolescent's point of view: Approval from others or liking oneself?* Paper presented at the annual meeting of the Society for Research in Child Development, Seattle.

Rogers, C. R. (1951). *Client-centered therapy.* Boston: Houghton Mifflin.

Rosenberg, M. (1979). *Conceiving the self.* New York: Basic Books.

Rosenberg, M. (1986). Self-concept from middle childhood through adolescence. In J. Suls & A. G. Greenwald (Eds.), *Psychological perspectives on the self* (Vol. 3, pp. 107-136). Hillsdale, NJ: Lawrence Erlbaum.

Sarbin, T. R. (1962). A preface to a psychological analysis of the self. *Psychological Review, 59,* 11–22.

Seligman, M. E. P. (1975). *Helplessness: On depression, development, and death.* San Francisco: Freeman.

Seligman, M. E. P., & Peterson, C. (1986). A learned helplessness perspective on childhood depression: Theory and research. In M. Rutter, C. E. Izard, & P. B. Read (Eds.), *Depression in young people: Developmental and clinical perspectives* (pp. 223–249). New York: Guilford Press.

Shaffer, D. (1974). Suicide in childhood and early adolescence. *Journal of Child Psychology and Psychiatry, 32,* 275–291.

Shaffer, D. (1985). Depression and suicide in children and adolescents. In M. Rutter & L. Hersov (Eds.), *Child and adolescent psychiatry: Modern approaches* (2nd ed.). Oxford: Blackwell Scientific Publications.

Shaffer, D., & Fisher, P. (1981). The epidemiology of suicide in children and young adolescents. *Journal of the American Academy of Child Psychiatry, 21,* 545–565.

Simmons, R. G., & Blyth, D. A. (1987). *Moving into adolescence: The impact of pubertal change and school context.* New York: Aldine DeGruyter.

Taylor, S. E., & Brown, J. D. (1988). Illusion and well-being: A social psychological perspective on mental health. *Psychological Bulletin, 103,* 193–210.

Tesser, A. (1988). Toward a self-evaluation maintenance model of social behavior. In L. Berkowitz (Ed.), *Advances in experimental social psychology* (Vol. 21). New York: Academic Press.

Tesser, A., & Campbell, J. (1983). Self-definition and self-evaluation maintenance. In J. Suls & A. G. Greenwald (Eds.), *Psychological perspectives on the self* (Vol. 2, pp. 1–32). Hillsdale, NJ: Lawrence Erlbaum.

Wylie, R. C. (1979). *The self concept: Vol. 2. Theory and research on selected topics.* Lincoln: University of Nebraska Press.

Zumpf, C. L., & Harter, S. (1989). *Mirror, mirror on the wall: The relationship between appearance and self-worth in adolescent males and females.* Paper presented at the annual meeting of the Society for Research in Child Development, Kansas City, MO.

Zumpf, C. L., & Harter, S. (1991). *Social comparison processes among the gifted.* Unpublished manuscript, University of Denver.

School and Family Effects on the Ontogeny of Children's Interests, Self-Perceptions, and Activity Choices

Jacquelynne S. Eccles
University of Colorado and
University of Michigan

in collaboration with Amy Arberton, Christy Miller Buchanan, Janis Jacobs, Constance Flanagan, Rena Harold, Douglas Mac Iver, Carol Midgley, David Reuman, and Allan Wigfield

Why do children choose such different activities and have such different goals? Why do some invest time and energy in developing their intellectual skills while other children, often with comparable intellectual abilities, invest their time and energy in developing physical or musical skills or no particular skills at all?

Why do children with fairly similar grades in school have different opinions of their intellectual abilities and place different value on various activities? Why, for example, do girls develop lower estimates of their math ability and lower math achievement expectancies than boys, even though they get equivalent grades? And why are girls less likely to take advanced math courses when they reach high school?

Why do children's self-perceptions and interests change as they get older? For example, why do many adolescents seem to lose confidence in their intellectual abilities and lose interest in school as they move into secondary school?

These questions, and others like them, lie at the heart of achievement and self-perception theory and have been the focus of our re-

Work for this paper was funded by grants to the first author from NICHD, NSF, and the Spencer Foundation.

search over the past fifteen years. Using a longitudinal approach, we have studied the determinants of both activity and course choices, as well as actual performance, during the early to middle adolescent years. We have explored children's perceptions of their various abilities and interests and have looked at how these perceptions are affected by experiences at school and at home. This work has demonstrated (1) that perceptions of one's abilities, of the probability of success, and of the value of these competencies are important mediators of activity and course choice and performance; (2) that parents' attitudes, beliefs and perceptions about their children's abilities are critical mediators of children's academic self and task beliefs—more critical in some instances than either the children's own academic performance or classroom experiences; and (3) that changing classroom characteristics have a significant impact on the developmental trajectory of early adolescents' motivational orientation in school, as well as on their self beliefs and task beliefs (see Eccles & Midgley, 1989; Eccles, Midgley, & Adler, 1984; Eccles et al., 1987; Eccles, Jacobs, Harold-Goldsmith, Jayaratne, & Yee, 1989; and Eccles Parsons et al., 1983). This work is summarized here. The chapter focuses on the social contextual influences on the ontogeny of a specific set of motivational constructs—the set associated with the following achievement-related self-perceptions and task perceptions: perceptions of one's competence in achievement-related activities (activities that involve skill acquisition and potential performance evaluation); the value one attaches to competence in these activities; and one's intrinsic interest in these activities. We have documented elsewhere that these constructs are important because they influence individuals' actual involvement and performance in various achievement-related activities (e.g., Eccles, Adler, & Meece, 1984). The chapter is organized around two general themes: individual differences and developmental change. Within each of these major sections, we present a general theoretical framework along with empirical evidence documenting the proposed links. In both of these major sections, evidence is given for family and school influences: family influences are highlighted in the discussion of individual differences; school influences are highlighted in the discussion of developmental changes.

Social Contextual Influences on the Ontogeny of Individual Differences in Motivation

Figure 1 summarizes the major categories of influence discussed in this section. First we discuss how these characteristics have been operationalized in the family context and how they might relate to each other. We present some of our findings in detail to illustrate the relation of parents' specific beliefs and practices to the ontogeny of motivation. These findings will focus primarily on the socialization of gender differences, but we believe that similar processes underlie the ontogeny of other individual differences as well. Then we briefly summarize how these same categories can be used to describe the work on classroom influences.

The Family as a Context for Socializing Individual Differences in Self Beliefs and Task Beliefs and in Activity Choices

COMMUNITY-BASED AND DEMOGRAPHIC CHARACTERISTICS

Sociological work on the relation between social class and school achievement has documented the importance of such factors as family structure, parents' financial resources and education, competing demands on parents' time, community characteristics, and dramatic changes in the family's economic resources in shaping children's motivation (e.g., Coleman et al., 1966; Kohn, 1969; Laosa, 1984; Marjoribanks, 1980; Sampson, in press; Thompson, Alexander, & Entwisle, 1988). Factors such as these are associated both with different parent beliefs and practices and with different opportunity structures in the child's environment. For example, Eccles, in collaboration with Furstenberg, Cook, Elder, and Sameroff, has been studying the relation of family management strategies to neighborhood characteristics. These investigators are interested in how families try to provide both good experiences and protection for their children, especially when the families live in high-risk neighborhoods— neighborhoods with few resources and many risks and hazards. To

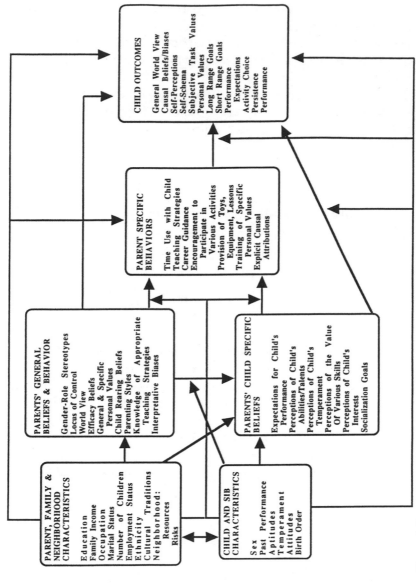

FIGURE 1: General model of relations among various possible paternal influences on the ontogeny of children's motivation.

study this issue, they are conducting a survey interview study of approximately 500 families living in high- to moderate-risk neighborhoods in inner-city Philadelphia. Initial results suggest that families who are actively involved with their children's development use different strategies depending on the resources available in their neighborhoods. As one would expect, families living in high-risk, low-resource neighborhoods rely more on in-home management strategies both to help their children develop talents and skills and to protect them from the dangers in the neighborhood; families in these neighborhoods also focus more attention on protecting their children from danger than on helping them develop specific talents. In contrast, families in less risky neighborhoods focus more on helping their children develop specific talents and are more likely to use neighborhood resources, such as organized youth programs, to accomplish this goal—perhaps because such resources are more readily available and accessible and because there are fewer dangers in their neighborhoods. In addition, many families appeared to be quite disengaged from their children's lives, and these highly disengaged families were equally likely to live in low-risk and high-risk neighborhoods (e.g., Eccles, Furstenberg, McCarthy, & Lord, 1992; Furstenberg, 1992).

Demographic and economic factors also influence how successfully parents can translate their general beliefs, goals, and values into effective practices. Several studies suggest that it is harder to do a good job of parenting if one lives in a high-risk neighborhood or is financially stressed (e.g., Elder & Caspi, 1989; Elder, Caspi, & Van Nguyen, 1985; Furstenberg, 1992; Garbarino & Sherman, 1980; McLoyd, 1990; Sampson, in press). Not only do such parents have limited resources available, they also have to cope with more external stressors than middle-class families living in stable, resource-rich neighborhoods. Being confronted with these stressors may force parents to adopt a less effective parenting style because they do not have the energy or the time to use more effective but more demanding strategies. For example, several investigators have found that economic stress in the family (e.g., loss of one's job or major financial change) has a negative affect on the quality of parenting (e.g., Elder, 1974; Elder & Ardelt, 1992; Elder, Conger, Foster, & Ardelt, 1992; Flanagan, 1990a, 1990b; Goldsmith, 1986; Harold-Goldsmith, Radin, & Eccles, 1988). High levels of stress may also hamper parents' ability to adapt their parenting strategies to developmental changes in their children's needs. For example, they may either remain too controlling or become too detached as their children move through adolescence, making it more difficult for their children to adapt effectively to this stressful period of life.

General Child-Rearing Climate and General Beliefs

Historically, most studies of parental influence have focused on the impact of general patterns of child rearing on children's overall orientation toward achievement. These studies have related a broad array of general behaviors and beliefs to the development of self-esteem, achievement motivation, locus of control, sense of personal efficacy, and so forth. For example, studies have focused on general emotional warmth and supportiveness in the home (e.g., Estrada, Arsenio, Hess, & Holloway, 1987; Maccoby & Martin, 1984); the timing and magnitude of independence training (e.g., McClelland & Pilon, 1983; Winterbottom, 1958); the valuing of achievement (Hess & Holloway, 1984); general parental child-rearing beliefs and theories, values and goals, as well as specific beliefs, goals, and values linked to sex-role and cultural ideologies (Crandall & Battle, 1970; Crandall, Dewey, Katkovsky, & Preston, 1964; Eccles & Hoffman, 1984; Goodnow, 1988; Goodnow & Collins, 1990; Hess, Chih-Mei, & McDevitt, 1987; Kohn, 1969; McGillicuddy-DeLisi, 1982; Rosen & D'Andrade, 1959; Sameroff & Feil, 1985; Stevenson, Lee, Chen, & Stigler, 1990); general child-rearing style as well as authority structure, discipline tactics, and general interaction patterns (Baumrind, 1971, 1989, 1991; Hess & McDevitt, 1984; Lamborn, Mounts, Steinberg, & Dornbusch, 1991); parental locus of control and personal efficacy (Maccoby & Martin, 1984); communicative style and teaching style (McGillicuddy-DeLisi, 1982; Sigel, 1982); and the quality of organizational management of household activities.

The recent work by Grolnick, Ryan, and their colleagues combines many of these features; they suggest the importance of three general components: involvement, support for autonomous behaviors, and structure (e.g., Grolnick & Ryan, 1989). Within this framework, involvement is defined as "the parents' active interest in the child, knowledge about the child, and dedication of time and resources to the childrearing process"; autonomy support is defined as encouraging "children to figure answers for themselves" and allowing children "some choice and latitude rather than assigning actions to them"; and structure is defined as "the extent to which parents provide clear and consistent guidelines, expectations, and rules for behaviors, without respect to the style in which they are enforced or encouraged" (Grolnick & Ryan, in press).

Although the magnitude of the effects of these various constructs varies by race, sex, socioeconomic class, nationality, and other family and community characteristics, there is consensus that these parental beliefs and practices do affect children's general orientation toward mastery and global self-esteem (Coleman et al., 1966; Hess & Holloway, 1984; Marjoribanks, 1980). What seems important is the right match of control and structure in a warm and supportive environment with positively motivated role models. These results are consistent with three general principles: appropriate scaffolding, good and consistent parenting, and observational learning. Families who know enough about their children to provide the right amount of challenge with the right amount of support seem more likely to produce highly competent and motivated children. Families who provide a positive emotional environment are more likely to rear children who want to internalize the parents' values and goals and therefore imitate the behaviors they model. Finally, children growing up in such homes should be more likely to develop a positive achievement orientation if the parents themselves provide a model of a positive general achievement orientation.

Much less is known about how these general factors might relate to specific behaviors and beliefs across various achievement-related activity domains. This issue, however, is beginning to attract attention. For example, it is one of the central foci of a recent book by Goodnow and Collins (1990; see also Eccles, 1989; Goodnow, 1988; Jacobs & Eccles, 1985). Figure 1 depicts a general overview of how one might think about these interrelationships. It suggests several important questions. First, what is the relation of general parental beliefs and practices to domain and child-specific parental beliefs, values, and practices? For example, do parents' gender-role stereotypes affect their perceptions of their own children's abilities in various activity domains? This will be discussed later.

Second, do cultural beliefs about the nature of ability affect how parents explain their children's successes and failures? Recent work by Hess and his colleagues (e.g., Holloway, Kashiwagi, Hess, & Azuma, 1986; Hess et al., 1987) and by Stevenson and his colleagues (Stevenson et al., 1990) have focused on this question. They have provided consistent evidence that Japanese and Chinese parents make different causal attributions than Euro-American parents for their children's performance on schoolwork: Japanese and Chinese parents are more likely to attribute success at schoolwork to effort and hard work than to natural talent. In contrast, Euro-American parents give natural talent much greater weight. These investigators also suggested that this difference results from a cultural difference in beliefs regarding the nature of ability and competence.

Third, do parents' general developmental theories affect the specific teaching strategies they use with their children? Some of the best work related to this question has been done by Sameroff and by Sigel, McGillicuddy-DeLisi, and their colleagues. McGillicuddy-DeLisi (1982), for example, has shown that fathers' general developmental theories do affect the teaching strategy they use with their children in a specific laboratory setting, though mothers' specific teaching strategies are not related to their general developmental theories to the same extent.

Fourth, are there other factors, such as mental health and social support, that influence parents' beliefs and practices? Evidence from the depression literature suggests that parents who are depressed feel less efficacious in implementing their parenting goals (see Elder & Ardelt, 1992). Similarly, work on the impact of neighborhoods and of economic stress suggests that these demographic characteristics may affect parenting through their influence on the parents' mental health and social support networks (e.g., Elder & Ardelt, 1992; Elder et al., 1992; Goldsmith, 1986; Harold-Goldsmith et al., 1988; McLoyd, 1990).

Fifth, how do general beliefs and practices interact with more specific practices in shaping children's preferences and beliefs? Are the effects of the parents' general beliefs on their children's development mediated primarily by their impact on specific practices and beliefs, or do these general beliefs and practices have substantial direct effects themselves? If so, do general beliefs particularly influence some types of motivational outcomes while specific beliefs and practices have more influence on other outcomes? One might predict, for example, that parents' general beliefs and practices will affect traitlike aspects of motivation, whereas specific beliefs and practices are more likely to affect the specific domains in which the traitlike characteristics are manifest.

Finally, what is the relation of these general beliefs and practices to children's integration of self and task beliefs in the process of maintaining self-esteem over time and in response to experiences outside the home? For example, what happens when a child finds out he or she either does not want to or cannot fulfill the parents' goals? Or what happens when children discover their peers have a different set of general beliefs than their parents do?

ROLE MODELS

Experimental research has established the importance of adults' behavior as a standard or model for children's behavior. "Observational learning" has been suggested as one of the mechanisms accounting for the efficiency with which children absorb a variety of social norms (cf. Bandura & Walters, 1963; Parsons, Adler, & Kaczala, 1982). There are several ways parents as models might influence their children's attitudes toward various activities. At the most basic level, they could influence their children's attitudes simply by engaging in different pursuits. If children want to be like their parents, they are likely to place high value on the activities their parents value. Similarly, within a family, boys and girls may develop differential preferences as a result of sex differences in the behavior patterns of their mothers and fathers. Status-attainment models of occupational choice provide good support for this type of effect (e.g., see Marjoribanks, 1980).

Parents might also influence children's beliefs through the messages they provide about their own abilities and preferences. For example, if mothers and fathers differ in their estimates of their own intellectual or athletic abilities, then boys and girls might develop different ability self-concepts and different preferences by incorporating their parents' beliefs into their own self-perceptions (Eccles Parsons et al., 1983). We know of few studies that have assessed these hypotheses. Our own work (Parsons, Adler, & Kaczala, 1982) suggests that parents have less of an effect on their children's academic beliefs as role models of math achievement than as interpreters of their children's experience. But this work has been done only within the academic achievement domain and only among families with a narrow range of variation in parents' self-perceptions and interests. The role modeling effect of parents may be more evident when we look at younger children and a wider range of activities and families.

Role models outside the home are also likely to influence children's interests and self-perceptions. Observing powerful others engage in a particular activity or behavior increases the likelihood that a child will imitate the behavior or seek out the activity (Bandura & Walters, 1963). These powerful others can engage either in positive or in risky or less desirable behaviors and activities. Neighborhoods, and particular schools, for example, differ in the prevalence and salience of positive and negative role models. Parents must deal with the possible influence of such role models on their children. Very little research has looked at how they go about managing this aspect of their children's experience and what distinguishes effective parents from less effective ones.

SPECIFIC BELIEFS, VALUES, AND PERCEPTIONS: PARENTS AS INTERPRETERS OF REALITY

Parents hold a variety of specific beliefs about their children and about more general things such as the nature of talent. We assume these beliefs affect both parents' behavior vis-à-vis their children and the type of messages parents give as they help their children interpret their own experiences. Therefore we think it is important to understand these beliefs. Although work is just beginning in this area, the following parental beliefs and interpretative processes seem most promising: (1) parents' causal attributions concerning their children's performance in each domain; (2) parents' perceptions of the difficulty of various tasks for their children; (3) parents' expectations for their children's probable success at the task and their confidence in their children's ability; (4) parents' view of the value of the task for each particular child and the extent to which they believe they should encourage their children to master various tasks; (5) parents' achievement standards for their children for activities from each domain; (6) parents' beliefs regarding the stability of low competence and the strategies for increasing competence in various domains; (7) parents' beliefs about the origin of individual differences in competence in various domains; and (8) parents' beliefs about the external barriers to success for each child and about effective strategies to overcome these barriers as well as their own ability to implement these strategies for a particular child.

We assume that parents convey these beliefs to their children in a variety of ways. For example, they may make causal attributions concerning their children's performance—praising them for that A in math by pointing out either their natural talent or their great diligence. Similarly, they may make statements about the origins of individual differences in competencies in various domains—statements such as "You have to be born with math talent" or "Anyone can be good at sports if they just work hard enough." They also form impressions of their children's competencies and may communicate these impressions in both overt and subtle messages; for example, by explicitly telling children what they are good at or more subtly by encouraging or discouraging particular activities.

These messages do influence children's developing self beliefs and task beliefs. Evidence from several investigators suggests that parents' estimates of their children's academic abilities are important predictors of children's own self and task beliefs (Parsons et al., 1982; see also Alexander & Entwisle, 1988; Entwisle & Baker, 1983; Miller, Manhal, & Mee, 1991). In our earlier work, for example, parents' perceptions of their children's math ability had a significant effect on the children's view of their own math ability that was independent of the impact of their actual performance on both the parents' and children's perceptions (Parsons et al., 1982).

We have now replicated this effect in the Michigan Study of Adolescent Life Transitions (MSALT), a longitudinal study of adolescent development in the context of the family and the school. In 1983, approximately 2,000 sixth graders were recruited into this study. About 1,000 of their mothers also agreed to participate. (About 600 fathers participated too, but their data are not presented here owing to space limitations; their results mirror the findings based on the mothers' data.) These families represent a wide range of socioeconomic backgrounds. Parents were asked a series of questions regarding their perceptions of their children's competency and their expectations for the child's performance in math, English, and sports. All scales reported in this chapter had several items, and all scales had good reliabilities (Cronbach alphas > .65) and good predictive validity (see Parsons et al., 1982, for predictive validity information). In this chapter we present findings from the first two years of this study, when the children were in the sixth and seventh grades.

One of the path analyses we performed to test the relation of mothers' perceptions of their sixth-grade children's abilities to the children's own self-perceptions is shown in Figure 2. Although this figure illustrates the results for boys, the effects for girls are virtually identical. As you can see, mothers' ratings of their children's abilities in math and English are related to the teachers' ratings of the children's math ability. But more important, the parents' view of their children's ability in both math and English had an important predictive relation to the children's own self-perceptions (Eccles et al., 1989). Furthermore, we have tested the causal direction implied in this relationship using longitudinal cross-lagged panel analyses, done with structural equation modeling as specified by Rogosa (1979). The results for the math domain are illustrated in Figure 3 (similar results hold for the sports domain as well). The findings are consistent with the hypothesized causal direction. Clearly, parent and child perceptions are reciprocally related. Nonetheless, mothers' perceptions of their children's ability at this age do appear to influence change over time in the children's self-perceptions more strongly than vice versa (Eccles, Jacobs, et al., 1991, in press).

The path analysis shown in Figure 2 suggests two other important conclusions. First, mothers' perceptions of their children's math abilities also predict the children's interest in doing mathematics. Second, there is a negative effect of mothers' perceptions of their children's English ability on the children's perceptions of their own math ability. Individuals use a variety of information in making an inference about how good they are in various domains. We have suggested, for example, that they compare their relative performance across domains and generate a hierarchy of ability perceptions from these internal self-comparisons, that is, they decide they are very good at math because they do better, and find it easier to do better, at math than at other school subjects (Eccles, 1987; Eccles

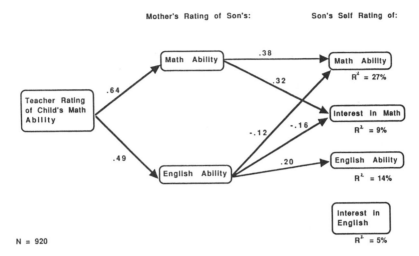

FIGURE 2: Mothers' influence on sons' self-perceptions. This is a path analysis using sequential columnwise multiple regression. Coefficients are standardized. *N* is approximately 900. Sons are in the sixth grade. Comparable results were obtained for daughters.

Parsons et al., 1983; see also Marsh, 1990). The results depicted in Figure 2 suggest that a similar phenomenon may characterize the impact of mothers' perceptions of their children's abilities on the development of the children's self-perceptions. If their mothers think they are very good in English, the children in this study have a lower estimate of their math ability than one would predict given their teachers' and their mothers' rating of their math ability. These findings suggest two conclusions: (1) mothers form, and communicate, a hierarchical view of their children's relative abilities, and (2) where math falls in this hierarchy has an impact on the children's conclusions regarding their math ability independent of their mothers' absolute assessment of it.

The messages parents provide regarding the value they attach to various activities should also influence their children's motivation. There are some data suggesting that parents convey differential task values through explicit rewards and encouragement for participating in some activities rather than others. For example, parents, teachers, and counselors are all more likely to encourage boys than girls to pursue math-related interests (see Eccles & Hoff-

DEVELOPMENTAL PERSPECTIVES ON MOTIVATION

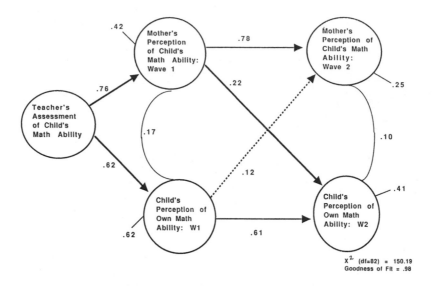

FIGURE 3: Cross-lagged structural equation model of causal directions and mediating influences on mothers' perceptions on sons' self-perceptions for the domain of mathematics. Measurement model coefficients have been omitted. Coefficients were generated with LISREL VI. N is approximately 900. Sons are in the sixth grade. Comparable results were obtained for daughters.

man, 1984). But whether this encouragement directly affects either the value the children attach to math or their participation in math activities has not been established. Our own work suggests rather weak relations between the values parents and adolescents place on math (Parsons, Adler, & Kaczala, 1982). Such relationships may be stronger for younger children and when a wider range of activities are included. The relationship may also be curvilinear. Work in the area of intrinsic motivation suggests that excessive attempts to influence children's interest in a specific activity can backfire and lead to a decrease in their interest and involvement (e.g., Deci & Ryan, 1985; Lepper & Greene, 1978).

We are also interested in the potential link between parents' activity-value hierarchy and children's general self-esteem. William James (1892/1963) suggested that perceptions of one's competence in a particular domain should influence one's self-esteem only if that particular domain is highly valued. A similar case has been made by Harter (1985, 1986). Extending this idea to more than one activity domain suggests that we need to know the hierarchy of a person's subjective task values as well as the hierarchy of her or his competence perceptions if we are to understand the link between competency self-perceptions and self-esteem. If James is correct, then children with high self-esteem should have congruent hierarchies for their competency assessments and their subjective task values. In contrast, children with discrepant hierarchies (that is, children who feel relatively incompetent at those activities that are relatively high in their task-value hierarchy) are likely to be at risk for low self-esteem. Individuals may protect their self-esteem over time by lowering the value they attach to those activities that they feel relatively less competent doing. For example, they may cope with being relatively incompetent in tennis by concluding that being good at tennis is not very important. But what happens when an individual cannot use this ego-protective strategy? For example, what happens if a child's parents' activity-value hierarchy is so rigid they do not adapt it to fit well with their child's strengths and weaknesses? In this case, the children should be at high risk for developing low self-esteem because their social environment will make it difficult for them to protect their self-esteem by lowering the value they attach to those activity domains that they feel relatively less "competent" doing.

Influences on the ontogeny of parents' perceptions of their children's competencies and interests. How do parents form their impressions of their children's abilities and interests? We have already noted that they appear to rely heavily on objective feedback, such as school grades. But it is also quite possible that their more general beliefs—beliefs linked to their culture or to their gender-role beliefs—play a role. Parents' gender-role stereotypes, for example, might lead them to distort their impression of their children's competencies in a stereotypic manner. We know, for example, that parents' perceptions of their children's abilities in math are related to the children's gender, despite the fact that gender differences in performance in mathematics are quite small and do not emerge with great regularity before secondary school. We have now replicated this effect in the Michigan Study of Adolescent Life Transition Study (MSALT) and have shown gender-role-congruent differences in these parents' perceptions of their children's ability in English and sports as well. These results are summarized in Table 1.

We have also replicated the results with a much younger sample in the Michigan Study of Middle Childhood, a four-year longitudinal study of the development of elementary-school-aged children, again in the context of the family and the school. In 1986 approximately 600 children and their families were recruited into this study. The children were in either kindergarten, first grade, or third grade at that time. The data summarized here were collected in the first year of the study (1987). We used scales and items similar to those in the MSALT study. The results for how children's sex affects parents' perceptions of the children's abilities and interests in math, reading, and sports are summarized in Table 1. Gender-role stereotypic differences emerged for both reading and sports. Parents of daughters rated their children as more competent in reading than parents of sons, and vice versa for sports. However, the children's sex did not significantly affect the parents' perceptions of the children's mathematical competence. Apparently this sex-of-child effect does not emerge until the children are somewhat older.

Why do these sex-of-child effects characterize parents' perceptions of, and goals for, their children? Many explanations have been offered to account for the gender-role stereotyping of people's ratings of males' and females' competencies in various domains. The most critical issue for this chapter is how far parents' stereotypical perceptions of their children either are accurate or reflect, at least in part, perceptual bias. It is true that parents' perceptions of their children's competence in academic subjects are highly correlated with indicators of the children's performance and achievement, such as school grades and standardized test scores (Alexander & Entwisle, 1988; Parsons, Adler, & Kaczala, 1982). But are the sex-of-child effects in their perceptions a reflection of "true" sex differences in either talent or competence? This question is difficult to answer because females and males are treated so differently by their parents and their peers from very early in their lives. Consequently it is impossible to get a good indicator of natural talent that is not influenced by the processes associated with gender-role socialization—the very processes we are trying to document. For example, can we conclude that parents' gender-role-stereotyped perceptions of their six-year-old children's talent in sports are accurate if we find that the male

Table 1
Sex-of-Child Effects on Parents' Perceptions

	Domains								
	Math			English/Reading			Sports		
Variables	Means Girls	Means Boys	F	Means Girls	Means Boys	F	Means Girls	Means Boys	F
Adolescent Transition Study[a]									
Parents' perception of current competence	5.45	5.40	< 1.00	5.65	4.99	101.71***	4.84	5.22	25.75***
Parents' perception of task difficulty	4.10	3.80	12.10***	3.73	4.24	39.20***	3.77	3.47	13.21***
Parents' perception of natural talent	4.76	5.01	9.85	5.03	4.51	46.76***	4.22	4.87	59.76***
Parents' perception of future performance	5.36	5.34	< 1.00	5.59	5.02	74.99***			
Parents' perception of performance in career	5.17	5.42	11.17***	5.41	4.87	54.91***	3.80	4.10	12.90***
Parents' perception of importance	6.38	6.50	9.21**	6.34	6.34	< 1.00			
Middle Childhood Development Study[b]									
Parents' perception of current competence	5.38	5.34	< 1.00	5.67	5.27	10.28***	4.50	4.98	16.41***
Parents' perception of task difficulty	2.08	2.02	< 1.00	1.64	2.01	8.33**	2.57	2.15	11.71***
Parents' perception of natural talent	5.01	5.15	1.45	5.41	5.11	7.00**	4.31	4.74	12.35***
Parents' perception of future performance	5.99	5.91	< 1.00	6.36	5.95	19.13***	5.02	5.52	19.91***
Parents' perception of importance	6.26	6.46	8.12**	6.65	6.63	< 1.00	4.20	4.72	20.00***

[a]Mothers of sixth graders, approximate $N = 900$.

[b]Parents of kindergarteners, first graders, and third graders, approximate $N = 500$.

*$p < .05$. **$p < .01$. ***$p < .001$.

children do, indeed, perform better than the female children on a standardized test of athletic skill at this age? Not really, because it is quite likely that the female and male children have already had different opportunities to develop their athletic skills. The best we can do at this point is to use the strategy proposed by Jussim (1986, 1989). This strategy involves assessing how closely the perceiver's judgments are related to the variables of interest (in this case the child's gender) after controlling for the possible association between the perceiver's judgment and more objective indicators of the child's actual performance level. If they are closely related, then we can begin to try to identify the mediating cognitive processes that account for the biased portion of these perceptions (i.e., the portion not due to actual differences in the performance levels of girls and boys).

In both our own work (see Parsons, Adler, & Kaczala, 1982; Eccles & Jacobs, 1986) and the work of Entwisle and her colleagues (see Alexander & Entwisle, 1988), it is clear that parents' perceptions of their children's competence in mathematics are influenced by the children's sex independent of their actual performance in mathematics. Comparable results appear to characterize other activity domains as well. For example, Jacobs and Eccles (in press) have found that a child's sex has an independent influence on parents' ratings of their sixth-grade children's athletic talent after controlling for the teachers' ratings of it. Thus it appears that something in addition to overt performance is influencing the formation of parents' perceptions of their children's competence in both math and sports. What might these factors be? This chapter presents evidence for two possible influences: (a) differential causal attributions—parents may attribute their children's performance to different causes, leading them to different conclusions regarding their daughters' versus their sons' "talents"; and (b) generalization of gender-role stereotypes— parents may generalize their category-based, gender-role stereotypes to their target-based judgments of their own children's competence.

Causal attributions. According to attribution theory (Weiner, 1972; Weiner et al., 1971), perceptions of another person's competence depend on the causal attributions made for the person's performance. If parents of boys make different attributions for their children's math performance than do parents of girls, it follows that these parents should develop different perceptions of their children's math competence. In a test of this hypothesis, Yee and Eccles (1988) found that parents of boys rated natural talent as a more important reason for their children's math successes than did parents of girls. In contrast, parents of girls rated effort as a more important reason for their children's math successes than did parents of boys (see also Holloway & Hess, 1985). In addition, to the extent that the parents attributed their children's success in mathematics to effort, they also rated them as less talented in mathematics. Conversely, to the extent that they attributed their child's success in mathematics to talent, they also rated them as more talented. Thus it appears that the gender-role-stereotyped attributions parents make for their children's performance may be important mediators of the parents' gender-differentiated perceptions of their math competence.

The sixth-grade data from MSALT provide a direct test of this conclusion. The mothers in this study were asked to imagine a time when their children had done very well in mathematics, reading, and sports and then to rate, on a seven-point Likert scale, the importance of the following six possible causes in determining this success: natural talent, effort, task ease, teacher help, parent help, and current skill level. Significant sex-of-child effects were obtained on attributions of success to natural talent in each domain; the pattern of these differences reflects the gender-role stereotyping of the domains: sons' successes in math and sports were more likely to be attributed to natural talent than daughters', while daughters' successes in English were more likely to be attributed to natural talent than sons'. These results confirm our earlier evidence of stereotypic sex-of-child effects on mothers' causal attributions.

To test the mediation hypothesis directly, we did a series of regression analyses on those mothers' perceptions that yielded a significant sex-of-child effect in each domain. Support for a mediational hypothesis consists of demonstrating that the relation between variables A and C is reduced or eliminated when the hypothesized mediating variable B is entered into the regression equation. We used a path-analytic procedure to test this effect. The results for math are illustrated in Figure 4; all significant paths ($p < .05$) are shown. Consistent with the mediational hypothesis, Figure 4 shows that the significant relation of child's sex to the relevant parent outcome variables reported in Table 1 (parents' perceptions of a child's natural

DEVELOPMENTAL PERSPECTIVES ON MOTIVATION

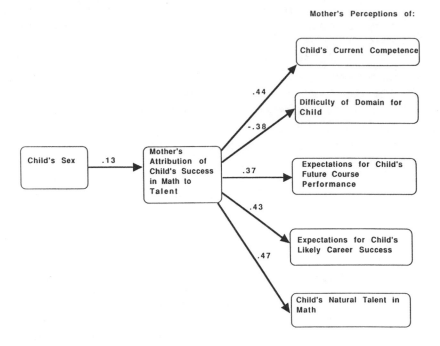

FIGURE 4: Path analysis testing mediating role of mothers' causal attributions of success to math talent. This path analysis uses sequential columnwise multiple regression. Coefficients are standardized. N is approximately 1,800. Children are in the sixth grade.

math talent, the difficulty of math for the child, and their expectations regarding the child's likely future success in both math courses and a math-related career) are no longer significant once the relation between the child's sex and the parents' attribution of the child's math success to talent are controlled (i.e., all the direct paths from the child's sex to the parent perception variables displayed in the far right column are nonsignificant). Comparable results for the talent attribution emerged in both the reading and sports domains. As predicted, children's sex influenced their mothers' causal attribution in each of these domains, which, in turn, influenced the mothers' perceptions of their children's talent. In these domains, however, we still found evidence of a direct effect of child's sex on parents' perceptions, even though the size of this effect was significantly reduced by including the mothers' causal attribution in the path analysis.

These data provide good preliminary support for the hypothesized biasing effect of causal attributions on parents' perceptions of their children's competencies. However, it is important to note that these beliefs are all highly interrelated, and the data are correlational in nature. The consistency of the findings across domains indicates that the relationships are reliable, but their actual causal direction is still at issue. We are just beginning the longitudinal analyses necessary to pin down the predominant causal directions of influence among these various beliefs; preliminary analyses support the direction illustrated in these figures: Causal attributions at time 1 do appear to influence parents' perceptions of their children's ability at time 2 (one year later) after controlling for the parents' time 1 perceptions of their children's abilities.

Biasing influence of gender-role stereotypes. We have hypothesized that parents' gender-role stereotypes regarding the extent to which males or females, in general, are likely to be more talented in a particular domain affect their perceptions of their own children's ability in this domain, leading to a distortion in the parents' perceptions of their ability in the gender-role-stereotyped direction (see Eccles, 1984; Eccles Parsons et al., 1983; Jacobs, 1987; Jacobs & Eccles, 1985). Evaluating this hypothesis requires testing two specific subhypotheses: (1) the impact of children's gender on parents' perceptions of their ability in any particular domain will depend partially on the parents' gender-role stereotypes regarding ability in that domain; and (2) this effect will be significant even after one has entered an independent indicator of the children's actual level of competence in the domain as a control. We have begun to test these hypotheses (see Jacobs, 1987, 1991; Jacobs & Eccles, in press). As reported earlier, parents hold gender-differentiated views of their children's academic and nonacademic abilities at a very early age, and these beliefs are more gender-differentiated than are objective indicators of the children's actual performance in these domains (e.g., Alexander & Entwisle, 1988; Eccles et al., 1989; Eccles & Harold, 1991; Jacobs & Eccles, 1985). But are these beliefs related to parents' more general gender-role stereotypes? The critical issue is not whether parents, on the average, give gender-differentiated estimates of their children's abilities. Instead, the issue is whether parents who endorse the culturally dominant gender-role stereotype regarding the distribution of talent between males and females distort their perception of their own children's abilities in a direction that is consistent with their gender-role stereotype to a greater extent than parents who do not endorse the stereotype. Evidence from both our studies supports this hypothesis.

In the Michigan Study of Middle Childhood, mothers were asked who they thought was naturally better at mathematics, reading, and sports—boys, girls, or neither. They were also asked on a separate questionnaire to state how much natural talent their children had in each of these three domains and how important they thought it was for them to be good in each domain. The interaction of children's sex with the parents' category-based gender-role stereotypes in predicting the parents' ratings of their own children's competency was tested in each domain. All nine interactions were significant at $p < .01$ (Eccles et al., 1989). The results for mathematics are particularly interesting. As you may recall, on the average the sex of their children did not affect these mothers' perceptions of either the children's math talent or the difficulty of math for them. But the children's sex did affect their rating of the children's competence in math when it was included in an interaction term with their gender-role stereotype of mathematical competence. As predicted, mothers who believed that males are naturally more talented in mathematics also rated sons as having more math talent than daughters; in contrast, the sex-of-child effect was not significant for those mothers who believed that males and females are equally likely to be talented at mathematics. Similar results were obtained for the importance ratings (Eccles et al., 1989, 1991, in press). Similar gender-role stereotypic effects characterized the mothers' reports on their children's talent in sports and English. Although it is possible that these effects are due to the impact of objective gender differences in the children's performance on the mothers' general gender-role stereotypes rather than vice versa, the extreme stability of gender-role stereotypes across time in a variety of populations makes this an unlikely alternative interpretation.

Jacobs and Eccles have more fully explored these effects in the domains of math and sports using data from the Michigan Study of Adolescent Life Transitions (Jacobs, 1987; Jacobs & Eccles, in press). Using path-analytic techniques, we tested the interaction of the sex of one's child and one's category-based gender-role stereotypes on

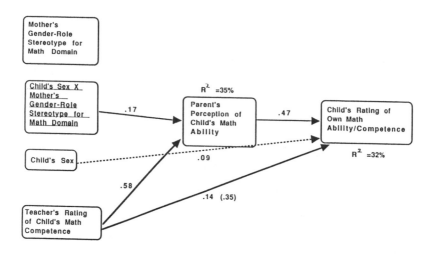

FIGURE 5. Path analysis showing moderating influence of mothers' gender-role stereotypes for the math domain on the effect of children's sex on mothers' perceptions of their abilities in math. This path analysis uses sequential columnwise multiple regression. Coefficients are standardized. *N* is approximately 1,800. Children are in the sixth grade.

mother's perceptions of their children's ability, controlling for the effect of an independent indicator of the child's actual ability level (the teacher's rating). The model tested is shown in Figure 5, which illustrates the results for the math domain. Comparable results characterized the sports and social domains (see Jacobs & Eccles, in press). The interaction term was created so that a positive coefficient indicates that the mother was distorting her impression of her child in the gender-role appropriate direction. That is, if she was talking about a son, her perception of her child's ability was higher than would have been predicted using only the teacher's rating; in contrast, if she was talking about a daughter, her perception was lower than would have been predicted using only the teacher's rating.

Once again the data are consistent with our hypothesis. The interaction term is significant, and the coefficient is positive. Thus, to the extent that these mothers endorsed the traditional gender-role stereotypic belief that males are naturally better than girls in math and sports, they distorted their perception of their children's competence in the gender-role stereotypic direction. In addition, consistent with the findings of Parsons, Adler, and Kaczala (1982), the mothers' perceptions of their children's competence in each domain had a significant influence on the children's own self-perceptions even after their actual performance in each domain was controlled. These results provide support for the hypothesis that general gender-role-stereotyped beliefs lead to a bias in parents' perceptions of their own children's competencies. Given the extensive exposure parents have to their children's actual performance levels, we would not expect the biasing effects to be large, and they are not. Nevertheless, the effects are both reliable and consistent across several activity domains, and they do appear to influence children's own self-perceptions in a manner consistent with the self-fulfilling prophecy hypothesis.

Evidence from these studies thus suggests that both parents' causal attributions for their children's successes and parents' category-based gender-role stereotypes lead to perceptual bias in their impressions of their children's competencies in gender-role-stereotyped activity domains. Although parents' perceptions of their children's competencies in various domains are strongly related to independent indicators of actual competence in these domains, the evidence clearly indicates that such perceptions are also influenced by the children's sex and by the parents' gender-role-stereotyped beliefs about which sex is naturally more talented in these domains. Furthermore, the evidence supports the conclusion that these influences are independent of any actual differences in the children's competencies. Thus our findings suggest that perceptual bias is operating in the formation of parents' impressions of their children's competencies in gender-role-stereotyped activity domains.

Other specific external factors should also affect the impressions parents form of their children's competencies. For example, teachers should play an important role. We have already noted that parents' perceptions of their children's academic abilities are strongly related to the grades teachers give them. But how teachers communicate and involve parents should also affect parents' and children's beliefs. Cultural factors, such as ethnic and religious heritage as well as their culture's view of the world should also affect parents' perceptions of their children.

In summary, in this section we have provided examples of how parents' general beliefs can affect their specific perceptions of their children. We have also shown how other types of experience can affect the ontogeny of these perceptions. In the next section we discuss how these specific and general beliefs affect parents' behaviors vis-à-vis their children.

PROVISION OF SPECIFIC EXPERIENCES AT HOME

Parents' behavior can influence their children's interests and activity choices in a number of ways. One way is through the pattern of reinforcements they provide for engaging in various behaviors. Negative reinforcement, especially, is likely to decrease the likelihood that the child will engage in the activity in the future. The effect of positive reinforcement is less clear. There is clear evidence that excessive positive reinforcement that is not linked to the quality of the child's performance can undermine children's intrinsic motivation for the activity and decrease the likelihood that they will engage in it in the future (e.g., Deci & Ryan, 1985).

Parents may also influence the ontogeny of their children's self and task beliefs by the things they do with them and by the types of experiences and toys they provide. In most families parents and children do many things together. It seems likely that parents' general and specific beliefs are related to which particular activities they choose and which experiences they try to provide for their children. For example, Katkovsky, Crandall, and Preston (1964) found that parents who value intellectual competence are more likely to become involved in their children's intellectual pursuits. Several studies have shown that parents' involvement in reading to their children and providing reading materials in the home predicts children's later reading achievement (e.g., Dix, 1976; Durkin, 1966). This work suggests that parents' involvement with their children and their attitudes toward the children's achievement have important consequences for achievement motivation and behavior. More recent confirmation of the importance of parents' involvement comes in the work of Grolnick and Ryan (e.g., 1989). Furthermore, these investigators have been able to show that the impact of parents' involvement on children's motivation is likely to be mediated by children's perceptions of their parents' behavior (Grolnick, Ryan, & Deci, 1991).

DEVELOPMENTAL PERSPECTIVES ON MOTIVATION

The socialization of gender roles provides a good example of these processes. It is likely that the sex differences we see in children's competencies, self-perceptions, interests, and aspirations result in part from sex differences in the types of experiences parents provide for them (Huston, 1984). For example, we have shown that parents have gender-role-biased perceptions of their children's competencies. Proponents of a self-fulfilling prophecy view of the socialization of gender differences would argue that these differences in parents' perceptions set in motion a series of events that ultimately create the very differences the parents originally believed to exist. But few studies have looked at the link between the experiences provided by parents and parents' beliefs. Our recent work has investigated how this differential provision of experiences is linked to general and specific beliefs, particularly with regard to gender-role socialization. The evidence suggests that general gender-role beliefs influence perceptions of individual children's competencies and interests, which in turn affect the kinds of experiences parents provide. This sequence is illustrated in Figure 6, which shows the theoretical model we have used to address this question. Essentially, we believe that parents' gender-role stereotypes, in interaction with their children's sex, affect the following mediators: (1) parents' causal attributions for the children's performance; (2) parents' emotional reaction to their children's performance in various activities; (3) the importance parents attach to their children's acquiring various skills; (4) the advice parents provide their children regarding involvement in various skills; and (5) the activities and toys parents provide. In turn, we predict that these subtle and explicit mediators influence the development of the following child outcomes across the various gender-role-stereotyped activity domains: (1) children's confidence in their ability; (2) children's interest in mastering various skills; (3) children's affective reaction to participating in various activities; and as a consequence of these self and task perceptions, (4) the amount of time and type of effort the children end up devoting to mastering and demonstrating various skills (see Eccles, Jacobs, & Harold, 1990).

We are just beginning to explore these links with the information we have gathered in the Michigan Study of Middle Childhood. In addition to questions regarding their perceptions of their children's abilities and interests, the parents in this study were asked for

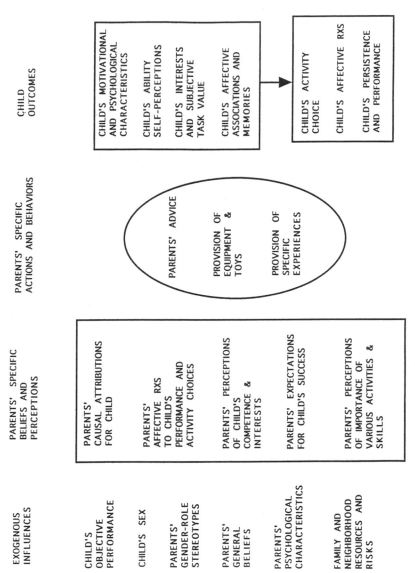

FIGURE 6: General model of relation of exogenous influences influences and parents' specific beliefs to parents' specific behaviors.

EXOGENOUS INFLUENCES

CHILD'S OBJECTIVE PERFORMANCE

CHILD'S SEX

PARENTS' GENDER-ROLE STEREOTYPES

PARENTS' GENERAL BELIEFS

PARENTS' PSYCHOLOGICAL CHARACTERISTICS

FAMILY AND NEIGHBORHOOD RESOURCES AND RISKS

PARENTS' SPECIFIC BELIEFS AND PERCEPTIONS

PARENTS' CAUSAL ATTRIBUTIONS FOR CHILD

PARENTS' AFFECTIVE RXS TO CHILD'S PERFORMANCE AND ACTIVITY CHOICES

PARENTS' PERCEPTIONS OF CHILD'S COMPETENCE & INTERESTS

PARENTS' EXPECTATIONS FOR CHILD'S SUCCESS

PARENTS' PERCEPTIONS OF IMPORTANCE OF VARIOUS ACTIVITIES & SKILLS

PARENTS' SPECIFIC ACTIONS AND BEHAVIORS

PARENTS' ADVICE

PROVISION OF EQUIPMENT & TOYS

PROVISION OF SPECIFIC EXPERIENCES

CHILD OUTCOMES

CHILD'S MOTIVATIONAL AND PSYCHOLOGICAL CHARACTERISTICS

CHILD'S ABILITY SELF-PERCEPTIONS

CHILD'S INTERESTS AND SUBJECTIVE TASK VALUE

CHILD'S AFFECTIVE ASSOCIATIONS AND MEMORIES

CHILD'S ACTIVITY CHOICE

CHILD'S AFFECTIVE RXS

CHILD'S PERSISTENCE AND PERFORMANCE

a detailed report of the types of activities and experiences they provide for their children in several activity domains. They were also asked what types of skills and activities they encourage their children to develop. Finally, they were asked what they do with their children. Longitudinal analysis of these data is under way. As a first step in this process, we tested whether parents provide different types of experiences for girls and boys. They clearly do in several of the activity domains we are studying. These results are summarized in Table 2 (adapted from Harold, Eccles, Yoon, Aberbach, & Freedman-Doan, 1991).

As the second step, we used path analysis to determine whether the sex-of-child effects on the types of activities parents provide and encourage are mediated by the parents' perceptions of their children's ability and interests in each domain. Consistent with the mediational hypothesis, the sex-of-child effect on parents' encouragement of participation becomes nonsignificant when the sex-of-child effect on parents' perceptions of their children's sports ability and interest is entered into the path analysis (Eccles, Jacobs, & Harold, 1990; Harold et al., 1991).

In summary, we have presented evidence of the influence of social factors on parents' perceptions of their children's abilities in various activity domains. We have focused on children's sex as one potentially critical social factor and have presented data showing how it might influence parents' perceptions of their children's ability independent of actual performance in the domain. We have summarized some work documenting the link of these parents' perceptions to the types of experiences parents provide for their children. Work by Miller and his colleagues (e.g., Miller, Manhal, & Mee, 1991) also provides important information about the connection between parents' specific beliefs regarding their children's abilities and their interactions with them. They argue that parents who have an accurate view of their children's level of competence are better at providing appropriate tasks and appropriate levels of scaffolding as the children go about mastering these tasks.

Wentzel and her colleagues are also looking at these connections and are finding less evidence that the influence of parents' expectations for their children's performance on the children's commitment to schoolwork is mediated via their effect on parenting behaviors (e.g., Wentzel & Feldman, 1991). Instead, the effect of parents'

Table 2

Sex-of-Child Effects on Parents' Time Use with Children
and Activity Encouragement

Activity	Mean for Daughters	Mean for Sons	F Value
Work with child on computer[a]	1.76	1.89	4.14*
Play computer games with child[a]	1.73	2.04	17.79***
Encourage child to do math/science activities[b]	4.78	5.04	11.44***
Have child read to you[a]	3.76	3.55	4.84*
Encourage child to read[b]	6.41	6.20	12.41***
Play sports with child[a]	2.72	3.37	38.07***
Take child to sports event[a]	1.61	1.91	53.14***
Encourage child to play competitive sports[b]	4.43	5.08	66.43***
Encourage child to watch sports on television[b]	3.97	4.29	24.19***

[a] Answered on seven-point time scale with 1 = never and 7 = almost every day for a long time.
[b] Answered on a seven-point Likert scale with following labeled points: 1 = discourage, 2 = neither encourage or discourage, 3 = slightly encourage, 5 = moderately encourage, and 7 = strongly encourage.   *$p < .05$ **$p < .01$ ***$p < .001$

expectations seems to be direct. We have also found that parents' beliefs have a direct influence on children's developing self-concepts, as well as on the experiences parents encourage their children to have in various activity domains. But like Wentzel and Feldman, we are having a hard time identifying all the specific mechanisms through which these experiences affect children's self-perceptions and interests.

Characteristics such as social class, family income, and ethnicity also affect the types of toys and other experiences children receive (e.g., Coleman et al., 1966; Laosa, 1984; Marjoribanks, 1980). As noted earlier, family economic resources clearly influence what experiences parents can afford to provide for their children. Economic distress is also likely to limit the psychological resources parents can bring to bear as they attempt to structure their children's experience. For example, Elder has found that economic distress leads to withdrawal from the parenting role as well as to erratic parenting (Elder et al., 1985). Social class also influences which neighborhood a family lives in. In turn, the neighborhood influences the kinds of resources readily available to the family and the children and also the kinds of stresses and the complexity of the family management tasks parents must cope with. Finally, the neighborhood is likely to influence the availability of social supports to help the parents cope with the demands of the environment and provide their children with opportunities and varied experiences. As a consequence of all of these factors, families living in poor neighborhoods will have an especially difficult time providing their children with rich and varied experiences both within and outside the home.

But how might exposure to toys and activities affect children's preferences and activity choices? Through the processes associated with channeling (Hartley, 1964), familiarity (Zajonc, 1968), and both operant and classical conditioning, children should come to prefer the toys and activities they are exposed to. However, the extent to which this is true should depend on the affective climate created by parents when the children are engaged in any particular experience. The affective climate is part of the experience parents provide. If learning a particular skill takes place in a positive affective setting, it is likely children will come to enjoy the activity. If, instead, learning takes place in a highly charged negative affective setting, it is likely that the children will develop an aversion to it. In addition, the controlling nature of the situation in which the child learns a particular skill has been shown to influence intrinsic interest in that skill domain in the future (e.g., Boggiano, Main, & Katz, 1988; Deci & Ryan, 1985).

But at a more specific level, exposure to different toys and activities also gives children the opportunity to develop different competencies and a differentiated set of task values. We know that exposure to reading materials predicts later reading achievement (e.g., see Hess & Holloway, 1984; Laosa, 1984). Similarly, exposure to manipulative toys and large-space play appears to affect the development of such basic cognitive skills as spatial facility (Connor, Schackman, & Serbin, 1978). Without the opportunity to try a particular activity, children will never get a chance to find out if they are good at it or if they enjoy it.

In this section we have presented several ways that socializers —in this case parents—might influence the ontogeny of individual differences in self and task perceptions, interests, and various indicators of involvement (e.g., activity choice, intensity of effort, and performance level). We have also presented data from our longitudinal studies to support several of the hypotheses. In the next section, we present a similar analysis of the school context.

Social Contextual Characteristics in the School

GENERAL PRACTICES AND BELIEFS

Historically, most studies of teacher influence have focused on the impact of their general personal characteristics and teaching style on children's overall achievement, motivation, satisfaction, and self-concept (see Dunkin & Biddle, 1974). As with parents, these studies document the importance of such characteristics as teacher warmth and positive classroom climate (e.g., Fraser & Fisher, 1982; Moos, 1979), efficient organization and management (e.g., Blumenfeld, Hamilton, Bossert, Wessels, & Meece, 1983; Moos, 1979), sense of personal efficacy (Ashton & Webb, 1986; Brookover, Beady, Flood, Schweitzer, & Wisenbaker, 1979), general focus on learning goals (Ames & Archer, 1988), and support for autonomous learning behavior (de Charms, 1980; Deci & Ryan, 1985; Lepper & Greene, 1978).

Recently several investigators have suggested that it is important to look at these characteristics in combination. For example, it has been suggested that there is a cluster of teaching practices (e.g., individualized/differentiated versus whole-group instruction; ability grouping practices; and reward structure and the publicness of feedback) that make ability differences in classrooms very salient to the students (see Rosenholtz & Rosenholtz, 1981; Rosenholtz & Simpson, 1984). These investigators assume that the salience of ability differences will affect students' motivation by focusing everyone's attention more on extrinsic motivators, social comparison information, and the perception of ability as a stable entity state rather than an incremental condition. Similarly, work on classroom organization has highlighted the importance of a cluster of characteristics linked to the open-classroom philosophy. This work suggests that students are more satisfied and motivated, and may develop more autonomy, have more positive self-concepts, and learn to capitalize better on their individual strengths and preferences in classrooms where many activities occur simultaneously, materials are varied in level and content, and they are given choice and control over what to work on and with whom (Horwitz, 1979). Evidence in this line of work also suggests that these motivational gains can be made without sacrificing rigor and learning provided the teacher is a very good classroom manager. Finally, evidence is emerging that there may be

sex differences as well as individual differences in children's preference for different learning contexts, and that these differences may
interact with subject area in such a way as to yield a sex difference in
interest in different subject areas. Our own work, and that of others
in the field (e.g., Casserly & Rock, 1980), suggests that females respond more positively to math and science instruction if it is taught
in a cooperative or individualized manner rather than a competitive
manner, if it is taught from an applied/person-centered perspective
rather than a theoretical/abstract perspective, if it is taught using a
hands-on approach rather than a "book learning" approach, and if
the teacher avoids sexism in its many subtle forms.

Thus, as was true for families, positive school environments
seem to be characterized by the integration of emotional support,
good management, and high teacher expectations and involvement
with the students. For example, many studies assume that warm relationships increase a teacher's influence by increasing children's
desire to do what the teacher says (owing either to identification or
to the increased power of teachers' social reinforcement properties).
If this is true, then variations in teacher warmth and supportiveness
should influence the value children attach to working hard in the
classroom only if the teacher also provides both clear guidelines on
what to do and sufficient opportunity for autonomous behavioral involvement. That is, the impact of teacher warmth and support on
motivation and performance should depend on the extent to which
the teacher also runs a well-managed but not overly controlling
classroom. This idea is analogous to Baumrind's conclusions regarding the greater effectiveness of authoritative parenting and to Ryan
and Grolnick's three components of effective parenting.

Recent work has extended this general approach to the climate
of the entire school. These researchers suggest, and provide some
evidence, that schools are like communities that can vary in their climate and general expectations for all students (e.g., Bryk & Driscoll,
1988; Comer, 1980). Furthermore, they suggest that this general climate affects both the teachers and the students in fundamental
ways. Taking this idea one step further, Simmons and Blyth (1987),
for example, suggest that there are widely shared differences between elementary schools and secondary schools in organizational
factors linked to climate. These differences, they say, may account

for the climate differences between these school levels and, in turn, may explain the motivational differences we see between students in elementary schools and secondary schools. We will discuss this perspective more fully later.

SPECIFIC BELIEFS, EXPECTATIONS, AND TASK VALUE SOCIALIZATION: TEACHERS AS INTERPRETERS OF REALITY

Teachers convey many particular messages to specific students that could influence children's beliefs, motivation, and self-perceptions. Evidence from the teacher expectancy literature provides the best example of this type of effect (see Eccles & Wigfield, 1985; Jussim, 1989). This work suggests that teachers convey their interpretations of children's ability more through subtle modes of interaction than through direct, overt statements. Generally, teachers make few explicit and public statements concerning the causes of success and failure in classwork (Blumenfeld et al., 1983; Parsons, Kaczala, & Meece, 1982). When they do, their comments focus almost exclusively on effort; they almost never refer to lack of ability. In addition, such statements most often concern the potential negative consequences of not finishing assignments rather than relating to the purpose, interest, or value of the work (Blumenfeld et al., 1983). Indeed, when teachers make statements about the purpose or value of a task, students often ignore or mistrust the information, believing it means the task will be too difficult. Instead, those teachers who produce expectancy effects in their students convey their expectations through the ways they interact with different children and the types of assignments they give different children (and not all teachers produce these effects). For example, these teachers give high-expectancy students more opportunity to answer questions in class, and if these students make a mistake, the teachers give them more opportunity to correct it. Consistent with this evidence, Weinstein and her colleagues have shown that teacher expectancy effects are most likely in classrooms where the students themselves believe the teacher treats high and low achievers differently (e.g., Weinstein & Middlestadt, 1971).

TEACHERS AS EXPERIENCE PROVIDERS

Teachers also affect children's self and task beliefs by the types of material presented, the amount of work assigned, frequency of coverage, and instructional style (Blumenfeld, Pintrich, Meece, & Wessels, 1982). If the teacher gives too much work, students are less likely to enjoy the task. And if topics are infrequently covered they decline in perceived value. Thus young children say they do not work hard on science or social studies because these subjects are not often dealt with and so are not thought of as important (Blumenfeld & Pintrich, 1982). In addition, if the teacher makes the subject matter interesting and provides variety, children are more likely to respond positively (Blumenfeld & Pintrich, 1983). In fact, teacher attitudes and enthusiasm are more important than particular curriculum materials in affecting student attitudes.

In summary, then, one can use the same approach as outlined earlier for studying family social context to identify and study the important social and structural characteristics of schools. But because schools are a more widely shared social environment than families, one can ask an even more interesting question about the school as a social context. We know there are fairly consistent age-related changes in various indicators of children's motivational orientation, interests, and activity involvement, particularly with regard to school-related achievement tasks. These changes are often interpreted as reflecting some developmental change going on in the individual. Is it possible that there are systematic changes in the social context of the school? Furthermore, is it possible that these changes could contribute to the age-related changes we see in children's school-related motivation? We turn to these questions in the next section.

Developmental Changes in Individuals' Self and Task Beliefs: The Effects of Stage-Environment Match

Several investigators have suggested that there are general developmental declines during early adolescence in such motivational constructs as interest in school (Epstein & McPartland, 1976); intrinsic motivation (Harter, 1981); theories about the nature of ability (Stipek

& Mac Iver, 1989); and self-concepts (Eccles, Adler, & Meece, 1984; Simmons & Blyth, 1987; see also Eccles & Midgley, 1989; Eccles, Midgley, & Adler, 1984). For example, Simmons and Blyth (1987) found a marked decline in some early adolescents' school grades as they moved into junior high school. Furthermore, the magnitude of this decline was predictive of subsequent school failure and drop-out. Similarly timed developmental declines have been documented for such motivational constructs as interest in school (Epstein & McPartland, 1976); intrinsic motivation (Harter, 1981); self-concepts/self-perceptions (Eccles, Midgley, & Adler, 1984; Simmons & Blyth, 1987); and confidence in one's intellectual abilities, especially after failure (Parsons & Ruble, 1977). There are also reports of age-related increases during early adolescence in such negative motivational and behavioral characteristics as test anxiety (Hill, 1980), focus on self-evaluation rather than task mastery (Nicholls, 1980), and both truancy and school dropout (Rosenbaum, 1976; see Eccles, Midgley, & Adler, 1984, for a full review). Although these changes are not extreme for most adolescents, there is sufficient evidence of a gradual decline in various indicators of academic motivation, behavior, and self-perception over the early adolescent years to make one wonder what is happening (see Eccles & Midgley, 1989, for a review).

A variety of explanations have been offered for these "negative" changes. Some have suggested that such declines result from the intraspsychic upheaval assumed to be associated with early adolescent development (e.g., Freud, 1969). Others have implicated the coincidence of the timing of multiple life changes. For example, Simmons and her colleagues have suggested that the coincidence of the junior high school transition with pubertal development accounts for the declines in the school-related measures and self-esteem (e.g., Blyth, Simmons, & Carlton-Ford, 1983; Simmons & Blyth, 1987). Drawing on cumulative stress theory, these theorists hypothesize that declines in motivation result because adolescents making the transition to junior high school at the end of grade six must cope with two major transitions: pubertal change and school change. And since coping with multiple transitions is more difficult than coping with only one, they conclude that these adolescents are at greater risk of negative outcomes than those who have to cope only with pubertal change during this developmental period. To test this hypothesis, Simmons and her colleagues compared the pattern of changes in school-related outcomes for early adolescents who moved from sixth to seventh grade in a K–8, 9–12 system with the pattern of change for those adolescents who made the same grade transition in a K–6, 7–9, 10–12 school system. This work separates the conjoint effects of age and transition operating in most developmental studies of this age period. These researchers find clear evidence, especially among girls, of greater negative change among those adolescents making the junior high school transition than among those remaining in the same school setting. We have obtained similar findings using the data from the National Educational Longitudinal Study (NELS). We compared eighth graders in a K–8 school system with eighth graders in either a K–6, 7–9 system or a K–5, 6–8 system. The students in the K–8 systems looked better on several motivational indicators such as self-esteem, preparedness, and attendance than the students in the other two systems (Eccles, Lord, & Midgley, 1991).

But are these differences due to the impact of a major school transition at the time of their pubertal changes, or are they due to differences in the nature of the school environments in these two educational structures? Or are the differences due to both sets of experiences? Simmons and her colleagues, as well as others, now argue for the last (see Carnegie Council on Adolescent Development, 1989; Simmons & Blyth, 1987). Other investigators have suggested that the changing nature of the educational environments many early adolescents experience is a plausible explanation for the declines in the school-related measures associated with the junior high school transition (e.g., Eccles & Midgley, 1989; Eccles, Midgley, & Adler, 1984; Lipsitz, 1981). Drawing upon person-environment fit theory (see Hunt, 1975), Eccles and Midgley (1989) proposed that these motivational and behavioral declines could result because junior high schools are not providing appropriate educational environments for early adolescents. According to person-environment fit theory, behavior, motivation and mental health are influenced by the fit between the characteristics individuals bring to their social environments and the characteristics of those social environments. Individuals are not likely to do very well, or be very motivated, if their social environments do not fit their psychological needs. If the social environments in the typical junior high school do not fit very well with the psychological needs of young adolescents, then person-environment fit theory predicts a decline in their motivation, interest, performance, and behavior as they move into this environment.

Hunt (1975) has suggested an even more interesting way to apply the person-environment fit perspective to the issues of declining motivation at early adolescence. Bringing a developmental perspective to the idea of person-environment fit, he argued that "maintaining a developmental perspective becomes very important in implementing person-environment matching because a teacher should not only take account of a student's contemporaneous needs by providing whatever structure he presently requires, but also view his present need for structure on a developmental continuum along which growth toward independence and less need for structure is the long-term objective" (Hunt, 1975, p. 221). In other words, teachers should provide the optimal level of structure for children's current levels of maturity while at the same time providing a sufficiently challenging environment to pull them along a developmental path toward higher levels of cognitive and social maturity. What we find especially intriguing about this suggestion is its application to an analysis of the motivational declines associated with the junior high school transition. If it is true that different types of educational environments may be needed for different age groups in order to meet developmental needs and to foster continued developmental growth, then it is also possible that some types of changes in educational environments may be especially inappropriate at certain stages of development. In fact, some changes in the educational environment may be "developmentally regressive." Exposure to such changes is likely to lead to a particularly poor person-environment fit, and this lack of fit could account for some of the declines in motivation seen at this developmental period. In essence, then, we are suggesting that it is the fit between the developmental needs of the adolescent and the educational environment that is important—we refer to this type of fit as a stage-environment fit. If this hypothesis is true, transition to a facilitative and developmentally appropriate environment, even at this vulnerable age, should have a positive effect on children's perceptions of themselves and their educational environment. In contrast, transition into a developmentally inappropriate educational environment should result in the types of motivational declines that have been identified as occurring with the transition into junior high school. This should be particularly true if the environment is developmentally regressive; that is, if it affords the children fewer opportunities for continued growth than previous environments.

Is there any evidence that such a regressive change in the social environment occurs with the transition to junior high school? Yes, and it occurs at both the macro and micro levels. For example, Simmons and Blyth (1987) enumerated the following types of macro changes: increased school size, increased bureaucratic organization, increased departmentalization, and decreased teacher-student individual contact and opportunity to have a close relationship with a particular teacher. In addition, the increased size, coupled with departmentalized teaching, can disrupt the students' opportunity to interact with their peer networks. Each of these changes could have a detrimental effect on early adolescents.

Although remarkably few empirical studies have been done on more micro-level changes in the classroom environment, there is evidence of regressive changes at this level as well. Looking across the various relevant studies, six patterns have emerged with a fair degree of consistency. First, junior high school classrooms, compared with elementary school classrooms, are characterized by a greater emphasis on teacher control and discipline and fewer opportunities for student decision making, choice, and self-management (e.g., Brophy & Evertson, 1976; Midgley & Feldlaufer, 1987; Midgley, Feldlaufer, & Eccles, 1988b; Moos, 1979). For example, Brophy and Evertson (1976) found evidence that junior high school teachers spend more time maintaining order and less time actually teaching than elementary school teachers. In our own work with the MSALT study, sixth-grade elementary school teachers reported less concern with controlling and disciplining their students than these same students' seventh-grade junior high school math teachers reported one year later (Midgley et al., 1988b). Similar differences emerge on indicators of students' opportunity to participate in decision making regarding their own learning. For example, Ward and his colleagues found that upper elementary school students are given more opportunities to take responsibility for various aspects of their schoolwork than seventh-grade students in a traditional junior high school (Ward et al., 1982). Similarly in the MSALT study, both seventh graders and their teachers in the first year of junior high school reported less opportunity for students to participate in classroom decision making than these same students and their sixth-grade elementary school teachers had one year earlier (Midgley & Feldlaufer, 1987).

Second, junior high school classrooms, compared with elementary school classrooms, are characterized by a less personal and positive teacher-student relationship (see Eccles & Midgley, 1989). For example, in Trebilco, Atkinson, and Atkinson (1977), students reported less favorable interpersonal relations with their teachers after the transition to secondary school than before. Similarly, in the MSALT study, both students and observers rated junior high school math teachers as less friendly, less supportive, and less caring than the teachers they had had one year earlier in the last year of elementary school (Feldlaufer, Midgley, & Eccles, 1988). In addition, the seventh-grade teachers in this study also reported that they trusted the students less than did these students' sixth-grade teachers (Midgley et al., 1988b).

Third, the shift to junior high school is associated with an increase in practices such as whole class task organization, between-classroom ability grouping, and public evaluation of the correctness of work (see Eccles & Midgley, 1989). For example, in the study by Ward and his colleagues mentioned above, whole-group instruction was the norm in the seventh grade, small-group instruction was rare, and individualized instruction was not observed at all. In contrast, the sixth-grade teachers mixed whole- and small-group instruction within and across subject areas (Rounds & Osaki, 1982). Similar shifts toward increased whole-class instruction with most students working on the same assignments at the same time, using the same textbooks, and receiving the same homework assignments were evident in the MSALT (Feldlaufer et al., 1988). In addition, several reports have documented the increased use of between-class ability grouping beginning at junior high school (e.g., Oakes, 1981).

Changes such as these are likely to increase social comparison, concerns about evaluation, and competitiveness (see Eccles, Midgley, & Adler, 1984; Rosenholtz & Simpson, 1984). They may also increase the likelihood that teachers will use normative grading criteria and more public forms of evaluation, both of which have been shown to negatively affect many early adolescents' self-perceptions and motivation. These changes may also make aptitude differences more salient to both teachers and students, leading to increased teacher expectancy effects and decreased feelings of efficacy among teachers.

Fourth, junior high school teachers feel less effective as teachers, especially for low-ability students. This was one of the largest differences we found between sixth- and seventh-grade teachers in the MSALT study. Seventh-grade teachers in traditional junior high schools reported much less confidence in their teaching efficacy than sixth-grade elementary school teachers in the same school districts (Midgley, Feldlaufer, & Eccles, 1988b, 1989).

Fifth, contrary to what one might expect, there is evidence that classwork during the first year of junior high school requires lower-level cognitive skills than classwork at the elementary level. One rationale often given for the large, departmentalized junior high school system is its efficiency in providing early adolescents with higher-level academic work and more varied academic courses taught by specialists in their fields. It is argued that early adolescents are ready for more formal instruction in the various subject areas and that such instruction can provide more intense and challenging training in higher-order learning skills. But evidence suggests that this is not occurring when students make the transition into secondary school. For example, in an observational study of 11 junior high school science classes, only a very small proportion of tasks required higher-level creative or expressive skills; the most frequent activity involved copying answers from the board or textbook onto worksheets (Mitman, Mergendoller, Packer, & Marchman, 1984). Similarly, Walberg, House, and Steele (1973) rated the level of complexity of student assignments across grades 6 to 12. The proportion of low-level activities peaked at grade 9, the first year after the students in this district made the transition into secondary school. Both of these studies, as well as other studies, suggest that the actual cognitive demands made on adolescents decrease rather than increase at this time.

Finally, junior high school teachers appear to use a higher standard in judging students' competence and in grading their performance than do elementary school teachers (see Eccles & Midgley, 1989). There is no stronger predictor of students' self-confidence and sense of personal efficacy for schoolwork than the grades they receive. If grades change, then we would expect to see a concomitant shift in the adolescents' self-perceptions and academic motivation.

There is evidence that junior high school teachers use stricter and more social-comparison-based standards than elementary school teachers to assess student competency and to evaluate student performance, leading to a drop in grades for many early adolescents as they make the junior high school transition. For example, Simmons and Blyth (1987) found a greater drop in grades between sixth and seventh grade for adolescents making the junior high school transition at this point than for adolescents enrolled in K–8 schools. That this decline in grades is not matched by a decline in the adolescents' scores on standardized achievement tests suggests that it reflects a change in grading practices rather than a change in the rate of the students' learning (Kavrell & Petersen, 1984). Imagine what this decline in grades might do to early adolescents' self-confidence, especially since the material they are being tested on is not likely to be more intellectually challenging.

Changes like these are apt to have a negative effect on many children's motivational orientation toward school at any grade level. But Eccles and Midgley (1989, 1990) have argued that these types of changes are particularly harmful during early adolescence, given what is known about psychological development at this stage of life. Evidence from a variety of sources suggests that early adolescent development is characterized by increases in desire for autonomy, peer orientation, self-focus and self-consciousness, salience of identity issues, concern over heterosexual relationships, and capacity for abstract cognitive activity. Simmons and Blyth (1987) have argued that adolescents need a reasonably safe, as well as an intellectually challenging, environment to adapt to these shifts—an environment that provides a "zone of comfort" as well as challenging new opportunities for growth. In light of these needs, the environmental changes often associated with the transition to junior high school seem especially harmful in that they emphasize competition, social comparison, and ability self-assessment at a time of heightened self focus; they decrease decision making and choice at a time when the desire for control is growing; they emphasize lower-level cognitive strategies at a time when the ability to use higher-level strategies is increasing; and they disrupt social networks at a time when adolescents are especially concerned with peer relationships and may be in special need of close adult relationships outside the home. We believe the nature of these environmental changes, coupled with the normal course of individual development, is likely to result in a developmental mismatch so that the "fit" between the early adolescent and the classroom environment is particularly poor, increasing the risk of negative motivational outcomes, especially for those who already have difficulty succeeding academically.

EFFECT OF ENVIRONMENTAL CHANGES ON EARLY ADOLESCENTS' MOTIVATION

To test these predictions, we conducted a large-scale two-year, four-wave longitudinal study of the effect of changes in the school and classroom environment on early adolescents' achievement-related beliefs, motives, values, and behaviors. These data comprise the first two years of the MSALT study. The sample was drawn from twelve school districts in middle-income communities in south-eastern Michigan. Approximately 1,500 early adolescents both participated in all four waves of the study and experienced the junior high school transition during the course of the study as they moved from sixth to seventh grade. Questionnaires were administered at school during the fall and spring terms of the two consecutive school years. In this section we summarize the results for changes in teacher efficacy, teacher support and warmth, and opportunities for involvement in autonomous decision making.

Teacher efficacy. As noted earlier, one of the largest differences we found between the sixth- and seventh-grade teachers was in their confidence in their teaching efficacy; the seventh-grade teachers reported less confidence. Several studies have documented a relation between teacher efficacy and student beliefs and attitudes (e.g., Ashton & Webb, 1986; Brookover et al., 1979; Eccles & Wigfield, 1985). Given these associations, differences in teachers' sense of efficacy before and after the transition to junior high school could contribute to the decline in early adolescents' beliefs about their academic competency and potential.

To test this hypothesis, we divided our adolescent sample into four groups based on median splits of their math teachers' ratings of their own personal teaching efficacy (see Midgley, Feldlaufer, & Eccles, 1989, for a full description of this study). The largest group (559 out of the 1,329 included in these analyses) moved from a high-efficacy sixth-grade math teacher to a low-efficacy seventh-grade math teacher. Another 474 adolescents had low-efficacy teachers in both years, 117 moved from low- to high-efficacy teachers, and 179 had high-efficacy teachers in both years. Thus, fully 78% of our sample of children moved to a low teacher-efficacy math classroom in the seventh-grade. As predicted, the adolescents who moved from high-efficacy to low-efficacy teachers during the transition (the most common pattern) ended their first year in junior high school with lower expectancies for themselves in math, lower perceptions of their performance in math, and higher perceptions of the difficulty of math than the adolescents who experienced no change in teacher efficacy or who moved from low- to high-efficacy teachers. Also as predicted, teacher-efficacy beliefs had a stronger impact on the low-achieving adolescents' beliefs than on the high-achieving adolescents' beliefs. The results for the low-achieving students are shown in Figures 7 and 8. By the end of the junior high school year, those low-achieving adolescents who had moved from high- to low-efficacy teachers experienced a dramatic decline in confidence in their ability to master mathematics. Note, however, that this same decline was not characteristic of the low-achieving adolescents who had moved to high-efficacy seventh-grade math teachers, suggesting that the decline is not a general feature of early adolescent development but rather a consequence of the fact that so many early adolescents experience a debilitating shift in their classroom environments as they make the junior high school transition.

Student-teacher relationships. As reported earlier, we also found that student-teacher relationships deteriorate after the transition to junior high school. Research on the effects of classroom climate indicates that the quality of student-teacher relationships is associated with students' academic motivation and attitudes toward school (e.g., Fraser & Fisher, 1982; Moos, 1979; Trickett & Moos, 1974). Consequently there is reason to believe that transition into a less supportive classroom will negatively affect early adolescents' interest in the subject matter being taught in that classroom. Using a strategy similar to that described for teacher efficacy, we divided the sample of students into four groups based on the pattern of change they experienced in teacher support and warmth as they made the junior high

DEVELOPMENTAL PERSPECTIVES ON MOTIVATION

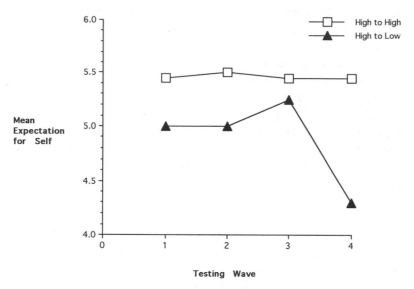

FIGURE 7. Expectations for one's own performance in math for the low-achieving students plotted across the transition into junior high school. "High to high" students had a high-efficacy teacher during both their sixth- (waves 1 and 2) and seventh-grade (waves 3 and 4) school years. "High to low" students had a high-efficacy teacher during their sixth-grade school year and a low-efficacy teacher during their seventh-grade school year.

school transition. As predicted, the early adolescents who moved from elementary teachers they perceived to be low in support to junior high school teachers they perceived to be high in support showed an increase in the value they attached to math; in contrast, the early adolescents who moved from teachers they perceived to be high in support to teachers they perceived to be low in support showed a decline in the value they attached to math. Again we found evidence that low-achieving students are particularly at risk when they move to less facilitative classroom environments after the transition (Midgley, Feldlaufer, & Eccles, 1988a).

Both of these studies show that the declines often reported in studies of early adolescents' motivational orientation to school subjects are not inevitable. Instead, these declines are associated with specific types of changes in the classroom environment experienced by many early adolescents as they make the junior high school transition. The studies also show that a transition into more facilitative

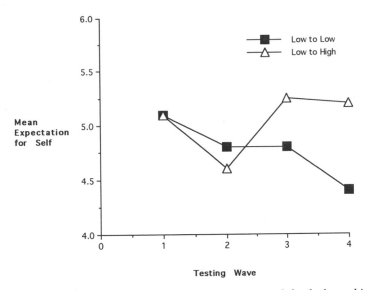

FIGURE 8. Expectations for one's own performance in math for the low-achieving students plotted across the transition into junior high school. "Low to low" students had a low-efficacy teacher during both their sixth- (waves 1 and 2) and seventh-grade (waves 3 and 4) school years. "Low to high" students had a low-efficacy teacher during their sixth-grade school year and a high-efficacy teacher during their seventh-grade school year.

classrooms can induce positive changes in early adolescents' motivation and self-perceptions. Unfortunately, our findings also indicate that most adolescents experience a negative change in their classroom experiences at this time.

Stage-environment fit in classroom decision making. Neither of these studies, however, directly tests our stage-environment fit hypothesis. To do this one must directly assess person-environment fit and relate this fit to changes in adolescents' self-perceptions and motivation. Using items developed by Lee, Statuto, and Kedar-Voivodas (1983), we asked both the adolescents and the teachers in this study to rate whether students were allowed input into classroom decisions regarding where to sit, classwork, homework, class rules, and what to do next, and whether students ought to be allowed input into each of these decisions. These questions can be used in the following ways: (1) to plot the developmental changes in adolescents' preferences for decision-making opportunities in the classroom; (2) to determine changes in the opportunity for them to participate in decision making; and (3) to determine the extent of match or mismatch between their preferences and the opportunities afforded them in the school environment. If developmental changes in this match are related to developmental changes in the adolescents' self-perceptions and school-related motivation, then we would have support for our stage-environment fit hypothesis.

As noted earlier, both the early adolescents and their teachers reported that there was less opportunity for participation in classroom decision making at the seventh-grade level than at the sixth-grade level. In contrast, there was a longitudinal increase over the school transition in the early adolescents' desire for more participation in classroom decision making. As a consequence of these two divergent patterns, the congruence between early adolescents' desire for the opportunity to participate in classroom decision making and their perception of how much these opportunities were available to them was lower when the adolescents were in the seventh grade than when they were in the sixth grade (Midgley & Feldlaufer, 1987).

How might the widening mismatch between the students' desire for autonomy and their perceptions of their opportunity for autonomy affect motivation? Person-environment fit theories suggest that a mismatch between one's needs and what the environment affords will lead to decline in motivation and engagement. Mac Iver, Klingel, and Reuman (1986) tested this prediction with the sixth-grade students by relating perceived congruence versus perceived incongruence to student motivation and behavior. Congruent children differed from incongruent children in several ways. They rated math as more useful and interesting; in general they liked the teacher and school better; they had higher expectations for their own performance in math; and they misbehaved less according to their own and their teachers' reports. Therefore it seems likely that this decline in the opportunity for decision making and this increase in the misfit between students' desire for autonomy and their perceptions of the opportunities for autonomy in their seventh-grade math classrooms could contribute to the decline we find in their motivation to study math.

But more specifically, given the general developmental progression toward increased desire for independence and autonomy during the early adolescent period, Eccles and Midgley (1989) predicted that adolescents who experience decreased opportunities for participation in classroom decision making along with increased desires for greater participation in such decisions (a "can't but should be able to" mismatch) should be most at risk for negative motivational outcomes. In a longitudinal analysis, Mac Iver and Reuman (1988) provide some support for this prediction. They compared the changes in intrinsic interest in math for adolescents reporting different types of changes in their responses to the actual and preferred decision-making items across the four waves of data. Consistent with our prediction, the adolescents who perceived their seventh-grade math classrooms as putting greater constraints on their preferred level of participation in classroom decision making than their sixth-grade math classrooms showed the largest and most consistent declines in their intrinsic interest in math as they moved from sixth grade into seventh grade. These are the students who are experiencing the type of developmental mismatch we outlined in our discussion of stage-environment fit.

MATURATIONAL DIFFERENCES IN THE DESIRE FOR AUTONOMY

Another way to look at developmental change is to look for interindividual differences between same-aged children of different maturational levels. At this age, the extent of pubertal development of the females provides a good indicator of individual differences in maturation. We related an indicator of maturational level to the female adolescents' desire for input into classroom decision making on the Lee et al. (1983) items. Consistent with the intraindividual longitudinal pattern of age-related change reported above, the more physically mature female adolescents expressed a greater desire for input into classroom decision making than their less physically mature female classmates (Miller, 1986). Unfortunately, as was true for the longitudinal results, the more physically mature females did not perceive greater opportunities for such participation. Although the females with varying degrees of pubertal development were in the same classrooms, the more physically mature females (the early de-

DEVELOPMENTAL PERSPECTIVES ON MOTIVATION

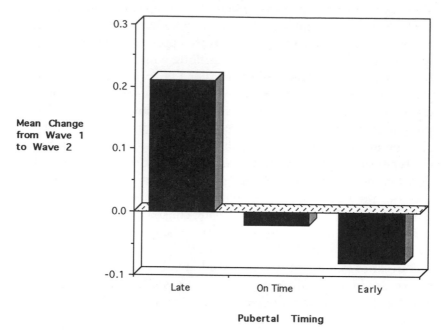

FIGURE 9. Mean change in girls' perception of the opportunities to participate in class-room decision making as a function of pubertal timing. Late-maturing girls are relatively less physically mature than the early-maturing girls.

velopers) reported fewer opportunities for participation in class-room decision making than did their less mature female peers (the on-time and late developers).

These maturational differences were even more striking when we looked at the within-year changes in these female adolescents' perceptions of their opportunities to participate in classroom decision making. We calculated the mean change in these females' perceptions of opportunities from fall to the spring testing. We then looked at this change as a function of their pubertal status. These results are shown in Figure 9. The early-maturing females showed a negative change (a decline) over the course of the school year in perceived opportunities to participate in classroom decision making. In contrast, the late-maturing females in these same classrooms showed a positive change (an increase) over the school year (Miller, 1986). How can this be, given that these adolescents were in the same classrooms? Did the teachers actually treat these adolescent females differently? (Did the teachers respond to earlier physical maturity with more controlling behavior?) Or did the adolescents perceive a similar environment differently? (Did the early-maturing adolescents perceive the same level of adult control as providing less opportunity for self-control than did the later maturing adolescents?) Evidence from educational psychology, developmental psychology, and general psychology suggests that either or both of these explanations could be accurate: Teachers do respond differently to various children in the same classroom depending on a variety of characteristics (Brophy & Evertson, 1976), and people do perceive similar environments differently depending on their cognitive or motivational orientation (see Baron & Graziano, 1991). More detailed classroom observations are needed to determine the exact nature of the relation between teachers' behavior and adolescents' perceptions.

But more important for the issues central to this chapter, the pubertal maturity of the female adolescents was related to the degree of mismatch between the adolescents' desires for input and their perceptions of these opportunities in their classroom environment: There was greater mismatch among the more physically mature female adolescents than among the less mature. In fact, by the end of the school year, almost twice as many early-maturing females as their less physically mature classmates reported experiencing the "can't but should" type of mismatch (e.g., answering "no" to the question, "Do you get to help decide what math you work on during math class?" but "yes" to the question "Should you have a say about this?").

We find this last set of results especially interesting in light of the findings of Simmons and her colleagues (e.g., Simmons & Blyth, 1987). They found that the pubertal status of female adolescents at the time of the junior high school transition is related to changes in the females' self-esteem and to the females' reports of truancy and school misconduct: the more physically mature females reported the higher amounts of truancy and school misconduct and lower self-esteem than their less mature classmates following the junior high school transition. Simmons and Blyth (1987) suggest that experiencing the school and pubertal transitions simultaneously puts these girls at risk for negative outcomes. Alternatively, it is possible that it is the mismatch between their desire for a less controlling adult environment and their perceptions of the actual opportunities for participation that puts them at risk for the most negative motivational outcomes.

We have begun to provide an in-depth description of the classroom environment changes most children experience as they make the transition from elementary school into junior high schools. In general, we find evidence of the types of changes we had predicted: an increase in the teachers' focus on student control and a decrease in teachers' feelings of efficacy and in the quality of student-teacher relationships. We have also begun to assess the effect of these changes on student motivation using a quasi-experimental approach. These results confirm the negative consequences of these changes and provide evidence that a different type of change would produce positive motivational effects at this developmental period. Together these two outcomes support our suggestion that the declines in motivation often assumed to be characteristics of the early adolescent period are less a consequence of the students' developmental stage than of the mismatch between their needs and the opportunities afforded them in the traditional junior high school environment. Is there any evidence of a comparable process going on in the family? Yes!

Stage-Environment Fit in Perceived Control in the Family and Its Link to School Achievement and School-Related Motivation

Evidence from several investigators suggests that adolescents' relationship with their parents also undergoes a stressful period during the early and middle adolescence (e.g., Collins, 1990; Paikoff & Brooks-Gunn, 1991; Steinberg, 1981). Furthermore, this stress is often focused on issues of control and autonomy within the family. Adolescence is a time for renegotiating power and authority relations within the family. When they are young, by necessity children's relationship with their parents is asymmetrical in terms of power and authority. But as children mature they need to take more and more responsibility for themselves until, ultimately, they leave their natal home and achieve full control over their own lives. In the optimal situation, parents will reinforce and stimulate this process of growing autonomy and independence. But it is very likely that the renegotiation processes associated with these developmental trajectories will not be perfectly smooth. It is not easy for parents to determine the optimal level of autonomy versus control for their children at all ages. And according to a stage-environment fit perspective, one would predict strained relationships whenever there is a poor fit between children's desire for increasing autonomy and the opportunities for independence provided by their parents. These strains may affect school-related motivation.

We are in the process of examining these issues in the MSALT study . We assessed decision making in the family in two ways: both the adolescents and their parents responded to two items derived from the Epstein and McPartland (1976) scale of family decision making (e.g., "In general, how do you and your child arrive at decisions?" [1 = I tell my child just what to do; 3 = We discuss it and then we decide; 5 = I usually let my child decide]; and "How often does your child take part in family decisions that concern her/himself?" [1 = never; 4 = always]). The adolescents were also asked to rate how they thought decisions ought to be made in their family and the extent to which they thought "their parents treated them more like a kid than like an adult."

Consistent with the analyses reported earlier, we found both a longitudinal increase in adolescents' desire for greater participation in family decision making and positive associations between participation in family decision making and indicators of both intrinsic school motivation and positive self-esteem (Flanagan, 1986, 1989; Yee, 1986, 1987; Yee & Flanagan, 1985). Even more interesting from the stage-environment fit perspective, the parents reported that they included their early adolescents more in family decision making than the early adolescents themselves perceived to be true (Flanagan, 1986; Yee, 1987). Furthermore, for girls in particular, the discrepancy between the adolescents' and the parents' perception of the opportunities for the adolescents to participate in family decision making increased over the four waves in our study (Yee, 1987). Finally, and most important, the pattern of changes in early adolescents' self-esteem and intrinsic versus extrinsic motivation for schoolwork were systematically, and predictably, related to changes in their perceptions of the opportunity to participate in decision making at home. As our developmental stage-environment fit perspective on adult control implies, the adolescents who reported decreasing opportunities to participate in family decision making showed a decrease in their self-esteem and intrinsic motivation over the period of this study; the opposite pattern of change occurred for those who reported increasing opportunities to participate (Flanagan, 1989; Yee, 1987). In addition, the opportunity to participate in family decision making also predicted more positive motivation at each wave (Flanagan, 1985; Yee, 1986) and better adjustment to the junior high school transition (Eccles, Lord, & McCarthy, 1991; Eccles, McCarthy, et al., 1990). Thus, not only may a mismatch between authority relationships in the home precipitate increased conflict, it may also be detrimental to the adolescents' self-esteem and school-related motivation.

Summary and Conclusions

In this chapter we have presented two perspectives on the link between social context and the following motivational constructs: self-concept of ability and sense of personal efficacy in specific activity domains; perceptions of the value of skills in various domains; interest in various activities; activity choice; persistence; performance; and general self-esteem. In the first section, we discussed how social-contextual variables in both the family and the home could produce individual differences in the motivational constructs of interest. We presented a general framework for thinking about this issue and summarized our recent empirical work. In the second section, we discussed how systematic changes in the social environments that confront children as they develop could explain age-related changes in the motivational constructs of interest. Again we presented a general framework for thinking about this issue and summarized our empirical work testing the hypotheses generated from this framework.

Throughout this section we have argued that optimal development takes place when there is good stage-environment fit between the needs of developing individuals and the opportunities afforded in their social environments. Furthermore, we suggested that the negative changes in motivational variables often associated with early adolescent development result from regressive changes in school and home environments. For example, the transition to junior high school, in particular, often confronts early adolescents with regressive environmental changes such as a decrease in the opportunity to participate in classroom decision making, a decrease in teacher support and teacher efficacy, and an increase in teaching styles and reporting practices likely to induce a focus on relative ability and comparative performance as well as excessive social comparison. Not surprisingly, there is also a decrease in intrinsic motivation and an increase in school misbehavior associated with this transition, and these changes are most apparent among adolescents who report regressive changes in the characteristics of classroom and school social environment. Such motivational changes are not apparent in adolescents who report the more developmentally appropriate shifts in the social context at school. Although our analysis of the family data is not as complete as our analysis of the classroom data, we have found evidence that a similar process may be going on in the family in relation to issues of control and autonomy. Excessive parental control is linked to lower intrinsic school motivation, to more negative changes in self-esteem following the junior high school transition, to more school misbehavior, and to relatively greater investment in peer social attachments. Clearly, these results point out the importance of designing educational and family environments for early adolescents that provide a better match to their growing desire for control over their own lives as well as providing the type of supportive environment necessary to explore this control and autonomy with minimal risk (see also Simmons & Blyth, 1987). However, many junior high schools, and some families, do not seem to be providing such an environment. Why? One explanation seems especially relevant to the position outlined in this chapter: beliefs and stereotypes regarding the nature of adolescence. Many adults in this culture hold negative stereotypes about adolescence. They see it as a stressful time and a time of great risk, and they see adolescents themselves as troublesome and untrustworthy (see Miller et al., 1990). Finally, they tend to feel there is little they can do to make the situation better. Consequently, it is not surprising that they resort to increased control. Unfortunately, this response may be creating the very behavior they are so worried about.

A second explanation is also relevant for the school findings. Work in the field of organizational psychology suggests that supervisors tend to use more controlling strategies and to trust their workers less if they have many workers to supervise and if there is a general ethic of mistrust in the organizational setting (Lawler, 1976). Two of the major differences between elementary schools and junior high schools are school size and departmentalization. As a result of these two characteristics, junior high school teachers have to interact with and teach many more students than elementary school teachers. In addition, there are many more students in general that have to be monitored. If the work in organizational psychology can be generalized to the school setting, then one would predict that junior high school teachers (supervisors in this case) would trust their students less than would elementary school teachers and would use more controlling strategies. This outcome should be especially likely given the negative stereotypes teachers typically hold about early adolescents.

REFERENCES

Alexander, K. L., & Entwisle, D. R. (1988). Achievement in the first two years of school: Patterns and processes. *Monographs of the Society for Research in Child Development, 53* (Serial No. 218).

Ames, C., & Archer, J. (1988). Achievement goals in the classroom: Student learning strategies and motivational processes. *Journal of Educational Psychology, 80,* 260–267.

Ashton, P., & Webb, R. (1986). *Making a difference: Teachers' sense of efficacy and student achievement.* New York: Longman.

Bandura, A., & Walters, R. H. (1963). *Social learning and personality development.* New York: Holt, Rinehart, and Winston.

Baron, R. M., & Graziano, W. G. (1991). *Social psychology.* Chicago: Holt, Rinehart, and Winston.

Baumrind, D. (1971). Current patterns of parental authority. *Developmental Psychology Monograph, 4* (1, Pt. 2).

Baumrind, D. (1989). Rearing competent children. In W. Damon (Ed.), *Child development today and tomorrow* (pp. 349–378). San Francisco: Jossey-Bass.

Baumrind, D. (1991). The influence of parenting style on adolescent competence and substance use. *Journal of Early Adolescence, 11,* 35–95.

Blumenfeld, P., Hamilton, V. L., Bossert, S., Wessels, K., & Meece, C. (1983) Teacher talk and student thought: Socialization into the student role. In J.

Levine and U. Wang (Eds.), *Teacher and student perceptions: Implications for learning.* Hillsdale, NJ: Lawrence Erlbaum.

Blumenfeld, P., & Pintrich, P. (1982). *Children's perception of school and school-work: Age, sex, social class, individual and classroom differences.* Paper presented at the annual meeting of the American Educational Research Association, New York.

Blumenfeld, P., & Pintrich, P. R. (1983, April). *The relation of student characteristics and children's perception of teachers and peers in varying classroom environments.* Paper presented at the annual meeting of the American Educational Research Association, Montreal.

Blumenfeld, P., Pintrich, P., Meece, J., & Wessels, K. (1982). The formation and role of self perceptions of ability in elementary school classrooms. *Elementary School Journal, 82,* 401–420.

Blyth, D. A., Simmons, R. G., & Carlton-Ford, S. (1983). The adjustment of early adolescents to school transitions. *Journal of Early Adolescence, 3,* 105–120.

Boggiano, A. K., Main, D. S., & Katz, P. A. (1988). Children's preference for challenge: The role of perceived competence and control. *Journal of Personality and Social Psychology, 54,* 134–141.

Brookover, W., Beady, C., Flood, P., Schweitzer, J., & Wisenbaker, J. (1979). *School social systems and student achievement: Schools can make a difference.* New York: Praeger.

Brophy, J. E., & Evertson, C. M. (1976). *Learning from teaching: A developmental perspective.* Boston: Allyn and Bacon.

Bryk, A. S., & Driscoll, M. E. (1988). *The high school as community: Contextual influences, and consequences for students and teachers.* Unpublished manuscript, University of Chicago.

Carnegie Council on Adolescent Development. (1989). *Turning points: Preparing American youth for the 21st century.* New York: Carnegie Corporation.

Casserly, P. L., & Rock, D. A. (1980). *Factors related to young women's persistence and achievement in mathematics.* (Final report). Washington, DC: National Institute of Education.

Coleman, J. S., Campbell, E., Hobson, C., McPartland, J., Mood, A., Weinfeld, F., & York, R. (1966). *Equality of educational opportunity.* U.S. Department of Health, Education, and Welfare. Washington, DC: U.S. Government Printing Office.

Collins, W. A. (1990). Parent-child relationships in the transition to adolescence: Continuity and change in interaction, affect, and cognition. In R. Montemayor, G. Adams, & T. Gullotta (Eds.), *Advances in adolescent development: Vol. 2. From childhood to adolescence: A transitional period?* (pp. 85–106). Newbury Park, CA: Sage.

Comer, J. 1980. *School power.* New York: Free Press.

Connor, J. M., Schackman, M., & Serbin, L. A. (1978). Sex-related differences in response to practice on a visual-spatial test and generalization to a related test. *Child Development, 49,* 24–29.

200

DEVELOPMENTAL PERSPECTIVES ON MOTIVATION

Crandall, V. C., & Battle, E. S. (1970). The antecedents and adult correlates of academic and intellectual achievement effort. In J. P. Hill (Ed.), *Minnesota symposia on child psychology* (Vol. 4). Minneapolis: University of Minnesota Press.

Crandall, V. J., Dewey, R., Katkovsky, W., & Preston, A. (1964). Parents' attitudes and behaviors and grade school children's academic achievements. *Journal of Genetic Psychology, 104,* 53–66.

deCharms, R. (1980). The origins of competence and achievement motivation in personal causation. In L. J. Fyans, Jr. (Ed.), *Achievement motivation: Recent trends in theory and research* (pp. 22–23). New York: Plenum Press.

Deci, E. L., & Ryan, R. M. (1985). *Intrinsic motivation and self determination in human behavior.* New York: Plenum Press.

Dix, M. (1976). *Are reading habits of parents related to reading performance of their children?* Paper presented at the annual meeting of the National Council of Teachers of English.

Dunkin, M., & Biddle, B. (1974). *The study of teaching.* Holt, Rinehart, and Winston.

Durkin, D. R. (1966). *Children who read early.* New York: Teachers College Press.

Eccles, J. S. (1984). Sex differences in achievement patterns. In T. Sonderegger (Ed.), *Nebraska symposium on motivation, 1983* (pp. 97–132). Lincoln: University of Nebraska Press.

Eccles, J. S. (1987). Gender roles and women's achievement-related decisions. *Psychology of Women Quarterly, 11,* 135–172.

Eccles, J. S. (1989). Bringing young women to math and science. In M. Crawford and M. Gentry (Eds.), *Gender and thought: Psychological perspectives* (pp. 36–57). New York: Springer-Verlag.

Eccles, J. S., Adler, T. F., & Meece, J. L. (1984). Sex differences in achievement: A test of alternate theories. *Journal of Personality and Social Psychology, 46,* 26–43.

Eccles, J. S., Flanagan, C., Goldsmith, R., Jacobs, J., Jayaratne, T., Wigfield, A., & Yee, D. (1987, April). *Parents as socializers of achievement attitudes.* Symposium paper, Society for Research in Child Development, Baltimore.

Eccles, J. S., Furstenberg, F., McCarthy, K. A., & Lord, S. E. (1992, March). *How parents respond to risk and opportunity.* Paper presented at the Biennial Meeting of the Society for Research on Adolescence, Washington, DC.

Eccles, J. S., & Harold, R. D. (1991). Gender differences in sport involvement: Applying the Eccles' expectancy-value model. *Journal of Applied Sport Psychology, 3,* 7–35.

Eccles, J. S., & Hoffman, L. W. (1984). Socialization and the maintenance of a sex-segregated labor market. In H. W. Stevenson & A. E. Siegel (Eds.), *Research in child development and social policy* (Vol. 1, pp. 367–420). Chicago: University of Chicago Press.

Eccles, J. S., & Jacobs, J. E. (1986). Social forces shape math attitudes and performance. *Signs, 11,* 367–380.

Eccles, J. S., Jacobs, J. E., & Harold, R. D. (1990). Gender-role stereotypes, expectancy effects, and parents' role in the socialization of gender differences in self perceptions and skill acquisition. *Journal of Social Issues, 46,* 182–201.

Eccles, J. S., Jacobs, J., Harold, R. D., Yoon, K. S., Aberbach, A., & Freedman-Doan, C. (1991, August). *Expectancy effects are alive and well: Gender-role socialization.* Invited address at the Annual meeting of the American Psychological Association, San Francisco.

Eccles, J. S., Jacobs, J., Harold, R., Yoon, K. S., Arberton, A., & Freedman-Doan, C. (in press). Parents and gender-role socialization. In S. Oshkamp (Ed.), *Gender and social psychology.* Beverly Hills, CA: Sage.

Eccles, J. S., Jacobs, J., Harold-Goldsmith, R., Jayaratne, T., & Yee, D. (1989, April). *The relations between parents' category-based and target-based beliefs: Gender roles and biological influences.* Symposium paper, Society for Research in Child Development, Kansas City.

Eccles, J. S., Lord, S., & McCarthy, K. (1991, April). *Protective and risk factors for coping with the transition to junior high school.* Symposium presentation at the annual meeting of the Society for Research in Child Development, Seattle.

Eccles, J. S., Lord, S., & Midgley, C. M. (1991). What are we doing to adolescents? The impact of educational contexts on early adolescents. *American Journal of Education, 99,* 521–542.

Eccles. J. S., McCarthy, K. A., Lord, S. E., Harold, R., Wigfield, A., & Aberbach, A. (1990, April). *The relationship of family factors to self-esteem and teacher-rated adjustment following the transition to junior high school environment.* Paper presented at the meeting of the Society for Research on Adolescence, Atlanta.

Eccles, J. S., & Midgley, C. (1989). Stage/environment fit: Developmentally appropriate classrooms for early adolescents. In R. E. Ames & C. Ames (Eds.), *Research on motivation in education* (Vol.3). New York: Academic Press.

Eccles, J. S., & Midgley, C. (1990). Understanding motivation: A developmental approach to person-environment fit. *Transition from childhood to adolescence* (Vol. 2). Sage Monographs. Newbury Park, CA: Sage.

Eccles, J., Midgley, C., & Adler, T. (1984). Grade-related changes in the school environment: Effects on achievement motivation. In J. G. Nicholls (Ed.), *The development of achievement motivation* (pp. 283–331). Greenwich, CT: JAI Press.

Eccles, J. S., & Wigfield, A. (1985). Teacher expectations and student motivation. In J. Dusek (Ed.), *Teacher expectancies* (pp. 185–217). Hillsdale, NJ: Lawrence Erlbaum.

Eccles Parsons, J., Adler, T. F., Futterman, R., Goff, S. B., Kaczala, C. M., Meece, J. L., & Midgley, C. (1983). Expectancies, values, and academic behaviors. In J. T. Spence (Ed.), *Achievement and achievement motivation.* San Francisco, CA: W. H. Freeman.

Elder, G. H., Jr. (1974). *Children of the Great Depression.* Chicago: University of Chicago Press.

202

DEVELOPMENTAL PERSPECTIVES ON MOTIVATION

Elder, G. H., Jr., & Ardelt, M. (1992, March). *Families adapting to economic pressure: Some consequences for parents and adolescents.* Paper presented at the biennial meeting of the Society for Research on Adolescence, Washington, DC.

Elder, G. H., Jr., & Caspi, A. (1989). Economic stress in lives: Developmental perspectives. *Journal of Social Issues, 44,* 25–45.

Elder, G. H., Jr., Caspi, A., & Van Nguyen, T. (1985). Linking family hardship to children's lives. *Child Development, 56,* 361–375.

Elder, G. H., Jr., Conger, R. D., Foster, E. M., & Ardelt, M. (1992). Families under economic pressure. *Journal of Family Issues, 13,* 5–37.

Entwisle, D. R., & Baker, D. P. (1983). Gender and young children's expectations for performance in arithmetic. *Developmental Psychology, 19,* 200–209.

Epstein, J. L., & McPartland, J. M. (1976). The concept and measurement of the quality of school life. *American Educational Research Journal, 13,* 15–30.

Estrada, R., Arsenio, W. F., Hess, R. D., & Holloway, S. D. (1987). Affective quality of the mother-child relationship: Longitudinal consequences for children's school-relevant cognitive functioning. *Developmental Psychology, 23,* 210–215.

Feldlaufer, H., Midgley, C., & Eccles, J. S. (1988). Student, teacher, and observer perceptions of the classroom environment before and after the transition to junior high school. *Journal of Early Adolescence, 8,* 133–156.

Flanagan, C. (1985, April). *The relationship of family environments in early adolescence and intrinsic motivation in the classroom.* Paper presented at the meeting of the American Educational Research Association, Chicago.

Flanagan, C. (1986, April). *Early adolescent needs and family decision-making environments: A study of person-environment fit.* Paper presented at the meeting of the American Educational Research Association, San Francisco.

Flanagan, C. (1989, April). *Adolescents' autonomy at home: Effects on self-consciousness and intrinsic motivation at school.* Paper presented at the meeting of the American Educational Research Association, Montreal.

Flanagan, C. A. (1990a). Families and schools in hard times. In V. C. McLoyd and C. A. Flanagan (Eds.), *New directions for child development* (Vol. 46, pp. 7–26). San Francisco: Jossey-Bass.

Flanagan, C. A. (1990b). Change in family work status: Effects on parent-adolescent decision-making. *Child Development, 61,* 163–177.

Fraser, B. J., & Fisher, D. L. (1982). Predicting students' outcomes from their perceptions of classroom psychosocial environment. *American Educational Research Journal, 19,* 498–518.

Freud, A. (1969). Adolescence as a developmental disturbance. In G. Kaplan & S. Lebovici (Eds.), *Adolescence: Psychosocial perspectives* (pp. 5–10). New York: Basic Books.

Furstenberg, F. (1992, March). *Adapting to difficult environments: Neighborhood characteristics and family strategies.* Paper presented at the biennial meeting of the Society for Research on Adolescence, Washington, DC.

Garbarino, J., & Sherman, D. (1980). High-risk neighborhoods and high-risk families: The human ecology of child maltreatment. *Child Development, 51,* 188–198.

Goldsmith, R. H. (1986). The effects of paternal employment status on fathering behaviors, cognitive stimulation, and confidence in the child's future (Doctoral dissertation, University of Michigan). *Dissertation Abstracts International, 8702736,* 4710A.

Goodnow, J. J. (1988). Parents' ideas, actions, and feelings: Models and methods from developmental and social psychology. *Child Development, 29,* 286–320.

Goodnow, J. J., & Collins, W. A. (1990). *Development according to parents: The nature, sources, and consequences of parents' ideas.* Hillsdale, NJ: Lawrence Erlbaum.

Grolnick, W. S., & Ryan, R. M. (1989). Parent styles associated with children's self-regulation and competence in school. *Journal of Educational Psychology, 81,* 143–154.

Grolnick, W. S., & Ryan, R. M. (in press). Parental resources and the developing child in school. In M. Procidano & C. Fisher (Eds.), *Families: A handbook for school professionals.* New York: Teachers College Press.

Grolnick, W. S., Ryan, R. M., & Deci, E. L. (1991). Inner resources for school achievement: Motivational mediators of children's perceptions of their parents. *Journal of Educational Psychology, 83,* 508–517.

Harold, R. D., Eccles, J. S., Yoon, K. S., Aberbach, A., & Freedman-Doan, C. (1991, April). *Parents hold a key to "the land of opportunity."* Poster presentation at the annual meeting of the Society for Research in Child Development, Seattle.

Harold-Goldsmith, R., Radin, N., & Eccles, J. S. (1988). Objective and subjective reality: The effects of job loss and financial stress on fathering behaviors. *Family Perspective, 22,* 309–326.

Hartley, R. E. (1964). A developmental view of female sex-role definition and identification. *Merrill-Palmer Quarterly, 10,* 3–16.

Harter, S. (1981). A new self-report scale of intrinsic versus extrinsic orientation in the classroom: Motivational and informational components. *Developmental Psychology, 17,* 300–312.

Harter, S. (1985). Competence as a dimension of self-evaluation: Toward a comprehensive model of self-worth. In R. L. Leahy (Ed.), *The development of the self* (pp. 55–151). New York: Academic Press.

Harter, S. (1986). Processes underlying the construction, maintenance, and enhancement of the self-concept in children. In J. Suls and A. G. Greenwald (Eds.), *Psychological perspectives on the self* (Vol. 3, pp. 137–181). Hillsdale, NJ: Lawrence Erlbaum.

Hess, R. D., Chih-Mei, & McDevitt, T. M. (1987). Cultural variations in family beliefs about children's performance in mathematics: Comparisons among People's Republic of China, Chinese-American, and Caucasian-American families. *Journal of Educational Psychology, 79,* 179–188.

Hess, R. D., & Holloway, S. D. (1984). Family and school as educational institutions. In R. D. Parke (Ed.), *Review of child development and research:*

Vol. 7. The family (pp. 179–222). Chicago: University of Chicago Press.

Hess, R. D., & McDevitt, T. M. (1984). Some cognitive consequences of maternal intervention techniques: A longitudinal study. *Child Development, 55,* 2017–2030.

Hill, K. T. (1980). Motivation, evaluation, and educational test policy. In L. J. Fyans (Ed.), *Achievement motivation: Recent trends in theory and research.* New York: Plenum Press.

Holloway, S. D., & Hess, R. D. (1985). Mothers' and teachers' attributions about children's mathematics performance. In I. E. Sigel (Ed.), *Parental belief systems: The psychological consequences for children.* Hillsdale, NJ: Lawrence Erlbaum.

Holloway, S. D., Kashiwagi, K., Hess, R. D., & Azuma, H. (1986). Causal attributions by Japanese and American mothers and children about performance in mathematics. *International Journal of Psychology, 21,* 269–286.

Horwitz, R. A. (1979). Psychological effects of the open classroom. *Review of Educational Research, 49,* 71–85.

Hunt, D. E. (1975). Person-environment interaction: A challenge found wanting before it was tried. *Review of Educational Research, 45,* 209–230.

Huston. A. (1984). Gender-role socialization. In E. M. Hetherington (Ed.), P. H. Mussen (Series Ed.), *Handbook of Child Psychology: Vol 4. Socialization, personality, and social development* (pp. 387–467). New York: John Wiley.

Jacobs, J. (1987). *Parents' gender role stereotypes and perceptions of their child's ability: Influences on the child.* Unpublished dissertation. University of Michigan, Ann Arbor.

Jacobs, J. E. (1991). Influence of gender stereotypes on parent and child mathematics attitudes. *Journal of Educational Psychology, 83,* 518–527.

Jacobs, J. E., & Eccles, J. S. (1985). Gender differences in math ability: The impact of media reports on parents. *Educational Researcher, 14,* 20–25.

Jacobs, J. E., & Eccles, J. S. (in press). The impact of mothers' gender-role stereotypic beliefs on mothers' and children's ability perceptions. *Journal of Personality and Social Psychology.*

James, W. (1963). *Psychology.* New York: Fawcett. (Original work published 1892)

Jussim, L. (1986). Self-fulfilling prophecies: A theoretical and integrative review. *Psychological Review, 93,* 429–445.

Jussim, L. (1989). Teacher expectations: Self-fulfilling prophecies, perceptual biases, and accuracy. *Journal of Personality and Social Psychology, 57,* 469–480.

Katkovsky, W., Crandall, V. C., & Preston, A. (1964). Parent attitudes toward their personal achievements and toward the achievement behavior of their children. *Journal of Genetic Psychology, 104,* 67–82.

Kavrell, S. M., & Petersen, A. C. (1984). Patterns of achievement in early adolescence. In M. L. Maehr (Ed.), *Advances in motivation and achievement* (pp. 1–35). Greenwich, CT: JAI Press.

Kohn, M. L. (1969). *Class and conformity.* Homewood, IL.: Dorsey Press.

Lamborn, S. D., Mounts, N. S., Steinberg, L., & Dornbusch, S. M. (1991). Patterns of competence and adjustment among adolescents from authoritative, authoritarian, indulgent, and neglectful families. *Child Development, 62,* 1049–1065.

Laosa, L. M. (1984). Social policies toward children of diverse ethnic, racial, and language groups in the United States. In H. W. Stevenson and A. E. Siegel (Eds.), *Child developmental research and social policy* (pp. 1–109). Chicago: University of Chicago Press.

Lawler, E. E. (1976). Control systems in organizations. In M. D. Dunnette (Ed.), *Handbook of industrial and organizational psychology.* Chicago: Rand McNally.

Lee, P., Statuto, C., & Kedar-Voivodas, G. (1983). Elementary school children's perceptions of their actual and ideal school experience: A developmental study. *Journal of Educational Psychology, 75,* 838–847.

Lepper, M., & Greene, D. (1978). *The hidden costs of rewards: New perspectives on the psychology of human motivation.* Hillsdale, NJ: Lawrence Erlbaum.

Lipsitz, J. (1981). Educating the early adolescent: Why four model schools are effective in reaching a difficult age group. *American Education,* 13–17.

Maccoby, E. E., & Martin, J. A. (1984). Socialization in the context of the family: Parent-child interaction. In E. M. Hetherington (Ed.), P. H. Mussen (Series Ed.), *Handbook of Child Psychology: Vol 4. Socialization, personality, and social development* (pp. 1–101). New York: John Wiley.

Mac Iver, D., Klingel, D. M., & Reuman, D. A. (1986, April). *Students' decision-making congruence in mathematics classrooms: A person-environment fit analysis.* Paper presented at the meeting of the American Educational Research Association, San Francisco.

Mac Iver, D., & Reuman, D. A. (1988, April). *Decision-making in the classroom and early adolescents' valuing of mathematics.* Paper presented at the annual meeting of the American Educational Research Association, New Orleans.

Marjoribanks, K. (1980). *Ethnic families and children's achievements.* Sydney: Allen and Unwin.

Marsh, H. W. (1990). Influences of internal and external frames of reference on the formation of math and English self-concepts. *Journal of Educational Psychology, 82,* 107–116.

McClelland, D. C., & Pilon, D. A. (1983). Sources of adult motives in patterns of parent behavior in early childhood. *Journal of Personality and Social Psychology, 44,* 564–574.

McGillicuddy-DeLisi, A. V. (1982). Parental beliefs about developmental processes. *Human Development, 25,* 192–200.

McLoyd, V. C. (1990). The impact of economic hardship on black families and children: Psychological distress, parenting, and socioemotional development. *Child Development, 61,* 263–266.

Midgley, C., & Feldlaufer, H. (1987). Students' and teachers' decision-making fit before and after the transition to junior high school. *Journal of Early Adolescence, 7,* 225–241.

Midgley, C., Feldlaufer, H., & Eccles, J. S. (1988a). Student/teacher relations and attitudes toward mathematics before and after the transition to junior high school. *Child Development, 60,* 375–395.

Midgley, C., Feldlaufer, H., & Eccles, J. S. (1988b). The transition to junior high school: Beliefs of pre- and post-transition teachers. *Journal of Youth and Adolescence, 17,* 543–562.

Midgley, C., Feldlaufer, H., & Eccles, J. S. (1989). Change in teacher efficacy and student self- and task-related beliefs during the transition to junior high school. *Journal of Educational Psychology, 81,* 247–258.

Miller, C. L. (1986, April). *Puberty and person-environment fit in the classroom.* Paper presented at the meeting of the American Educational Research Association, San Francisco.

Miller, C. L., Eccles, J. S., Flanagan, C., Midgley, C., Feldlaufer, H., & Harold, R. D. (1990). Parents' and teachers' beliefs about adolescents: Effects of sex and experience. *Journal of Youth and Adolescence, 19,* 363–394.

Miller, S. A., Manhal, M., & Mee, L. L. (1991). Parental beliefs, parental accuracy, and children's cognitive performance: A search for causal relations. *Developmental Psychology, 27,* 267–276.

Mitman, A. L., Mergendoller, J. R., Packer, M. J., & Marchman, V. A. (1984). *Scientific literacy in seventh-grade life science: A study of instructional process, task completion, student perceptions and learning outcomes.* (Final report). San Francisco: Far West Laboratory.

Moos, R. H. (1979). *Evaluating educational environments.* San Francisco: Jossey-Bass.

Nicholls, J. G. (1980, June). *Striving to develop and demonstrate ability: An intentional theory of achievement motivation.* Paper presented at Conference on Attributional Approaches to Human Motivation, Center for Interdisciplinary Studies, University of Bielefeld, West Germany.

Oakes, J. (1981). *Tracking policies and practices: School by school summaries.* A study of schooling: Technical report no. 25. Los Angeles: University of California Graduate School of Education.

Paikoff, R. L., & Brooks-Gunn, J. (1991). Do parent-child relationships change during puberty? *Psychological Bulletin, 110,* 47–66.

Parsons, J. E., Adler, T. F., & Kaczala, C. M. (1982). Socialization of achievement attitudes and beliefs: Parental influences. *Child Development, 53,* 310–321.

Parsons, J. E., Kaczala, C. M., & Meece, J. L. (1982). Socialization of achievement attitudes and beliefs: Classroom influences. *Child Development, 53,* 322–339.

Parsons, J. E., & Ruble, D. N. (1977). The development of achievement-related expectancies. *Child Development, 48,* 1975–1979.

Rogosa, D. (1979). Causal models in longitudinal research: Rationale, formulation, and interpretation. In J. R. Nesselroade & P. B. Baltes (Eds.), *Longitudinal research in the study of behavior and development* (pp. 263–302). New York: Academic Press.

Rosen, B. C., & D'Andrade, R. (1959). The psychosocial origins of achievement motivation. *Sociometry, 22,* 185–218.

Rosenbaum, J. E. (1976). *Making inequality: The hidden curriculum of high school tracking*. New York: John Wiley.

Rosenholtz, S. J., & Rosenholtz, S. H. (1981). Classroom organization and the perception of ability. *Sociology of Education, 54*, 132–140.

Rosenholtz, S. J., & Simpson, C. (1984). The formation of ability conceptions: Developmental trend or social construction? *Review of Educational Research, 54*, 301–325.

Rounds, T. S., and Osaki, S. Y. (1982). *The social organization of classrooms: An analysis of sixth- and seventh-grade activity structures*. (Report EPSSP-82-5). San Francisco: Far West Laboratory.

Sameroff, A. J., & Feil, L. (1985). Parental concepts of development. In E. E. Sigel (Ed.), *Parental belief systems* (pp. 83–105). Hillsdale, NJ: Lawrence Erlbaum.

Sampson, R. J. (in press). Family management and child development: Insights from social disorganization theory. In J. McCord (Ed.), *Advances in criminological theory* (Vol. 3). New Brunswick, NJ: Transaction.

Sigel, I. E. (1982). The relationship between parental distancing strategies and the child's cognitive behavior. In L. M. Laosa & I. E. Sigel (Eds.), *Families as learning environments for children* (pp. 47–86). New York: Plenum Press.

Simmons, R. G., & Blyth, D. A. (1987). *Moving into adolescence: The impact of pubertal change and school context*. Hawthorn, N.Y.: Aldine de Gruyter.

Steinberg, L. (1981). Transformation in family relations at puberty. *Developmental Psychology, 17*, 833–840.

Stevenson, H. W., Lee, S.-Y., Chen, C., & Stigler, J. W. (1990). Contexts of achievement: A study of American, Chinese, and Japanese children. *Monographs of the Society for Research in Child Development, 55* (Serial No. 221).

Stipek, D., & Mac Iver, D. (1989). Developmental changes in children's assessment of intellectual competence. *Child Development, 60*, 521–538.

Thompson, M. S., Alexander, K. L., & Entwisle, D. R. (1988). Household composition, parental expectations, and school achievement. *Social Forces, 67*, 424–451.

Trebilco, G. R., Atkinson, E. P., & Atkinson, J. M. (1977, November). *The transition of students from primary to secondary school*. Paper presented at the annual conference of the Australian Association for Research in Education, Canberra.

Trickett, E. J., & Moos, R. H. (1974). Personal correlates of contrasting environments: Student satisfactions in high school classrooms. *American Journal of Community Psychology, 2*, 1–12.

Walberg, H. J., House, E. R., & Steele, J. M. (1973). Grade level, cognition, and affect: A cross-section of classroom perceptions. *Journal of Educational Psychology, 64*, 142–146.

Ward, B. A., Mergendoller, J. R., Tikunoff, W. J., Rounds, T. S., Dadey, G. J., & Mitman, A. L. (1982). *Junior high school transition study: Executive summary*. San Francisco: Far West Laboratory.

DEVELOPMENTAL PERSPECTIVES ON MOTIVATION

Weiner, B. (1972). *Theories of motivation: From mechanism to cognition*. Chicago: Markham.

Weiner, B., Frieze, I., Kukla, A., Reed, A., Rest, S., & Rosenbaum, L. M. (1971). *Perceiving the causes of success and failure*. Morristown, NJ: General Learning Corporation.

Weinstein, R. S., & Middlestadt, S.E. (1971). Student perceptions of teacher interactions with male high and low achievers. *Journal of Educational Psychology, 71*, 421–431.

Wentzel, K. R., & Feldman, S. S. (1991). *Parenting styles, parental expectations, and boys' self-restraint as predictors of commitment to schoolwork: A longitudinal study*. Unpublished manuscript, Stanford University.

Winterbottom, M. R. (1958). The relation of need for achievement to learning experiences in independence and mastery. In J. W. Atkinson (Ed.), *Motives in fantasy, action, and society*. Princeton, NJ: Van Nostrand.

Yee, D. K. (1986, April). *Family decision-making, classroom decision-making, and student self- and achievement-related attitudes*. Paper presented at the meeting of the American Educational Research Association, San Francisco.

Yee, D. K. (1987, April). *Participation in family decision-making: Parent and child perspectives*. Paper presented at the meeting of the Society for Research in Child Development, Baltimore.

Yee, D., & Eccles, J. S. (1988). Parent perceptions and attributions for children's math achievement. *Sex Roles, 19*, 317–333.

Yee, D. K., & Flanagan, C. (1985). Family environments and self-consciousness in early adolescence. *Journal of Early Adolescence, 5*, 59–68.

Zajonc, R. B. (1968). Attitudinal effects of mere exposure. *Journal of Personality and Social Psychology, 9*, 1–27.

Motivation for Social Contact across the Life Span: A Theory of Socioemotional Selectivity

Laura L. Carstensen
Stanford University

Introduction

Social interaction patterns, social preferences, and social choices are of central interest to psychologists. Yet the developmental course of social behavior within a life-span context remains distinctly understudied. In this chapter I argue that the goal hierarchies that organize social motives change across the life span. Specifically I argue that, with age, interaction is increasingly motivated by the regulation of emotion and less motivated by the potential acquisition of information or fulfillment of affiliation needs with unfamiliar social partners.

I present this argument within the framework of a model of social aging I refer to as socioemotional selectivity theory (SST). In contrast to macro-level theories that explain age-related changes in social behavior at the societal level, SST focuses on psychological mechanisms that moderate such changes. Essentially the theory holds that social interaction is motivated by a wide range of goals. In

The writing of this chapter was helped by NIA grants RO1-AGO8816 and RO1-AGO7476. Work was completed in part while the author was a Visiting Fellow at the Max Planck Institute for Human Development and Education, Berlin. Much appreciation is expressed to Margret Baltes, Paul Baltes, Barbara Fredrickson, Frieder Lang, Yvonne Schütze, and Susan Turk for their comments and criticism on earlier drafts of the manuscript.

addition to the instrumental goals of social interaction are three principal psychological ones: the acquisition of information, the development and maintenance of self-concept, and the regulation of emotion. In SST, I contend that place in the life cycle influences the salience of specific social motives and the behavioral strategies people use to obtain social goals. As a result, preferences for social partners and social behavior change in predictable ways across the life span. According to SST, in late life a narrowing of the range of social partners and a reduction in social contact reflect the diminished significance of previously central goals and the increasing significance that emotion plays in the lives of older adults.

I should note that, unlike many life-span theories that begin with ideas about youth and proceed chronologically to include old age, my exploration of the life course of social relationships began with an interest in the social lives of very old people. Reductions in social contact in old age are prototypical, and the reduction has been interpreted in largely negative terms (e.g., Bromley, 1990; Looft, 1972). However, as I pursued a line of research initially aimed at identifying the psychopathological concomitants of social inactivity in the very old, I became increasingly convinced of the adaptive value of reduced social activity.

Gradually I enlarged the window of time to include more of the life span, eventually coming to include people as young as adolescents in my work. When I did, I observed a gradual trend toward decreasing interaction that begins early in life (Carstensen, 1992). I also found evidence that the social patterns typical of old people are seen in the behavior of young people when they encounter circumstances that mimic those endemic to old age (Carstensen & Fredrickson, 1992; Fredrickson & Carstensen, 1990). The nonlinearity of development, a fundamental stay of life-span theory (P. Baltes, 1987; P. Baltes & Goulet, 1970; P. Baltes, Reese, & Lipsitt, 1980; Heckhausen, Dixon, & P. Baltes, 1989), became increasingly apparent. It is unlikely that age-related changes in social behavior are simply a product of the passage of time. More likely they follow from a complex network of interactions representing the person's past, present, and future percepts as well as opportunities afforded in the environment to satisfy fundamental human needs.

In the following pages, I first provide some background about the general assumptions underlying research in gerontology. I then survey traditional views of social relationships and social interaction in old age, placing these views within a life-span context. Finally, I present SST, arguing that it provides a model of social aging that, while heretical to traditional thinking about social aging, is highly consistent with the fundamental tenets of life-span theory and best explains the set of empirical findings about social behavior at the end of life. SST represents a radical departure from the view of aging as a steady deteriorating process characterized by social withdrawal and emotional flattening. On the contrary, according to SST, in old age emotion is the *dominant* motivating factor in social interaction.

A COMMENT ON THE STATUS OF THEORY AND RESEARCH ON HUMAN AGING

Aging remains a mystery to gerontologists. Not only has the fountain of youth eluded its pursuers, but researchers do not know *why* we age (Hayflick, 1987). We know less about the last 30 years of life than we know about the first five. However, the current growth of the older population is creating an unprecedented interest in the aging process. Researchers and theorists of the biological and social sciences have begun to turn their attention to characteristics of human aging so that we, as a society, can adjust to the growing numbers of elderly citizens.

Yet science is not immune to social and cultural influences. The questions we ask and the framework within which we interpret our findings reflect well-ingrained beliefs about human behavior drawn from collective representations of the social world (Moscovici, 1984; Prilleltensky, 1989). Representations of old age—which have guided our thinking inside and outside the laboratory—are steeped in assumptions about the pervasiveness of deterioration in old age. Consequently, researchers have searched for problems, tacitly approaching the study of old age as a discrete period in life with little reference to the continuity of early and late life, and as a result have created a body of literature that reifies initial assumptions about decrement. The vast majority of research on aging addresses problems associated with old age (Rowe & Kahn, 1987). Granted, much good has come of our attention to the problems older people face. The past two decades have witnessed tremendous gains in behavioral

DEVELOPMENTAL PERSPECTIVES ON MOTIVATION

(Carstensen, 1988) and medical (Fries, 1980) treatments for seemingly intractable conditions common in late life. Yet the virtually exclusive focus on problems has led to a literature that suggests ubiquitous decrement.

Concerted attention to successful aging is relatively new in gerontology (M. Baltes & Carstensen, 1992; P. Baltes & M. Baltes, 1990; P. Baltes & Smith, 1990; P. Baltes, Smith & Staudinger, 1992; Rowe & Kahn, 1987; Vaillant & Vaillant, 1990), as is consideration of the adaptive value of presumed deficits of old age (M. Baltes, Wahl, & Reichert, 1991; M. Baltes & Silverberg, in press). Starkly different from earlier decremental models, these recent attempts to understand positive late-life aging focus on topics such as wisdom (P. Baltes et al., 1992), happiness (Ryff, 1982, 1989a) and control (M. Baltes et al., 1991; P. Baltes & M. Baltes, 1990). P. Baltes (1987) argues cogently that deficits inherent in the aging process do not preclude positive development. On the contrary, aging deficits in circumscribed domains can sometimes prompt growth in other domains.

P. Baltes and M. Baltes (1990) have presented a model of successful aging called selective optimization with compensation. They contend that three processes—selection, optimization and compensation—allow older people to maximize positive experience in old age. They argue that people who age successfully *select* life domains that hold greatest importance; *compensate* for intractable deficits by relying on preserved skills and supplemental aids; and *optimize* performance in selected life domains, in part by drawing on existing reserves or increasing the effort expended in these domains. Clearly, a viable science of gerontology will have to include, as an essential complement to the study of pathological aging, the study of adaptive, successful aging. The reader is cautioned, however, that such a science is in its infancy.

GERONTOLOGICAL VIEWS OF SOCIAL
RELATIONSHIPS AND SOCIAL INTERACTION

The most reliable, generalizable finding about the aging process is that it involves a general "slowing" in both biological and psychological processes (Salthouse, 1985). The most reliable finding about *social* aging is that rates of social interactions decline. Large-scale cross-sectional (Cumming & Henry, 1961; Gordon & Gaitz, 1976; Harvey & Singleton, 1989; Lawton, Moss, & Fulcomer, 1987) and longitudinal studies (Lee & Markides, 1990; Palmore, 1981) support this finding. Put simply, in old age people interact with others far less than in youth.

Insights into when and how age-related reductions in social contact occur have been elucidated by longitudinal studies. The Duke Longitudinal Study, for example, revealed a slow but steady decline in social activity from middle age on, intensifying in very old age (Palmore, 1981). This charting and most other descriptions in the literature, however, are based primarily on subjective reports about activity described at fairly gross levels. Dependent variables typically include indexes like the number of club memberships individuals hold or the overall frequency of contact with other people. We know very little about day-to-day contact, specific types of relationships, or qualitative changes in relationships; and we know next to nothing about the subjective experience of the activity changes that have been documented.

One refreshing exception to this trend is a study by Field and Minkler (1988). They analyzed intensive interviews that spanned a 14-year period based on the Berkeley Intergenerational Studies, focusing on contact and commitment to relationships from early old age to late old age. Considerable evidence for continuity was found. Contacts with adult children were highly stable, and satisfaction with these relationships increased over time. Contact with friends was somewhat reduced, more so for men than women. And contact with grandchildren declined in very old age even though satisfaction with such relationships remained stable.

Family contact seems to take on heightened importance in old age. The renewal of sibling ties is common (Cicirelli, 1989; Troll, 1971); in fact, a close bond with a sister seems to be protective against depression in old age (Cicirelli, 1989). Contact with children and grandchildren predicts satisfaction with interpersonal relationships (Kahn & Antonucci, 1984). And it appears that marriages become more affirming in old age, both more positive and less negative (Gottman, Levenson, & Carstensen, 1992; Guilford & Bengtson, 1979; Levenson, Carstensen, & Gottman, 1992a).

In old age, most friends are old friends (Field & Minkler, 1988; Palmore, 1981). Gender differences are found in the number and type of friendships. As during earlier years, women have relatively more close friends than men and see them more often (Candy, Troll, & Levy, 1981; Field & Minkler, 1988). Not surprisingly, widows and widowers report greater contact with friends than do married people (Field & Minkler, 1988).

Still, older people spend most of their time alone. In a community-based study conducted by M. Baltes, Wahl, and Schmid-Furstoss (1990), elderly respondents spent most of their time tending to basic personal essentials like eating, dressing, housework, and legal or financial matters. On average, socializing—most of which occurred within a family context—took only 9 percent of the day.

TRADITIONAL THEORIES ABOUT SOCIAL RELATIONSHIPS IN LATE LIFE

What explains this reduction in social interaction? The two most prominent theoretical accounts of this change are disengagement theory (Cumming & Henry, 1961) and activity theory (Havighurst, 1961; Havighurst & Albrecht, 1953; Maddox, 1963, 1965). More recently, social exchange theory also has been used to explain the age-related drop in activity level.

Disengagement theory is rooted in the functional theory of sociology. It holds that the reduction in social contact in old age represents an adaptive mechanism through which the person disassociates from society and society disassociates from the person. Fundamental tenets of the theory are that social withdrawal is mutual (originating in both society and the individual) and adaptive, and that emotional distancing from others is part of this normative process. At the individual level, disengagement theory invokes psychodynamic processes that represent a symbolic preparation for death. In short, the theory contends that emotional and social disengagement allows societies to prepare for the loss of individuals and individuals to prepare for death.

In stark contrast, activity theory—presuming that older people do desire social contact—holds social and physical *barriers* to interaction accountable for declining rates of interaction. Citing age-related losses, from mandatory retirement to the deaths of friends and loved ones, activity theorists argue that lowered rates of interaction are symptomatic of problems and pressures independent of the needs and wishes of individuals themselves.

Social exchange theorists contend that limited resources in old age confine social relationships to a narrower range than is available in youth and that an increased need for assistance undermines the equitable power balance necessary for mutually strong relationships (Bengtson & Dowd, 1980–81; Dowd, 1980). Essentially the argument is that older members of a social network contribute less to their interpersonal relationships, and subsequently the basic foundations of relationships erode away and social ties are weakened.

Each of these models can account for *some* of the findings published in the literature, yet none provides a cohesive explanation for the larger body of empirical findings. For example, activity theory and social exchange theory lead to predictions of subjective dissatisfaction in old age. Indeed, for many years gerontologists assumed that reduced social contact was a central reason for the inordinately high rates of depression and anxiety in old age (Gurland, 1976). Yet rates of social contact do not predict dissatisfaction in old age (Chapell & Badger, 1989; Lee & Markides, 1990). And recent large-scale epidemiological studies have shown that—with the exception of the dementias—older people suffer *lower* rates of mental health problems than their younger counterparts (George, Blazer, Winfield-Laird, Leaf, & Fischback, 1988; Weissman, Bruce, Leaf, Florio, & Holzer, 1991). By and large, older people report being happier with their lives than younger people do (Herzog & Rodgers, 1981). Thus reduced rates of interaction do not appear to stem from or lead to a basic dissatisfaction with life.

Moreover, even when efforts have been made to ensure access to social contact, most older people do not "take advantage" of the opportunity. Elaborate interventions aimed at increasing contact have not had lasting effects (Carstensen, 1986; Carstensen & Erickson, 1986). And senior centers—designed to provide easy access to social contact in the United States—are utilized by only 15% of the aged population.

The implicit assumption of the social exchange model is that older people are dependent. Yet even this assumption is equivocal. First, although there is no doubt that some older people require assistance from their social networks, empirical evidence suggests that as a group they need no more assistance than younger network members (Antonucci & Akiyama, 1987); and in terms of financial aid, more money flows down through the generations than up (Johnson, 1988). Second, at least some of the dependency observed in older people appears to be the product of social scripts that require dependent behavior in order to gain social contact. In a series of studies of nursing-home residents, M. Baltes and her colleagues (Baltes & Wahl, 1987; Baltes et al., 1991) show clearly that staff members reinforce dependent behavior and ignore independent behavior, suggesting that if older people are indeed dependent, younger people play a role, at least, in its etiology. One final problem with the social exchange model is that, on average, older people report *increasing* satisfaction with their relationships in late life (Field & Minkler, 1988), calling into question assumptions about decaying relationships.

Indeed, most of the empirical findings reviewed thus far are compatible with predictions of disengagement theory. Rates of contact decline, but this does not appear to affect people negatively. However, the essential premise of disengagement theory—that reduced rates of activity are fueled by an *emotional* distancing from others—has not withstood empirical tests. Meaningful social relationships are central to lay formulations of successful aging among both women and men (Ryff, 1991). And there is strong evidence that even though overall rates of interaction fail to predict satisfaction in old age, social connectedness predicts mental (Antonucci & Jackson, 1987; Lowenthal & Haven, 1968) and physical health and longevity (Berkman & Syme, 1979; Blazer, 1982), thus contradicting the cardinal assumption of disengagement theory.

RETHINKING TRADITIONAL MODELS WITHIN
A LIFE-SPAN FRAMEWORK

A tacit assumption underlying all the traditional models of social aging is that the changes we see in late life are uniquely late-life phenomena. For disengagement theorists, closeness to death leads to a flattening of emotional attachments; for activity theorists, ageism leads to changes; and for social exchange theorists, age-related health and social losses threaten the reciprocality of relationships. Yet virtually all of the literature comprises either cross-sectional comparisons of different age groups or longitudinal studies that began when subjects were just on the threshold of old age.

There is evidence in the developmental literature that a selective narrowing of the range of social partners may begin early in life. Toddlers negotiate social interaction with virtually any prospective social partner (Corsaro, 1985). "Friendships" are generally based more on proximity than on personal characteristics of others. Over time, however, preferences for certain types of social partners over others become evident. Maccoby (1988, 1990) has demonstrated strong preferences for same-sex play partners and avoidance of opposite-sex partners in childhood, starting about the age of 3 or 4 and lasting until adolescence. Sociological trends show that during the middle-school years, children separate into two primary subgroups, holding strong preferences for one group over the other (Eder, 1985). Social cliques, steeped in strong preferences for a select group of people over others, typify adolescence (Dunphy, 1963).

Taken together, the child and aging literatures hint that there may be a life-span progression of reduced social interaction. Could the narrowing of social partners in old age represent the culmination of a lifelong phenomenon in which people gradually interact with fewer and fewer people? If in fact these patterns are evinced early in life, they provide serious challenge to theories that explain social narrowing as a function of circumstances unique to old age. Moreover, they force reconsideration of the adaptive value of diminished social contact beyond a symbolic withdrawal from life.

Since the issues in question are about intraindividual change, the only way to systematically address the change is through longitudinal analysis. The fundamental issue is not whether older people, on average, are more or less active than younger people, but whether older people decline in relative activity level compared with themselves at earlier ages.

Ready answers to questions requiring longitudinal analysis are always limited by practical constraints. Several years ago I had the opportunity to reanalyze data from a longitudinal study initiated by Jean Mcfarlane in 1930 (Mcfarlane, 1938) and maintained by a core group of researchers who continue to follow subjects today.[1]

DEVELOPMENTAL PERSPECTIVES ON MOTIVATION

Housed at the Institute for Human Development at the University of California–Berkeley, the data provide a rich source of information about the nature of social relationships.

When subjects who had been followed since 18 months of age turned 17 or 18 years old, 30 years old, 40 years old, and 50 years old, they were interviewed intensively by clinical psychologists about their personal and social lives. Interviews included questions ranging from inquiries about acquaintances to highly intimate questions about close relationships. Questions focused on subjects' satisfactions and sorrows as well as their feelings of closeness and isolation. Because the interviews included questions about a variety of relationships, they allowed for the examination of changes within specific types of relationships. If people interact with fewer social partners because they become increasingly selective, such patterns should be evinced by declines in certain relationships but not others.

I designed a research project to investigate adulthood change in (a) the frequency of interaction; (b) emotional closeness in these relationships; and (c) satisfaction, with each of six types of social relationships—acquaintances, siblings, parents, close friends, children, and spouses (Carstensen, 1992). Two hypotheses were explored. First, I hypothesized that the frequency of social contact with acquaintances would be highest in early adulthood and would decline gradually throughout middle adulthood. I expected that contact with acquaintances would show the greatest decline; in other words, I expected that the decrease in contact would be selective. Second, I hypothesized that emotional closeness would increase in significant relationships throughout adulthood *even when rates of interaction declined*. Recall that the premise of earlier theories has been that rates of interaction are legitimate proxies for emotional investment. In this longitudinal data set, I was able to examine empirically the relation between emotional closeness and frequency of contact.

Interview materials were reviewed and rated by research assistants who were blind to the hypotheses under study. Results supported the hypotheses. In general, rates of interaction with friends and acquaintances declined from early to middle adulthood (Figure 1). During these same years, however, interaction rates with spouses remained constant (Figure 2). Emotional closeness to close friends also remained stable, despite a reliable decline in interaction rate.

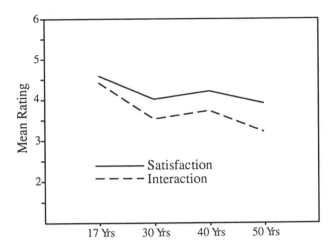

FIGURE 1. Acquaintances. Means, and SDs, respectively, for interaction frequency (IF) and satisfaction (S) (N = 50). At 17, IF = 4.39, 1.26; S = 4.63, 1.01. At 30, IF = 3.47, 1.09; S = 3.96, 0.98. At 40, IF = 3.79, 1.07; S = 4.12, 1.20. At 50, IF = 3.30, 1.18; S = 3.95, 1.01. From L. L. Carstensen, "Social and Emotional Patterns in Adulthood: Support for Socioemotional Selectivity Theory," *Psychology and Aging, 7*, 331–338. Copyright 1992 by the American Psychological Association. Reprinted by permission.

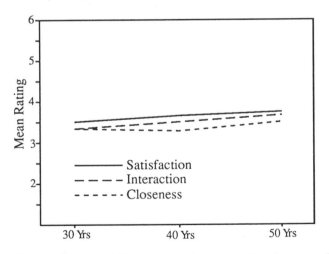

FIGURE 2. Spouses. Means and SDs, respectively, for interaction frequency (IF), emotional closeness (EC), and satisfaction (S) (N = 42). At 30, IF = 3.68, 0.79; EC = 4.11, 1.09; S = 4.12, 1.31. At 40, IF = 3.93, 0.89; EC = 4.39, 0.74; S = 4.33, 1.39. At 50, IF = 3.83, 1.06; EC = 4.68, 0.80; S = 4.92, 0.76. From L. L. Carstensen, "Social and Emotional Patterns in Adulthood: Support for Socioemotional Selectivity Theory," *Psychology and Aging, 7*, 331–338. Copyright 1992 by the American Psychological Association. Reprinted by permission.

DEVELOPMENTAL PERSPECTIVES ON MOTIVATION

Thus the picture that emerged suggested that although rates of interaction drop precipitously in some relationships, they remain stable in others.

This longitudinal analysis clarified three important issues. First, enlarging the window of time to include late adolescence through middle age illustrated that reductions in social contact were evident long before failing health or closeness to death could be likely instigators. People begin to reduce social contact *early* in adulthood, calling into question the causal role of old age. Second, reductions in social contact occur only in more peripheral relationships. In some intimate relationships contact increases. And third, frequency of contact is a poor proxy for emotional closeness. In some close relationships, subjects experienced greater closeness over time even when rates of contact declined over the same period.

A model of social aging, very different from traditional models, began to emerge. On the one hand, social contact diminishes with age. On the other hand, social relationships are very important, predicting psychological well-being (Antonucci & Jackson, 1987), health and longevity (Berkman & Syme, 1979; Blazer, 1982). Viewed within a life-span context, it appears that declining rates of contact can be accounted for by *selective* drops in contact in some relationships but not in others. In this light, none of the traditional theoretical accounts—emotional disengagement, ageism, or the weakening of social bonds—accounts persuasively for empirical findings. The nature and patterns of change suggest that people play a volitional role in the reduction. Thus the motivational basis for age-related changes must be considered.

Socioemotional Selectivity Theory

Socioemotional selectivity theory (SST) is a life-span theory of social behavior rooted in motivational and functional properties of social interaction (Carstensen, 1987, 1991). The theory assumes that social interaction is motivated both by fundamental human needs, like hunger and sex, and by the social modulation of psychological and affective states. In addition to serving basic survival functions, social interaction allows people to acquire information, develop and maintain self-concept, and regulate emotion states.

Even though the same basic motives probably operate throughout life, effective satisfaction of social goals requires increasing selectivity in the choice of social partners. A basic tenet of selectivity theory is that reduced social interaction is not imposed on older individuals but, rather, that older people themselves play an active role in narrowing the social environment. Consistent with disengagement theory, SST assumes that people actively reduce social contact. In stark contrast to disengagement theory, however, I believe that emotion regulation assumes increasing centrality among social motives.

Below I review three of the most prominent psychological goals that motivate social interaction—information acquisition, self-concept development and maintenance, and the regulation of emotion—and illustrate how each is influenced by place in the life cycle. Following relatively brief reviews of the ways that information acquisition and self-concept motivate social behavior, I focus on life-span changes in emotion experience and regulation.

Before proceeding, allow me to clarify two points. First, in SST I define psychological goals broadly. Information acquisition includes gathering not only objective facts, but also self-relevant information like social standing and social norms; emotions include feelings of accomplishment and purposefulness in addition to basic emotion states. Second, the three general classes of social motives I address are not mutually exclusive. Acquiring information about professional standing, for example, may occasion an affective response and, similarly, may have implications for self-concept. Nevertheless, I contend that there is heuristic value in considering different functional aspects of social interaction to be motivated by distinct social goals; and in this chapter I present empirical evidence that people represent social partners along dimensions related to such goals.

SOCIAL CONTACT AND THE ACQUISITION OF INFORMATION

Whether we are instructed explicitly or learn through observation, we derive much of our knowledge about the world through social interaction. Indeed, the transmission of culture (e.g., knowledge, morals, beliefs, art, customs) from generation to generation occurs largely through social means (D'Andrade, 1981).

At no point in life does the social transmission of information cease. However, there is a developmental trajectory for the efficacy of obtaining information through social means. In infancy and early childhood most of the information we seek is easily (arguably, best) obtained through social interaction. Older people provide young children with information about the world out there. Even interaction with same-age mates, whose stores of knowledge are comparably limited, provides important information about other people and the consequences of our own behavior.

With age, two things change. First, our stores of information steadily increase, making information-rich social contact less likely. Second, we acquire skills that permit information acquisition through nonsocial means. Reading is perhaps the best example of a skill that opens doors to nonsocial learning. Scientific exploration is another example of the use of nonsocial means to discover completely original information.[2]

Over the life course people become increasingly different from one another (Dannefer & Perlmutter, 1990) and increasingly expert in relatively circumscribed areas. As a result, increasingly fewer social partners can serve as resources for new information. It is important to point out that there is no reason to think that information becomes less rewarding with age; it is just harder to come by via social interaction. Information seeking requires contact with people who have greater expertise; whereas in youth such individuals are plentiful, over time fewer relative experts can be found.

Because information is more likely to be derived from social interaction earlier in life rather than later, the extent to which social contact is motivated by information acquisition varies across the life course. Consider early adolescence. During the teenage years, a great deal of heterosocial contact is motivated by information acquisition. Largely through face-to-face contact, teenagers learn the likes and dislikes of prospective social partners, how to demonstrate their interest in another person, and how to talk to people of the opposite sex. Social gatherings, such as parties, serve an extremely important socializing function, in which social facts are acquired and social comparison runs rampant. Such gatherings are not necessarily affectively positive; nevertheless, they assume larger-than-life importance. Most adolescents opt for attending these social functions even though the affective payoff is limited because of the potential for acquiring information. By middle age, social functions involving highly diverse groups are less compelling because the potential information gain is less. That is, once basic information about social interaction with peers is acquired, it no longer broadly motivates social contact, so that by middle age informal gatherings tend to comprise people from a much more restricted range of social partners.

The changes I note are age graded (i.e., normative), but not inevitable or age caused. Rather, they are related to conditions that commonly co-occur with age. Although—on average—information acquisition motivates less social contact with age, there are conditions under which information seeking will appear at any age. I predict, for example, that older people first relocating to a senior housing project may be highly social, recognizing that other residents hold information they do not have. More sinister situations, like receiving the diagnosis of a serious disease, may also provoke information seeking. But generally speaking, the acquisition of novel information motivates less social interaction over time. Moreover, in instances where social contact *is* motivated by information seeking, social partners must be selected using more exacting strategies.

SOCIAL CONTACT AND THE SELF

The self is a unifying principle that organizes diverse beliefs and motives (Hilgard, 1949). Operationally, self-concept is a collection of beliefs about the self, essentially embodied in private or public statements that begin with "I" or include "me" (Triandis, 1989). Although in many ways the self is highly stable (McCrae & Costa, 1984, 1988), it is not a static entity. On the contrary, the self is dynamic. According to Markus and Herzog (1991, p. 110), "The self-concept integrates an individual's experiences across time and provides continuity and meaning to them. As such, it is centrally implicated in all aspects of psychological experience—in emotion, well-being, and coping; in goal setting, striving, motivation and control; and in ability, efficacy, and competence."

There is an intimate, reciprocal influence between the self and the social world. Self theorists argue that social relatedness is a basic human need, integrally interwoven with self-concept and motivation (Deci & Ryan, 1985, 1991; Ryan, this volume; Steele, 1988). In the words of Deci and Ryan (1991, p. 238), the self entails "intrinsic growth processes whose tendency is toward the integration of one's own experience and actions with one's sense of relatedness to others." Two broad, and in some ways opposing, processes are involved in the development of self: differentiation and integration (Csikszentmihalyi, 1990). Through differentiation people define themselves as unique individuals; through integration they unite with other people and society at large.

Much social behavior operates in the service of defining the self and maintaining a consistent, well-integrated view over time. The process is clearly not passive. People do not simply mirror the images others offer (Bandura, 1978; Kilhstrom & Cantor, 1984; Markus & Sentis, 1982). Instead they actively seek social partners who affirm their self-perceptions (Cantor, Mackie, & Lord, 1984; Swann, 1987; Swann & Hill, 1982). Thus, although people ultimately come to see themselves as other people see them, they also play an active role in selecting the people who provide feedback.

Social comparison theory maintains that people need to have stable representations of themselves and, toward that end, evaluate themselves against others (Festinger, 1954). Here again the selection of social partners with whom one compares oneself is not arbitrary. Festinger asserted that similar others were the best candidates for comparison purposes and further hypothesized that, owing to an inherent desire for improvement, there is a tendency to compare "upward" to people who perform slightly better along the dimension of interest. More recently, Taylor and her colleagues have demonstrated that upward social comparison is not uniformly preferred. Whereas the desire to affiliate with others and the desire for information about others lead to upward social comparison, self-evaluation in the service of self-esteem enhancement leads to downward social comparison (Taylor & Lobel, 1989). Under conditions of threat, for example, people consistently compare themselves with less fortunate others (Collins, Dakof, & Taylor, 1988; Taylor, 1983; Taylor, Falke, Shoptaw, & Lichtman, 1986; Wills, 1981; Wood, Taylor, & Lichtman, 1985).

What is the developmental trajectory of self-concept? Some have claimed that with age the self becomes more elaborated and complex (Labouvie-Vief & DeVoe, 1991; Neugarten, 1968) and that increasing self-knowledge leads to what we consider wisdom and maturity (Jung, 1934). However, role changes such as retirement, health problems, and negative attitudes and stereotypes may challenge self-concept in later life. If the task of youth is the development of self-concept, surely the task of late life is its maintenance. In SST I argue that social strategies optimal for the development of self-concept are different from the social strategies involved in its maintenance.

Early in life, the differentiation and integration of the self with the world at large is promoted by exposure to a wide range of people. Exposure to others, similar or different, helps people understand who they are and who they are not. The development of the self typically involves "trying on" an assortment of values and beliefs. Some are internalized, others are discarded; either way, social interaction helps to crystallize self-concept. Once self-concept is firmly developed, however, comparisons with people who are very different hold little information relevant to the self and may occur less frequently (Suls & Mullen, 1982).

Indeed, effective social comparison may become more difficult with age because, as people become increasingly differentiated from one another and increasingly expert in circumscribed areas, fewer social partners can serve social comparison functions. For example, a young boy may first become aware of his artistic talents by comparing himself with a wide range of children in his age cohort. When the boy has grown into an accomplished artist, there will be fewer people with whom comparisons will yield useful information. When he is an elderly man, he may compare himself only with other artists who achieved similar status and are now in similar health. In other words, even though social comparisons may serve the same functions in old age as they do in youth—self-enhancement or self-improvement—fewer appropriate comparisons may be possible.

The priorities of certain aspects of self-concept may also change with age. Assumptions about an inherent desire for self-improvement, for example, may not hold across the life span. Older people appear to be more accepting of their current abilities than younger people (Cross & Markus, 1991; Ryff, 1989b).

Finally, when social goals shift from the development of self to the maintenance of self, social selectivity about partners is clearly demanded. Intimates, with whom we share a developmental history, are best able to assist in laying out the consistencies between then and now. Antonucci and Jackson (1987) have shown that over the life course people come to rely on social "convoys" that comprise people who reliably provide instrumental support and emotional sustenance. SST predicts that such convoys will become increasingly important with age, in large part because they help people integrate past selves with current and future selves in ways that maintain self-consistency.

At the same time that interactions with familiar social partners become increasingly important and predictable, interactions with novel social partners become increasingly unpredictable and pose possible threats to self-concept— a point to which I now turn.

Threats to self-concept. Social interactions can foster the positive development of self-concept, but they also pose threats. Although this is true at any age, it is particularly true for older people. In a sample of elderly women, Rook (1984) showed that negative aspects of social interactions predicted general well-being better than positive aspects. Strained social relationships subtracted substantially from overall well-being.

If we are to fully understand changes in social behavior in older people, we must also appreciate changes in the behavior of their social partners. In the domain of self-concept a basic tenet of SST converges with a basic tenet of activity theory: we live in an ageist society. In old age, ageism begins to erode possibilities for self-enhancing contact with unfamiliar social partners. I once interviewed a retired English professor in a nursing home. She mentioned the irritation she felt at being called "dearie" by staff members half her age with half her education. The blatant disregard for her identity made interactions with others quite toxic. When people grow old, they become part of a stigmatized group, and subsequently interaction with others, particularly interaction with unfamiliar social partners, risks threats to self-concept and self-esteem.

A sizable literature in social psychology demonstrates the deleterious effects stereotypes can have on stigmatized groups (Allport, 1954; Darley & Fazio, 1980). An important difference between age stereotypes and stereotypes of other kinds, however, is that Western stereotypes of the elderly typically include both positive (e.g., kindly) and negative (e.g., incompetent) characteristics (Lutsky, 1980). Still, a recent study by Crocker, Voelkl, Testa, and Major (1991) portends negative effects even when interactions are highly positive. Crocker et al. found that African American college students who received positive feedback from Caucasian peers benefited only when it was clear that students providing the feedback were blind to race. When feedback was delivered face-to-face, African American students' self-esteem declined even when the information they received was *positive.* Apparently they assumed that feedback was influenced by their race and thus discounted the content of the message. One can imagine a host of comparable situations in old age in which the behavior of some social partners is highly positive, even though underlying motives are questionable. Generalizing from Crocker et al.'s findings, either positive or negative extremes may have similarly nefarious effects.

My students and I recently began investigating changes in interactional dynamics when young people interact with old people. In a laboratory study focused on interactions between college-aged subjects and healthy community elderly, young subjects interact with either elderly or age-matched confederates (Tsai & Carstensen, 1992). In the experimental paradigm, subjects are asked to complete a preference questionnaire indicating their opinions about a wide range of topics on a rating scale. Next, two subjects are introduced and asked to discuss, for ten minutes, a topic we know they disagree about. Subjects are told that at the end of ten minutes they must provide a rating that represents their joint opinion on the topic, thereby forcing either compromise or deference on the part of one member. After the joint rating is obtained, just before subjects leave the laboratory, we ask them once again to indicate their opinions independently on the preference questionnaire. This last step is included so that we can examine whether opinions actually changed or whether the compromise represented only momentary deference. Discussions are also videotaped, and nonverbal behavior is coded.

Our findings suggest that young people's behavior is not overtly negative when they interact with older people. By self-report, young people are equally positive about interactions with old and young confederates. However, younger people are more likely to defer to older confederates than to younger ones. As predicted, however, opinions tapped on the follow-up preference questionnaire indicated that they do not, in fact, change their opinions. Differences in interaction style were also observed on videotape. When interacting with old confederates young subjects, although very polite, were more distanced, formal, and reticent than when they interacted with young confederates.

It seems that qualitative aspects of the social interactions older people have with younger people may change with age. Our preliminary findings suggest that although social interactions with younger adults may be pleasant and respectful, they also may take on a rather artificial quality. The potential for information-rich, highly energized conversations with acquaintances may become rare in old age.[3] We know very little about the effects this type of interaction has on self-concept, but it is unlikely that they are uniformly positive.

To summarize, self-concept is intimately embedded within a web of social relationships. Early in life the development of self-concept benefits from interaction with a wide range of social partners. Over the life course a select group of social partners becomes increasingly able to affirm the self, allowing for the interweaving of past, present, and future selves. At the same time familiar social partners become better able to provide self-definition, novel social partners begin to pose potential threats to self-concept. Even positive stereotypes about the elderly can change interactional dynamics in ways that threaten self-concept. Subsequently, as we age, interactions motivated by the maintenance of self-concept require that social partners be more carefully selected.

SOCIAL CONTACT AND THE REGULATION OF EMOTION

Emotion and motivation are so closely intertwined that debate continues about how far one subsumes the other. Some argue that emotion underlies motivation; others argue that emotion is epiphenomenal to motivation (see Hansell, 1989). Conceptual distinctions aside, few disagree with Darwin's (1872) basic observation that emotion is intimately associated with social behavior. In SST I argue that the hedonic properties of social contact become increasingly salient with age, such that by the very end of life social contacts are evaluated, and subsequently approached or avoided, based almost entirely on their affective quality.

This argument diverges sharply from traditional thinking about emotion in old age. Emotions in late life have been described as flattened, rigid (Banham, 1951), increasingly negative in valence, and less well controlled (Bromley, 1990). Indeed, the fundamental premise of disengagement theory is that the social withdrawal that typifies old age reflects a basic emotional disengagement from life. Given past thinking about old age, the association of reduced social activity with diminished emotionality was not far-fetched. Stage models of late life also assume that at the end of life people turn inward toward more internal, interior concerns (Buhler, 1933; Erickson, 1968, 1982; Jung, 1933). However, a small but growing empirical literature suggests that such a picture is at best incomplete. Below I review recent research focused on developmental features of emotion and then return to a discussion of the salience of emotion in old age.

The social nature of emotion in early life. Considerable attention has been focused on developmental aspects of emotion in infancy and early childhood. Findings from this literature underscore the social embeddedness of emotion from the beginning of life. Newborns show greater interest in social than nonsocial stimuli (Fantz, 1973) and within months come to display differential responses to distinct emotion faces; and they vicariously activate emotion through social referencing (Izard, 1971). Social referencing of emotion also appears to serve important informational functions. Campos and his colleagues, for example, showed that under conditions of uncertainty, even preverbal infants read and respond to the emotion faces and voices of their caregivers before acting (Campos, Barrett, Lamb, Goldsmith, & Stenberg, 1983). Moreover, social referencing of the emotions of others influences personal efficacy, which subsequently influences both the course of action and the amount of effort recruited to pursue goals (Bandura, 1982, 1987).

Relatively recently, developmental researchers have concluded that cognitive understanding of emotion appears much earlier than once thought (cf. Bridges, 1930, 1932). Stein and her colleagues have shown that children as young as 3 or 4 years understand emotion signals and emotion activation; they understand that external events cause emotions and that goals motivate action aimed at changing internal emotion states, thus laying the groundwork for emotion regulation (Stein & Levine, 1987; Stein & Trabasso, 1990).

The regulation of emotion is clearly embedded in a social context. At first children rely on other people—typically parents—to help them regulate feelings. Increasingly they come to rely on self-control strategies, such as cognitive distraction, reframing, or disclosure, to quell negative emotional states and elicit positive ones (Thompson, 1990). Although with age people shift from a primary reliance on external sources of emotion regulation to internalized strategies, social contact remains a primary vehicle for emotion regulation throughout the life course. People seek social contact during times of distress and rely on social partners to instigate positive emotions. Indeed, our greatest joys, as well as our greatest sorrows, are elicited in social contexts.

The experience of emotion in old age. Compared with the relative explosion of interest in emotion in infancy and childhood over the past two decades, little attention has been paid to emotion in old age. It was only about eight years ago that several laboratories began to focus concerted attention on emotion in old age. Below, I review recent empirical findings that begin to provide a clearer picture of emotion in later life.

Acknowledging gaps in our empirical knowledge base, Richard Schulz (1985) published a seminal review on affect and aging, in which he articulated important questions about emotion in old age and offered preliminary answers. Following a review and synthesis of relevant empirical and theoretical findings from sociology, biology, and psychology, Schulz concluded tentatively that the existing evidence suggested that older people experience emotions at about the same level of intensity as do younger people, but that older people may experience more negative emotions (given the negative life events associated with aging). He also reasoned that, owing to decreased efficiency in the regulatory mechanisms of the central nervous system, older people would experience emotions longer and show less variability in emotional states from day to day. Finally, he surmised that emotional responses would become less unidimensional with age and that the types of events that elicit emotions would change as well. At this point, some of his postulates have been confirmed and others disconfirmed.

One of the most compelling and, at the same time, provocative suggestions Schulz raised was that diminished integrity of the central nervous system results in heightened arousability and decreased homeostatic control over physical features of emotion. The relevance of biological functioning to emotion is obvious. In all theories of emotion, neurophysiological involvement is considered a central feature (Cannon, 1927; James, 1884; Levenson, 1992). Modern debates center on questions of autonomic specificity (Levenson, 1992) and mechanisms of activation (Lazarus, 1991; Zajonc, 1985), but there is no argument that physiological changes accompany emotion. If aging exerts a negative effect on the integrity of the biological system that modulates arousal, there may well be behavioral and subjective changes in the experience of emotion in old age.

Despite evidence for reduced homeostatic control, however, experimental and clinical studies show that aging is associated with a *decrease* in sympathetic and parasympathetic innervation (Frolkis, 1977). At the end-organ level, activation thresholds are higher (Shmavonian, Miller, & Cohen, 1970), and extinction occurs more rapidly than in younger controls (Botwinick & Kornetsky, 1960). It is true, however, that *smaller* doses of catecholamines, acetycholine, and serotonin affect hemodynamics in older subjects (Bogatskaya, 1972). Older subjects show greater norepinephrine and blood pressure response to cold pressor tasks and isometric exercise (Palmer, Ziegler, & Lake, 1978). Thus, neurophysiological changes in late life do not follow a consistent path. Although underarousal is generally characteristic of older adults, it does not uniformly occur (Eisdorfer, 1978).

To the best of my knowledge, the first direct examination of emotion-elicited arousal of the autonomic nervous system (ANS) in an elderly sample was published in 1991. Robert Levenson, Paul Ekman, Wallace Friesen, and I decided to examine physiological reactivity and subjective experience of emotion in a sample of healthy elderly adults (mean age 77 years) (Levenson, Carstensen, Friesen, & Ekman, 1991). Two central questions guided the research. The first concerned whether emotion-specific ANS activity, found in younger samples (Ekman, Levenson, & Friesen, 1983; Levenson, Ekman, Heider, & Friesen, 1992), also would be seen in an elderly sample. Our second question focused on the level of arousal that was occasioned by two very different eliciting tasks, a facial posing task and a relived emotions task, both of which have been shown to recruit

ANS activity in previous research. The facial posing task involved voluntary posing of muscle-by-muscle facial configurations associated with distinct emotions. The relived emotions task involved remembering and reexperiencing emotional events.

Overall, our older subjects showed great similarity to younger subjects. Older subjects were able to perform the experimental tasks with little apparent trouble. Evidence for emotion-specific ANS activity was found, and the intensity of the subjective experience of emotion was not unlike that reported by younger subjects. However, results of the study failed to support Schulz's suspicion of heightened arousability. The magnitude of ANS activity was much reduced in the old sample. Given clear evidence, both by subjective reports and by ANS specificity, that our subjects did respond to the experimental manipulations, our results suggest that hypoarousal rather than hyperarousal may characterize emotion in old age.[4]

Of course most emotions occur in a social context. Would results be similar using a different eliciting task, in which subjects discussed emotionally charged issues embedded in an important social relationship? In our ongoing study of long-term marriages, Robert Levenson, John Gottman, and I have been able to examine physiological reactivity in middle-aged and older couples while they discuss a conflict in their relationship as well as a pleasant topic and a more neutral topic. Half of the couples we study are happily married; the other half are unhappily married. In this research paradigm, couples come to the laboratory, agree upon a problem in their marriage (with the help of a research assistant), and then discuss the topic while physiological measures of major organ systems are recorded.

In all three of the conversations older couples show lower physiological arousal than middle-aged couples. In addition, older couples are more positive and less negative in their affective expressions, even when discussing a conflict (Gottman, Levenson, & Carstensen, 1992; Levenson, Carstensen, & Gottman, 1992a; 1992b).

Thus, although there are age-related changes in the physiological domain that theoretically could lead to hyperarousal in response to emotion, empirical investigations directly examining emotion arousal fail to support this prediction. On the contrary, arousal appears to be reduced in old people relative to their younger counterparts. It is possible, of course, that older people actively suppress emotional reactions in order to limit their responses, but comparable levels of self-reported intensity argue against this position.

Another component process of emotion that could theoretically change with age is facial expression. The face is the primary communicative tool for felt emotions (Ekman & Friesen, 1969; Tomkins, 1963, 1970). If wrinkles and sagging skin, inevitably associated with the aging process, obscure the signal value of the face (Ekman, 1978), one could expect changes in the behavior of social partners and possibly even in the experience of emotion itself (see Ekman et al., 1983; Zajonc, Murphy, & Inglehart, 1989).

Over the past several years, Carol Malatesta and her colleagues have pursued a series of studies aimed at illuminating the ways age may influence both encoding and decoding of facial expressions of emotion. In one study Malatesta, Izard, Culver, and Nicholich (1987) compared the accuracy of young, middle-aged, and older people in decoding the emotion faces of young, middle-aged, and older people. Although they failed to find reliable evidence that older faces were harder to decode, they noted a trend in that direction. And older people were poorer at decoding faces than younger people. They also observed that each of the age groups was most accurate at decoding the faces of age-matched peers, suggesting that there may be age-by-cohort interaction effects in decoding accuracy such that people of similar generations are best able to decode one another's facial expressions.

Of course errors in emotional decoding are common at any age. Malatesta contends that there may be a pattern to decoding errors such that errors in decoding neutral faces are consistent with personality characteristics in old age (Malatesta, Fiore, & Messina, 1987). Malatesta et al. contend that by the time people reach late life, expressions of prevalent emotions have become ingrained in static features of the face. Subsequently, personality characteristics associated with emotions come to be visible to the casual observer and may even obscure transient emotions expressed by the older person.

Still another domain of emotion functioning is the subjective experience, and here again an increasingly strong case can be made for age-related change. The cognitive appraisal of events clearly influences the experience of emotion and resulting coping responses (Folkman, Lazarus, Pimley, & Novacek, 1987; Lazarus & Folkman,

1984; Schulz, 1985; Stein & Trabasso, 1990; Yarrow, 1979). Age-related changes in cognitive appraisal processes could hypothetically influence emotion in many ways. Schulz (1985) speculated that there may be comparison processes inherent in the appraisal of events such that after a person has experienced a lifetime of events, fewer elicitors are viewed as extremely positive or negative. If a person has experienced very few losses, for example, a relatively minor loss may be experienced as extremely intense. After major losses, however, the same type of loss may elicit much less emotion. In the same way, extremely positive events could have a diminishing effect on the experience of future positive events. In other words, there may be a continuous recalibrating of intensity that accommodates events that have occurred. A young girl whose dog dies, for example, may feel the most intense sadness she has ever experienced. When that same girl is a 50-year-old woman and has undergone the death of several people who were emotionally close to her, a similar event might elicit far less sadness.

Although Schulz's very interesting hypothesis has yet to be tested, there is growing empirical evidence for cognitive change leading to improved emotion self-regulation across adulthood. In recent years Labouvie-Vief and her colleagues have extended developmental models about the integration of emotion and cognition in childhood to middle adulthood and old age (Labouvie-Vief & De-Voe, 1991; Labouvie-Vief, DeVoe, & Bulka, 1989; Labouvie-Vief, Hakim-Larson, DeVoe, & Schoeberlein, 1989). They argue that the experience of emotion changes across adulthood as people come to represent the world with increasingly complex cognitive categories that integrate affective and cognitive modes of thought. Whereas "decentering" from the self is at the core of widely accepted models of child development (e.g., Piagetian theory), Labouvie-Vief et al. believe that the task of adulthood maturation is to reintegrate cognition with more relational, affective reasoning processes. Essentially, they argue that in youth it is adaptive to acquire a epistimological structure that emphasizes external shared reality and deemphasizes the inner, more emotional, and relative world. Mature adult thought, in their view, deemphasizes the distinction between these modes of reason and leads to improvement in emotion self-regulation. Labouvie-Vief and her colleagues have conducted several studies that suggest greater understanding and control of basic emotion states, predicted by both age and ego level (Blanchard-Fields, 1986; Labouvie-Vief, DeVoe, & Bulka, 1989; Labouvie-Vief, Hakim-Larson, DeVoe, & Schoeberlein, 1989), and they find indirect support for the model in studies suggesting that people use increasingly more mature defense mechanisms across adulthood·(Vaillant, 1977).[5]

Recently Lawton, Kleban, Rajagopal, and Dean (1992) reported findings from a cross-sectional study of healthy adults, spanning better than a 40-year age range, which provide further support for ideas about improved self-regulatory capacity in late adulthood. Based on questionnaires that broadly tap affective experience, from the perception of basic physical and psychological changes to the degree of volitional control exerted over emotional responses, older subjects expressed relatively less sensation seeking and emotional lability and more moderation of affective responsiveness. Evidence was found for improved self-regulation through effective coping efforts as well as proactive strategies involving the design of affect-friendly environments (Lawton, 1989; Lawton et al., 1992). Thus there is strong converging evidence that older people perceive themselves as having greater control over their emotions.

Are older people less happy than younger people? For many years the answer to this question was believed to be yes. It was assumed that age-related losses, such as deaths of friends and loved ones and personal illness, must lead to reductions in happiness. However, recent evidence suggests that this is not necessarily so. On some surveys of well-being and happiness, older people report being happier than their younger counterparts (e.g., Herzog & Rodgers, 1981). Within the context of marriage, our research suggests clear evidence for greater positivity and reduced negativity (Gottman et al., 1992; Levenson et al., 1992a, 1992b).

What about the intensity of emotion? In several ongoing investigations in my laboratory as well as collaborative investigations with Robert Levenson's laboratory, we find the self-reported intensity of emotions in old subjects to be indistinguishable from reports of young subjects (Carstensen, 1992; Carstensen & Fredrickson, 1992; Levenson et al., 1991). Malatesta and her colleagues report similar results (Malatesta & Kalnok, 1984; Malatesta et al., 1987).

In their recent paper Lawton and his colleagues (Lawton et al., 1992) take a different position, arguing for a decrease in emotional surgency and a leveling of positive affect in older cohorts. I expect that apparent discrepancies may result from definitional matters regarding constructs of surgency and positive affect. In Lawton et al.'s work, emotional surgency is based on items like "When I'm happy, I feel like bursting with joy," and "I sometimes get emotionally involved in things even when I don't want to." Similarly, evidence for a subjective leveling of positive affect in older subjects is based in part on questionnaire items that measure "interest" (e.g., "Fewer novel or interesting things happen as I get older, compared with when I was in my twenties"). In our research, and Malatesta's, subjects are asked directly about the level of intensity they experienced when they felt a specific emotion, whereas Lawton et al. ask subjects about more general views of emotional experiences and include interest and excitement in their conceptualization of positive affect.

Are there qualitative differences in emotion experience? Definitive answers to this question are clearly lacking at this time, but I anticipate that the answer ultimately will be proved affirmative. In talking with subjects in our studies, we regularly hear anecdotes that suggest a high level of complexity and richness in emotion experience. Many times subjects mention spontaneously that, as one nears the end of life, emotional experience involves a composite of positive and negative feelings. Poignancy, an affective response virtually absent in childhood, appears to be very common in old age. The following example provides a particularly eloquent illustration. As noted above, in the Levenson et al. (1991) study we used an emotion-induction procedure that involves asking subjects to recall times when they felt specific emotions, gathering information about the eliciting events, and asking subjects to reexperience one particular emotion as strongly as they can. As part of a happiness induction, we had asked an elderly woman to identify a time when she felt very happy. She told about a recent visit from her sister, smiling and laughing as she spoke. As requested, she focused on the moment when she first saw her sister's face through a crowd of passengers leaving an airplane. We then asked her to reexperience the emotion, focusing on the feelings of happiness. As we monitored her expressions via video monitor, amid smiles, we noticed a tear run down her cheek. Afterward, when we asked her to explain, she told us that seeing her sister reminded her of the recent death of her brother-in-law, who had accompanied her sister on previous visits. She commented further that her sister was older than she was and so she could not know for certain that she would see her again. Thus, as happy as she was to see her sister, the event elicited a complicated set of emotions.

Although anecdotal, such observations fit well into Labouvie-Vief's life-span view of emotional experience (Labouvie-Vief et al., 1989) in which the acceptance and embrace of opposing fields represents maturation; they are also consistent with wisdom theory, which stresses an appreciation for the uncertainties of life (Baltes et al., 1992; Staudinger, Smith, & Baltes, 1992).

Thus, the emerging profile of emotion in old age suggests gains and losses. On the one hand, there is evidence of decreased skill in some domains, such as decoding emotion faces, and perhaps a greater likelihood that facial configurations of emotions will be mistaken by unfamiliar observers. Relative to younger people, the magnitude of autonomic arousal is reduced in older people, who seem to find fewer things novel and interesting and experience excitement less frequently. On the other hand, older people subjectively experience specific emotions at about the same levels of intensity as younger people. They are not reliably less happy than younger people and may even come to experience emotion in richer, more complex ways than in earlier years. In regard to emotion self-regulation, there is clear evidence for growth in old age. Older people appear to control their emotions better than younger people and invest more energy in proactively moderating emotional experience.

Quite possibly the changes in various domains of emotion functioning are interrelated. Lower autonomic arousal may allow people to approach potentially toxic situations with greater self-efficacy about emotion control, which may subsequently influence the cognitive appraisal of events and the actions of others. Alternatively, reduced autonomic arousal may be the *consequence* of changed cognitive appraisals and beliefs. Certainly, however, it would be a mistake at this point to assume that lowered levels of autonomic arousal reflect the diminished importance of emotion in the lives of older adults. Old people report about the same subjective experience as young people and say that emotion is central to their lives (Malatesta & Kalnok, 1984).

Speculating even further, along the lines of Lawton's proactivity stance, it may be that older people are highly conscious of the hedonic qualities of social relationships and interactions and take special care to ensure the positivity of emotion experience in day-to-day life. In my laboratory we have recently conducted two studies that suggest emotion is *more* salient to older people than to their younger counterparts.

In the first study, Susan Turk and I postulated that if emotion were more salient for older than for younger people, memory for emotional material should be enhanced relative to memory for emotionally neutral information (Turk & Carstensen, 1991). At the beginning of an hour-long experimental session, subjects aged 18–85 were asked to read a two-page segment from an Agatha Christie detective novel that contained equivalent amounts of emotional and neutral information. At the end of the hour, subjects were asked to recollect everything they could about the story they had read. Responses were tape-recorded and transcribed verbatim. Phrases were then parsed and coded as either emotional or neutral.

Our hypothesis was confirmed. We observed a significant linear trend in which successive age cohorts recollected proportionately more emotional memories than neutral memories. It is important to point out that older people did not remember more emotional phrases than younger people remembered. Rather, a greater *proportion* of the older subjects' memories were emotional ones.

In a second investigation focused on the salience of emotion, Nancy Stein, Chantal Piot-Ziegler, and I designed an experimental paradigm that we could use with young children as well as adults (Piot-Ziegler, Carstensen, & Stein, 1992). Rather than using texts as experimental stimuli, we developed a set of 30 photographs that featured children, adults, and elderly people either expressing a specific emotion or assuming a neutral expression. The people featured in the photographic stimuli also varied by sex, physical attractiveness, apparel, and other subtle characteristics that could potentially differentiate them from one another. Subjects, aged 6 to 85 years, completed a forced classification task in which they were asked, on two consecutive trials, to classify the photographs along any dimension they wished. Older adults, more than any other age group, relied on emotion cues in completing the task. Once again, our findings suggest that emotion is highly salient to older people.

The salience of emotion in social contexts. In SST I argue that emotional experience and regulation assume greater prominence among social motives late in life. In part, this simply reflects the decreasing salience of other social goals discussed earlier, which leads to an increase in the *relative* importance of emotion. In part, however, I contend that limited time —implicitly imposed by old age—results in a shift away from long-term goals to more proximal ones,[6] and that when this occurs emotion regulation is afforded central importance.

Early in adulthood social goals are defined and developed with little attention to time constraints. Long-term career goals are formulated. Life partners are identified; families are conceived and raised. And new acquaintances hold the promise of becoming old friends. At this point in life, a tremendous amount of social behavior is geared toward the realization of long-term goals; toward that aim, it is highly adaptive to afford the regulation of emotion states relatively low priority. For example, it would obviously be maladaptive for young college students to speak only to professors who make them feel good. Despite negative affective consequences in the short term, receiving highly critical feedback may hold great benefits in the long run. Similarly, heatedly contentious interactions with a well-informed colleague may yield substantial future gains. And working through conflicts with a spouse or a child—although painful in the short term—may prevent years of emotional turmoil. This is not to say that the regulation of emotion is unimportant early in life, only that other goals often take priority.

Old age, however, imposes a ceiling on the realization of long-term goals. A 90-year-old woman will not make new old friends. An aversive interaction with an acquaintance may not be justified as leading to some long-term good. Even conflicts with a spouse may be better set aside than discussed, because the future payoff is limited. At this time in life it makes far better sense to shift focus from long-term social goals to more proximal ones—and the most proximal of all is the regulation of emotion.

In recent years Barbara Fredrickson and I have tested postulàtes, derived from SST, about the relative salience of emotion regulation and information seeking in people's thinking about and preferences for social partners (Fredrickson & Carstensen, 1990). We developed a classification procedure in which subjects sort a set of 18 cards, each containing a brief description of a prospective social partner, according to how similarly they would feel interacting with the person described on the card. Examples are the author of a book

DEVELOPMENTAL PERSPECTIVES ON MOTIVATION

you've read, an attractive person you do not know, a sibling, a person you know but dislike, and so on. By using this approach, we avoid asking subjects directly about their likes or dislikes of particular people, which we suspect would be heavily influenced by demand characteristics. Data are submitted to analysis by three-way multidimensional scaling (MDS) in order to identify cognitive dimensions people use to represent prospective social partners and examine differences among subgroups in the importance of specific dimensions.

In our first study using this paradigm, 80 people—adolescents, middle-aged adults, and older adults—completed the procedure. Three dimensions emerged from the MDS analysis, accounting for 77% of the variance in the solution. The dimensions were interpreted (and verified by an independent sample) as affective potential, information seeking, and future possibilities. The first two dimensions correspond directly with the social motives identified by SST. The third, future possibilities, suggests that there is an awareness of time in people's cognitive representations of social partners.

As predicted, the importance of the dimensions varied by age group. Older people placed greatest emphasis on the affective potential of prospective social partners, with relatively little regard for information seeking or future possibilities. This was particularly true for our frail elderly subjects, for whom the affective potential was given almost exclusive consideration. In contrast, adolescents placed greatest emphasis on future contact but were also influenced by information seeking and affect.

We found further evidence for SST when we asked subjects to tell us which of the persons described on the cards they would most like to spend their social time with. Younger people were likely to include novel social partners among the most preferred. With age, subjects were increasingly likely to list only people they already knew. To our surprise, when one adolescent boy was asked which of the prospective social partners he would like to get to know better, he responded "the person I know but dislike." Asked why, he responded, "So I could figure out why I dislike him." In this example there was clear evidence for information gain at the expense of negative affect. None of the older subjects made such choices. Especially among frail older subjects, novel social partners were simply not compelling. There was little evidence of future planning in their responses and very little tolerance for social interaction without immediate affective yield. If a social interaction felt good, it was positive; if it felt bad or simply neutral, it was not worth the effort.

Research subjects in this initial study were a fairly homogeneous group of educated, middle-class Caucasians. Recently, we replicated our findings using a larger ($N = 240$), more representative sample of the San Francisco Bay area, in which we oversampled African Americans and included blue- and white-collar workers (Carstensen & Fredrickson, 1992). The same three dimensions—affect, information seeking, and future contact—emerged as the principal dimensions along which people classified prospective social partners. And once again older people based their classification more on the affective potential of the interaction than the other two dimensions; this was true within both the African American subsample and the sample overall.

As we listened to our older subjects talk about social memories, partners, and preferences, we became increasingly convinced that limited time rather than chronological age per se was responsible for the differences we were observing. Older people, particularly those who were the oldest or the most infirm, said they had no time for people they did not know well. The influence we were observing seemed to be better conceptualized as time until death than as time since birth. We decided to test the hypothesis that anticipated endings—as opposed to age per se—drive preferences for interaction. We hypothesized that when endings are anticipated, the affective potential of interactions is the primary consideration in selecting social partners.

We expected that very old adults would be less interested in new relationships, in part owing to their closeness to death. But we predicted that a similar phenomenon would be observed in younger people under conditions in which they too believed they would not have the opportunity for future contact with novel social partners. In a within-subjects design we manipulated anticipated social endings.

In this study 380 people, ranging in age from 11 to 92, were randomly selected from the telephone directory and called by phone. They were asked to respond to two scenarios. In the first, they were asked to imagine that they had 30 minutes free, with no pressing commitments, and that they decided to spend this time with an-other person. They were presented with three prospective social partners, representing the three cognitive dimensions uncovered in our previous work—a member of their immediate family, a recent acquaintance with whom they seemed to have much in common, and the author of a book they had read—and asked to select their preferred social partner. The second scenario was only slightly dif-ferent. In this case they were asked to imagine that in a few weeks they would be moving across the country, unaccompanied by family or friends. Then they were presented with the same three social partners described above and asked to choose among them. Results confirmed our hypotheses. Under both specified and unspecified circumstances, older people preferred familiar social partners. Un-der unspecified conditions, younger people preferred novel social partners, but in the anticipated ending condition, their choices were strikingly similar to those of older people, demonstrating strong preferences for familiar social partners.

Of course, in life chronological age and time until death are nearly always confounded. Yet, sadly, there are exceptions to this rule. Young people with terminal illnesses also anticipate limited fu-tures. We wondered whether young people living with a terminal illness would make choices similar to those made by older people in our studies. That is, if the future is perceived as limited, do younger people also minimize future contact and information gain in their thinking about social partners and place greatest emphasis on the af-fective potential of social contacts?

We recently completed a modified replication of our original card-sort procedure with a relatively young sample of gay men liv-ing in the San Francisco Bay area (Carstensen & Fredrickson, 1992). Of a total of 120 men, 40 tested negative for the HIV virus, 40 tested positive but were not experiencing symptoms, and 40 were HIV positive and had symptoms of AIDS. Although comparable in age, the three groups had quite different life expectancies. We hypothe-sized that (a) the HIV-negative group would perform similarly to an age-matched group of healthy peers from the general population; (b) the HIV-positive, asymptomatic group would perform similarly to our middle-aged subjects; and (c) foreseeing a limited future, the HIV-positive symptomatic group would perform similarly to our el-derly subjects. Results confirmed our hypotheses.

In short, cognitive changes surrounding the appraisal of events and construals of the future seem to influence the salience of emotion. Although age related, these influences are not age caused. Essentially, when future social opportunities are perceived as limited, the salience of emotion increases and long-term goals diminish in importance.

Summary and Conclusion

Older people engage in social interaction less frequently than their younger counterparts. As I mentioned at the start, the change has been interpreted in largely negative terms. Yet when asked about their social relationships, older people describe them as satisfying, supportive, and fulfilling. Marriages are less negative and more positive. Close relationships with siblings are renewed, and relationships with children are better than ever before. Even though older people interact with others less frequently than younger people do, old age is not a time of misery, rigidity, or melancholy.

Rather than present a paradox, I argue here that decreasing rates of contact reflect a reorganization of the goal hierarchies that underlie motivation for social contact and lead to greater selectivity in social partners. This reorganization does not occur haphazardly. Self-definition, information seeking, and emotion regulation are ranked differently depending not only on past experiences, but on place in the life cycle and concomitant expectations about the future.

I contend that the emphasis on emotion in old age results from a recognition of the finality of life. In most people's lives this does not appear suddenly in old age but occurs gradually across adulthood. At times, however, life events conspire to bring about endings more quickly. Whether as benign as a geographical relocation or as sinister as a fatal disease, endings heighten the salience of surrounding emotions. When each interaction with a grandchild or good-bye kiss to a spouse may be the last, a sense of poignancy may permeate even the most casual everyday experiences.

When the regulation of emotion assumes greatest priority among social motives, social partners are carefully chosen. The most likely choices will be long-term friends and loved ones, because they are most likely to provide positive emotional experiences and affirm the

DEVELOPMENTAL PERSPECTIVES ON MOTIVATION

self. Information seeking will motivate some social behavior, but for reasons discussed previously, this will also require judicious choices of social partners. Narrowing the range of social partners allows people to conserve physical and cognitive resources, freeing time and energy for selected social relationships. As such, SST is highly consistent with the selective optimization with compensation model of successful aging formulated by P. Baltes and M. Baltes (1990) described above.

SST is meant to describe and explain the underlying mechanisms for age-related changes in social behavior. It is not intended to be prescriptive. Although most of the subjects we have studied have been healthy and relatively happy, we do not know whether selection processes contribute to successful aging or if all people engage in them. No doubt there are individual differences in the degree to which older adults perceive the future as limited; it will be interesting to examine whether this relates to individual differences in social preferences and behavior. Moreover, although SST is a far more optimistic interpretation of reduced social contact in old age than previous theoretical models, there are potential losses involved in selectivity as well. If people come to avoid negative emotions in an effort to promote positive relationships, a certain emotional texture to life could be lost. If people limit social partners too much, they could pass by potentially rewarding relationships or end up alone in very old age. Especially at a time in life when emotional salience is at its peak, this could have very negative consequences.

However, the potential for positive outcomes also exists. It may well be that old age, more than any other period in life, liberates people from the need to pursue social contacts devoid of emotional rewards, in which complex emotions dominate the affective sphere and a final integration of meaning and purpose in life can be achieved.

NOTES

1. These researchers, to whom developmental psychologists owe a great debt, include Jack Block, John Clausen, Carol Huffine, Dorothy Eichorn, Norma Haan, Paul Mussen, Majorie Honzik, Eliane Aerts, Dorothy Field, and Arlene Skolnick.

2. Clearly, science is not an asocial endeavor (see Knorr-Cetina, 1984). My point is simply that face-to-face contact becomes a less efficient means by which to pursue information, even if that information is generated in a social manner.

3. I am regularly reminded of a passage in a book I once read in which the very elderly protagonist—referring to the deference paid her by others—comments that you know you are old when no one calls you by your first name any more.

4. Robert Levenson, Barbara Fredrickson, Jeanne Tsai, and I are currently exploring questions about the duration of emotion in old and young adults. Using films as emotion elicitors, we are measuring the duration of subjective and physiological reactivity.

5. We also have been including the question, "As you get older, do you control your emotions better?" in various surveys over the years, with samples ranging from blue-collar males to Catholic nuns, and approximately 86% of respondents answer affirmatively.

6. For a review of time perspective in the elderly see Bouffard, LaPierre, and Bastin (1989).

REFERENCES

Allport, G. (1954). *The nature of prejudice*. Reading, MA: Addison-Wesley.

Antonucci, T. C., & Akiyama, H. (1987). An examination of sex differences in social support in mid- and late-life. *Sex Roles, 17*, 737–749.

Antonucci, T. C., & Jackson, J. S. (1987). Social support, interpersonal efficacy, and health. In *Handbook of clinical gerontology* (pp. 291–311). New York: Pergamon Press.

Baltes, M. M., & Carstensen, L. L. (1992). *Successful aging*. Manuscript under review.

Baltes, M. M., & Silverberg, S. B. (in press). The dynamics between dependency and autonomy across the life span. In P. B. Baltes, D. Featherman, & R. Lerner (Eds.), *Life-span development and behavior* (Vol. 12). New York: Academic Press.

Baltes, M. M., & Wahl, H.-W. (1987). Dependence in aging. In L. L. Carstensen & B. A. Edelstein (Eds.), *Handbook of clinical gerontology* (pp. 204–221). New York: Pergamon Press.

Baltes, M. M., Wahl, H.-W., & Reichert, M. (1991). Institutions and successful aging for the elderly? In K. W. Schaie (Ed.), *Annual review of gerontology and geriatrics* (Vol. 11). New York: Springer.

Baltes, M. M., Wahl, H.-W., & Schmid-Furstoss, U. (1990). The daily life of elderly Germans: Activity patterns, personal control and functional health. *Journals of Gerontology: Psychological Science, 45*, P173-P179.

Baltes, P. B. (1987). Theoretical propositions of life-span developmental psychology: On the dynamics between growth and decline. *Developmental Psychology, 23*, 611–626.

Baltes, P. B., & Baltes, M. M. (1990). Psychological perspectives on successful aging: The model of selective optimization with compensation. In P. B. Baltes & M. M. Baltes (Eds.), *Successful aging: Perspectives from the behavioral sciences* (pp. 1–34). New York: Cambridge University Press.

Baltes, P. B., & Goulet, L. R. (1970). Status and issues of life-span developmental psychology. In L. R. Goulet & P. B. Baltes (Eds.), *Life-span developmental psychology: Research and theory* (pp. 4–21). New York: Academic Press.

Baltes, P. B., Reese, H. W., & Lipsitt, L. P. (1980). Life-span developmental psychology. *Annual Review of Psychology, 31*, 65–110.

Baltes, P. B., & Smith, J. (1990). The psychology of wisdom and its ontogenesis. In R. J. Sternberg (Ed.), *Wisdom: Its nature, origins and development* (pp. 87–120). New York: Cambridge University Press.

Baltes, P. B., Smith, J., & Staudinger, U. (1992). Wisdom and successful aging (pp. 123–167). *Nebraska symposium on motivation, 1991.* Lincoln: University of Nebraska Press.

Bandura, A. (1978). The self system in reciprocal determinism. *American Psychologist, 33*, 344–358.

Bandura, A. (1982). Self-efficacy mechanisms in human agency. *American Psychologist, 37*, 122–147.

Bandura, A. (1987). Self-regulation of motivation and action through goal systems. In V. Hamilton, G. H. Bower, & N. H. Frijda (Eds.), *Cognitive perspectives on emotion and motivation* (pp. 37–61). Dordrecht: Kluwer Academic Publishers.

Banham, K. M. (1951). Senescence and the emotions: A genetic theory. *Journal of Genetic Psychology, 78*, 183.

Bengtson, V. L., & Dowd, J. J. (1980–81). Sociological functionalism, exchange theory and life-cycle analysis: A call for more explicit theoretical bridges. *International Journal of Aging and Human Development, 12*, 55–73.

Berkman, L., & Syme, S. L. (1979). Social networks, host resistance and mortality: A nine year follow-up study of Alameda County residents. *American Journal of Epidemiology, 109*, 186–204.

Blanchard-Fields, F. (1986). Reasoning on social dilemmas varying in emotional saliency: An adult developmental perspective. *Psychology and Aging, 1*, 325–333.

Blazer, D. (1982). Social support and mortality in an elderly community population. *American Journal of Epidemiology, 115*, 684–694.

Bogatskaya, B. (1972). Age characteristics of energy metabolism in myocardium and its regulation. *Ninth International Congress of Gerontology, 2*, 77–79.

Botwinick, J., & Kornetsky, C. (1960). Age differences in the acquisition and extinction of the galvanic skin response. *Journal of Gerontology, 15*, 83–84.

Bouffard, L., LaPierre, S., & Bastin, E. (1989). Extension temporelle des projets personnels au cours de la viellesse. *International Journal of Psychology, 24*, 265–291.

Bridges, K. M. B. (1930). A genetic theory of the emotions. *Journal of Genetic Psychology, 37,* 514–527.

Bridges, K. M. B. (1932). Emotional development in early infancy. *Child Development, 3,* 325–341.

Bromley, D. B. (1990). *Behavioural gerontology: Central issues in the psychology of ageing* (pp. 263–316). Chichester, England: John Wiley.

Buhler, C. (1933). *Der menschliche Lebenslauf als psychologisches Problem.* Leipzig: Hirzel.

Campos, J., Barrett, K. C., Lamb, M. E., Goldsmith, H. H., & Stenberg, C. (1983). Socioemotional development. In P. H. Mussen (Ed.), *Handbook of child psychology: Vol. 2. Infancy and developmental psychobiology* (pp. 783–915). New York: John Wiley.

Candy, S. E., Troll, L. W., & Levy, S. O. (1981). A developmental exploration of friendship functions in women. *Psychology of Women Quarterly, 5,* 456–472.

Cannon, W. B. (1927). The James-Lange theory of emotions: A critical examination and an alternative theory. *American Journal of Psychology, 39,* 106–124.

Cantor, N., Mackie, D., & Lord, C. (1984). Choosing partners and activities: The social perceiver decides to mix it up. *Social Cognition, 3,* 256–272.

Carstensen, L. L. (1986). Social support among the elderly: Limitations of behavioral interventions. *Behavior Therapist, 6,* 111–113.

Carstensen, L. L. (1987). Age-related changes in social activity. In L. L. Carstensen & B. A. Edelstein (Eds.), *Handbook of clinical gerontology* (pp. 227–237). New York: Pergamon Press.

Carstensen, L. L. (1988). The emerging field of behavioral gerontology. *Behavioral Therapy, 19,* 259–281.

Carstensen, L. L. (1991). Selectivity theory: Social activity in life-span context (pp. 195–217). In *Annual review of gerontology and geriatrics* (Vol. 11). New York: Springer.

Carstensen, L. L. (1992). Unpublished data. Department of Psychology, Stanford University.

Carstensen, L. L. (1992). Social and emotional patterns in adulthood: Support for socioemotional selectivity theory. *Psychology and Aging, 7,* 331–338.

Carstensen, L. L., & Erickson, R. E. (1986). Enhancing the social environments of elderly nursing home residents: Are high rates of interaction enough? *Journal of Applied Behavior Analysis, 19,* 349–355.

Carstensen, L. L., & Fredrickson, B. F. (1992, July). *Aging, illness and social preferences.* Paper presented at the International Congress of Psychology, Brussels, Belgium.

Chapell, N. L., & Badger, M. (1989). Social isolation and well-being. *Journals of Gerontology: Social Sciences, 44,* S169–S176.

Cicerelli, V. (1989). Feelings of attachment to siblings and well-being in later life. *Psychology and Aging, 4,* 211–216.

Collins, R. E., Dakof, G., & Taylor, S. E. (1988). *Social comparison and adjustment to a threatening event.* Manuscript submitted for publication. As cited in Taylor, S., & Lobel, M. (1989). Social comparison activity under threat:

Downward evaluation and upward contacts. *Psychological Review, 96,* 569–575.

Corsaro, W. A. (1985). *Friendship and peer culture in the early years.* Norwood, NJ: Ablex.

Crocker, J., Voelkl, K., Testa, M., & Major, B. (1991). Social stigma: The affective consequences of attributional ambiguity. *Journal of Personality and Social Psychology, 60,* 218–228.

Cross, S., & Markus, H. (1991). Possible selves across the life span. *Human Development, 34,* 230–255.

Csikszentmihalyi, M. (1990). *Flow: the psychology of optimal experience.* New York: Harper and Collins.

Cumming, E., & Henry, W. E. (1961). *Growing old: The process of disengagement.* New York: Basic Books.

D'Andrade, R. G. (1981). The cultural part of cognition. *Cognitive Science, 5,* 179–195.

Dannefer, D., & Perlmutter, M. (1990). Development as a multidimensional process: Individual and social constraints. *Human Development, 33,* 108–137.

Darley, J. M., & Fazio, R. H. (1980). Expectancy confirmation processes arising in the social interaction sequence. *American Psychologist, 35,* 867–881.

Darwin, C. (1872). *The expression of the emotions in man and animals.* London: Murray.

Deci, E., & Ryan, R. (1985). *Intrinsic motivation and self-determination in human behavior.* New York: Plenum Press.

Deci, E., & Ryan, R. (1991). A motivational approach to self: Integration in personality (pp. 237–288). *Nebraska symposium on motivation, 1990.* Lincoln: University of Nebraska Press.

Dowd, J. J. (1980). Aging as exchange: A preface to theory. *Journal of Gerontology, 30,* 584–594.

Dunphy, D. C. (1963). The social structure of urban adolescent peer groups. *Sociometry, 26,* 230–246.

Eder, D. (1985). The cycle of popularity: Interpersonal relations among female adolescents. *Sociology of Education, 58,* 154–165.

Eisdorfer, C. (1978). Psychophysiologic and cognitive studies in the aged. In G. Usdin & C. K. Hofling (Eds.), *Aging: The process and the people* (pp. 96–128). New York: Bruner/Mazel.

Ekman, P. (1978). Facial signs: Facts, fantasies and possibilities. In T. Sebeok (Ed.), *Sight, sound, and sense* (pp. 124–156). Bloomington: Indiana University Press.

Ekman, P., & Friesen, W. (1969). The repertoire of nonverbal behavior. *Semiotica, 1,* 49–98.

Ekman, P., Levenson, R. W., & Friesen, W. V. (1983). Autonomic nervous system activity distinguishes among emotions. *Science, 221,* 1208–1210.

Erikson, E. H. (1968). *Identity: Youth and crisis.* New York: W. W. Norton.

Erikson, E. H. (1982). *The life cycle completed. A review.* New York: W. W. Norton.

Fantz, R. L. (1973). Pattern vision in newborn infants. In L. J. Stone, H. T.

Smith, & L. B. Murphy (Eds.), *The competent infant* (pp. 314–316). New York: Basic Books.

Festinger, L. (1954). A theory of social comparison processes. *Human Relations, 7,* 117–140.

Field, D., & Minkler, M. (1988). Continuity and change in social support between young-old, old-old, and very-old adults. *Journal of Gerontology, 43,* P100–P106.

Folkman, S., Lazarus, R. S., Pimley, D., & Novacek, J. (1987). Age differences in stress and coping processes. *Psychology and Aging, 2,* 171–184.

Fredrickson, B. L., & Carstensen, L. L. (1990). Choosing social partners: How old age and anticipated endings make people more selective. *Psychology and Aging, 5,* 335–347.

Fries, J. F. (1980). Aging, natural death and the compression of morbidity. *New England Journal of Medicine, 303,* 130–135.

Frolkis, V. V (1977). Aging of the autonomic nervous system. In J. E. Birren & K. W. Schaie (Eds.), *Handbook of the psychology of aging* (pp. 177–189). New York: Van Nostrand Reinhold.

George, L. K., Blazer, D. F., Winfield-Laird, I., Leaf, P. J., & Fischback, R. L. (1988). Psychiatric disorders and mental health service use in later life: Evidence from the Epidemiologic Catchment Area Program. In J. Brody & G. Maddox (Eds.), *Epidemiology and aging* (pp. 189–219). New York: Springer.

Gordon, C., & Gaitz, C. (1976). Leisure and lives. In R. Binstock & E. Shanas (Eds.), *Handbook of aging and the social sciences* (Vol. 1, pp. 310–341). New York: Van Nostrand Reinhold.

Gottman, J. M., Levenson, R. W., & Carstensen, L. L. (1992). *Emotional interaction in middle-aged and elderly long-term marriages.* Manuscript under review.

Guilford, R., & Bengtson, V. (1979). Measuring marital satisfaction in three generations: Positive and negative dimensions. *Journal of Marriage and the Family, 39,* 387–398.

Gurland, B. (1976). The comparative frequency of depression in various adult age groups. *Journal of Gerontology, 31,* 283–292.

Hansell, J. H. (1989). Theories of emotion and motivation: A historical and conceptual review. *Genetic, Social and General Psychology Monographs, 115,* 429–448.

Harvey, A. S., & Singleton, J. F. (1989). Canadian activity patterns across the life span: A time budget perspective. *Canadian Journal on Aging, 8,* 268–285.

Havighurst, R. J.(1961). Successful aging. *Gerontologist, 1,* 8–13.

Havighurst, R. J., & Albrecht, R. (1953). *Older people.* New York: Longmans.

Hayflick, L. (1987). The cell biology and theoretical basis of human aging. In L. L. Carstensen & B. A. Edelstein (Eds.), *Handbook of clinical gerontology* (pp. 3–17). New York: Pergamon Press.

Heckhausen, J., Dixon, R. A., & Baltes, P. B. (1989). Gains and losses in development throughout adulthood as perceived by different adult age groups. *Developmental Psychology, 25,* 109–121.

Herzog, A. R., & Rodgers, W. L. (1981). Age and satisfaction: Data from several large surveys. *Research on Aging, 3,* 142–165.

Higgins, E. T. (1987). Self-discrepancy: A theory relating self and affect. *Psychological Review, 94,* 319–340.

Hilgard, E. (1949). Human motives and the concept of the self. *American Psychologist, 4,* 374–382.

Izard, C. E. (1971). *The face of emotion.* New York: Appelton-Century-Crofts.

James, W. (1884). What is an emotion? *Mind, 9,* 188–205.

Johnson, C. L. (1988). *Ex familia.* New Brunswick, NJ: Rutgers University Press.

Jung, C. G. (1934). The stages of life. In *Modern man in search of a soul* (pp. 109–131). London: Paul, Trench, Trubner.

Kahn, R. L., & Antonucci, T. C. (1984). Supports of the Elderly final report. As cited in Antonucci, T. C., & Akiyama, H. (1987). Convoys of social support: Intergenerational issues. *Families: Intergenerational and Generational Connections, 20,* 103–123.

Kilhstrom, J., & Cantor, N. (1984). Mental representations of the self. In L. Berkowitz (Ed.), *Advances in experimental social psychology* (Vol. 17, pp. 2–47). New York: Academic Press.

Knorr-Cetina, K. (1984). *The manufacture of knowledge.* Frankfurt: Suhrkamp.

Labouvie-Vief, G., & DeVoe, M. (1991). Emotional regulation in adulthood and later life: A developmental view. In *Annual review of gerontology and geriatrics* (Vol. 11, pp. 172–194). New York: Springer.

Labouvie-Vief, G., DeVoe, M., & Bulka, D. (1989). Speaking about feelings: Conceptions of emotion across the life span. *Psychology and Aging, 4,* 425–437.

Labouvie-Vief, G., Hakim-Larson, J., DeVoe, M., & Schoeberlein, S. (1989). Emotions and self-regulation: A life span view. *Human Development, 32,* 279–299.

Lawton, M. P. (1989). Environmental proactivity and affect in older people. In S. Spacapan & S. Oskamp (Eds.), *Social psychology of aging* (pp. 135–164). Newbury Park, CA: Sage.

Lawton, M. P., Kleban, M. H., Rajagopal, D., & Dean, J. (1992). Dimensions of affective experience in three age groups. *Psychology and Aging, 7,* 171–184.

Lawton, M. P., Moss, M., & Fulcomer, M. (1987). Objective and subjective uses of time by older people. *International Journal of Aging and Human Development, 24,* 171–188.

Lazarus, R. S. (1991). *Emotion and adaptation.* New York: Oxford.

Lazarus, R. S., & Folkman, S. (1984). *Stress, appraisal and coping.* New York: Springer.

Lee, D. J., & Markides, K. S. (1990). Activity and mortality among aged persons over an eight-year period. *Journals of Gerontology: Social Sciences, 45,* S39-S42.

Levenson, R. W. (1992). Autonomic nervous system differences among emotions. *Psychological Science, 3,* 34–38.

Levenson, R. W., Carstensen, L. L., Friesen, W. V., & Ekman, P. (1991). Emotion, physiology, and expression in old age. *Psychology and Aging, 6,* 28–35.

Levenson, R. W., Carstensen, L. L., & Gottman, J. M. (1992a). *Long term marriage: Age, satisfaction, gender health, conflict and pleasure.* Manuscript under review.

Levenson, R. W., Carstensen, L. L., & Gottman, J. M. (1992b). *Marital interaction in old and middle-aged long-term marriages: Physiology, affect and their interrelations.* Manuscript under review.

Levenson, R. W., Ekman, P., Heider, K., & Friesen, W. V. (1992). Emotion and autonomic nervous system activity in the Minangkabau of West Sumatra. *Journal of Personality and Social Psychology, 62,* 972–988.

Looft, W. R. (1972). Egocentrism and social interaction across the life span. *Psychological Bulletin, 78,* 73–92.

Lowenthal, M., & Haven, C. (1968). Interaction and adaptation: Intimacy as a critical variable. In B. L. Neugarten (Ed.), *Middle age and aging: A reader in social psychology* (pp.390–400). Chicago: University of Chicago Press.

Lutsky, N. (1980). Attitudes toward old age and elderly persons. In C. Eisdorfer (Ed.), *Annual review of gerontology and geriatrics* (Vol. 1, pp. 287–336). New York: Springer.

Maccoby, E. E. (1988). Gender as social category. *Developmental Psychology, 24,* 755–765.

Maccoby, E. E. (1990). Gender and relationships. *American Psychologist, 45,* 513–520.

Maddox, G. L. (1963). Activity and morale: A longitudinal study of selected elderly subjects. *Social Forces, 42,* 195–204.

Maddox, G. L. (1965). Fact and artifact: Evidence bearing on disengagement theory from the Duke Geriatrics Project. *Human Development, 8,* 117–130.

Malatesta, C. Z., Fiore, M. J., & Messina, J. J. (1987). Affect, personality and facial expressive characteristics of older people. *Psychology and Aging, 2,* 64–69.

Malatesta, C. Z., Izard, C. E., Culver, C., & Nicholich, M. (1987). Emotion communication skills in young, middle-aged, and older women. *Psychology and Aging, 2,* 193–203.

Malatesta, C. Z., & Kalnok, M. (1984). Emotional experience in younger and older adults. *Journal of Gerontology, 39,* 301–308.

Markus, H. R., & Herzog, A. R. (1991). The role of the self-concept in aging. In K. W. Schaie (Ed.), *Annual review of gerontology and geriatrics* (Vol. 11, pp. 110–143). New York: Springer.

Markus, H. R., & Sentis, K. (1982). The self in social information processing. In J. Suls (Ed.), *Psychological perspectives on the self* (Vol. 1, pp. 41–70). Hillsdale, NJ: Lawrence Erlbaum.

McCrae, R. R., & Costa, P. T., Jr. (1984). *Emerging lives, enduring dispositions: Personality in adulthood.* Boston: Little, Brown.

McCrae, R. R., & Costa, P. T., Jr. (1988). Age, personality and the spontaneous self-concept. *Journals of Gerontology: Social Sciences, 43,* S177–S185.

Mcfarlane, J. (1938). Studies in child guidance: I. Methodology of data collection and organization. *Monographs of the Society for Research in Child Development, 3*, 1–254.

Moscovici, S. (1984). The phenomenon of social representations. In R. M. Farr & S. Moscovici (Eds.), *Social representations* (pp. 3–70). Cambridge: Cambridge University Press.

Nelson, E. A., & Dannefer, D. (1992). Aged heterogeneity: Fact or fiction? The fate of diversity in gerontological research. *Gerontologist, 32*, 17–23.

Neugarten, B. L. (1968). The awareness of middle age. In B. L. Neugarten (Ed.), *Middle age and aging* (pp. 93–98). Chicago: University of Chicago Press.

Palmer, G., Ziegler, M., & Lake, R. (1978). Response of norepinephrine and blood pressure to stress increases with age. *Journal of Gerontology, 33*, 482–487.

Palmore, E. (1981). *Social patterns in normal aging: Findings from the Duke Longitudinal Study.* Durham, NC: Duke University Press.

Piot-Ziegler, C., Carstensen, L. L., & Stein, N. L. (1992, Novermber). *The importance of emotion in the interpretation of faces: A life-span study developmental study.* Paper presented at the meetings of the Gerontological Society of America, Washington, D.C.

Prilleltensky, I. (1989). Psychology and the status quo. *American Psychologist, 44*, 795–802.

Rook, K. (1984). The negative side of social interaction: Impact on psychological well-being. *Journal of Personality and Social Psychology, 46*, 1097–1108.

Rowe, J. W., & Kahn, R. L. (1987). Human aging: Usual and successful. *Science, 237*, 143–149.

Ryff, C. D. (1982). Successful aging: A developmental approach. *Gerontologist, 22*, 209–214.

Ryff, C. D. (1989a). Beyond Ponce de Leon and life satisfaction: New directions in the quest for successful aging. *International Journal of Behavioral Development, 12*, 35–55.

Ryff, C. D. (1989b). In the eye of the beholder: Views of psychological well-being among middle-aged and older adults. *Psychology and Aging, 4*, 195–210.

Ryff, C. D. (1991). Possible selves in adulthood and old age: A tale of shifting horizons. *Psychology and Aging, 6*, 286–295.

Salthouse, T. A. (1985). Speed of behavior and its implications for cognition. In J. E. Birren & K. W. Schaie (Eds.), *Handbook of the psychology of aging* (2nd ed.) (pp. 400–426). New York: Van Nostrand Reinhold.

Schulz, R. (1985). Emotion and affect. In J. E. Birren & K. W. Schaie (Eds.), *Handbook of the psychology of aging* (2nd ed.) (pp. 531–543). New York: Van Nostrand Reinhold.

Shmavonian, B., Miller, L., & Cohen, S. (1970). Differences among age and sex groups with respect to cardiovascular conditioning and reactivity. *Journal of Gerontology, 25*, 87–94.

Staudinger, U. M., Smith, J., & Baltes, P. B. (1992). Wisdom-related knowledge in a life-review task: Age differences and the role of professional specialization. *Psychology and Aging, 7,* 271–281.

Steele, C. (1988). The psychology of self-affirmation: Sustaining the integrity of the self. In L. Berkowitz (Ed.), *Advances in experimental social psychology: Vol. 21. Social psychological studies of the self: Perspectives and programs* (pp. 261–302). San Diego, CA: Academic Press.

Stein, N., & Levine, L. J. (1987). Thinking about feelings: The development and organization of knowledge. In R. E. Snow & M. Farr (Eds.), *Aptitude, learning and instruction: Vol. 3. Cognition, conation and affect* (pp. 165–197). Hillsdale, NJ: Lawrence Erlbaum.

Stein, N., & Trabasso, T. (1990). Children's understanding of changing emotional states. In C. Saarni & P. L. Harris (Eds.), *Children's understanding of emotion* (pp. 50–77). New York: Cambridge University Press.

Suls, J., & Mullen, B. (1982). From the cradle to the grave: Comparison and self-evaluation across the life span. In J. Suls (Ed.), *Psychological perspectives on the self* (Vol. 1, pp. 97–128). Hillsdale, NJ: Lawrence Erlbaum.

Swann, W. B. (1987). Identity negotiation: Where two roads meet. *Journal of Personality and Social Psychology, 53,* 1038–1051.

Swann, W. B., & Hill, C. A. (1982). When our identities are mistaken: Reaffirming self-conceptions through social interaction. *Journal of Personality and Social Psychology, 43,* 59–66.

Taylor, S. E. (1983). Adjustment to threatening events: A theory of cognitive adaptation. *American Psychologist, 38,* 1161–1173.

Taylor, S. E., Falke, R. L., Shoptaw, S. J., & Lichtman, R. R. (1986). Social support, support groups and the cancer patient. *Journal of Consulting and Clinical Psychology, 54,* 608–615.

Taylor, S. E., & Lobel, M. (1989). Social comparison activity under threat: Downward evaluation and upward contacts. *Psychological Review, 96,* 569–575.

Thompson, R. (1990). Emotion and self-regulation. In *Nebraska symposium on motivation, 1988* (pp. 367–467). Lincoln: University of Nebraska Press.

Tomkins, S. S. (1963). *Affect, imagery, consciousness.* New York: Springer.

Tomkins, S. S. (1970). Affect as the primary motivational system. In M. B. Arnold (Ed.), *Feelings and emotions* (pp. 101–110). New York: Academic Press.

Triandis, H. (1989). The self and social behavior in differing cultural contexts. *Psychological Review, 96,* 506–520.

Troll, L. (1971). The family of later life: A decade of review. *Journal of Marriage and the Family, 44,* 263–290.

Tsai, J., & Carstensen, L. L. (1992). *Dyadic interactions among young and old Caucasian and Asian-Americans.* Unpublished manuscript, Department of Psychology, Stanford University.

Turk, S., & Carstensen, L. L. (1991). *Qualitative differences in recall: How emotional and informational saliency changes with age.* Paper presented at the November meetings of the Gerontological Society of America, San Francisco.

Vaillant, G. E. (1977). *Adaptation to life*. Boston: Little, Brown.

Vaillant, G. E., & Vaillant, C. O. (1990). Natural history of male psychological health, 12: A 45-year study of predictors of successful aging at age 65. *American Journal of Psychiatry, 147*, 31–37.

Weissman, M. M., Bruce, M. L., Leaf, P. J., Florio, L. P., & Holzer, C., III. (1991). Affective disorders. In L. N. Robins & D. A. Regier (Eds.), *Psychiatric disorders in America: The Epidemiological Catchment Area Study* (pp. 53–80). New York: Free Press.

Wills, T. A. (1981). Similarity and self-esteem in downward comparison. In J. Suls & T. A. Wills (Eds.), *Social comparison: Contemporary theory and research* (pp. 51–78). Hillsdale, NJ: Lawrence Erlbaum.

Wood, J. V., Taylor, S. E., & Lichtman, R. R. (1985). Social comparison in adjustment to breast cancer. *Journal of Personality and Social Psychology, 49*, 1169–1183.

Yarrow, L. J. (1979). Emotional development. *American Psychologist, 34*, 951–957.

Zajonc, R. B. (1985). Emotion and facial efference: A theory reclaimed. *Science, 228*, 15–21.

Zajonc, R. S., Murphy, S. T., & Inglehart, M. (1989). Feeling and facial efference: Implications of the vascular theory of emotion. *Psychological Review, 96*, 395–416.

Commentary on the Fortieth Nebraska Symposium on Motivation

Richard M. Ryan
University of Rochester

At some point during the 1992 Nebraska Symposium on Motivation, each of the speakers publicly acknowledged the personal significance of presenting at this conference. More than one noted that earlier papers in this series had strongly influenced them during their own development as scholars. Several also described how participating in a tradition that includes such figures as Harlow, Cattell, Heider, White, Rogers, Rappaport, Hunt, Maslow, and others was at the same time both an honor and a humbling experience.

The 40 years of the Nebraska Symposium on Motivation represent, indeed, a history of great theoretical essays. In most cases one finds in these volumes probing discussions that consider the philosophical assumptions underlying theories and empirical programs. I attribute the depth of the symposium at least in part to the nature of the concept of motivation itself, which generally has been its organizing theme.[1] Motivation, as has often been stated, concerns the "why" of behavior. A symposium on motivation thus challenges one to address the "why" surrounding one's focus of study—to unveil not only one's framework of inquiry, but also its underlying assumptions. This, I think, has shaped this symposium as a forum for important theoretical statements in behavioral sciences.

In light of this tradition, I was pulled to reflect on some of the assumptions and explanations underlying this year's papers. The 1992 conference theme, "motivation and development," presumably concerns the whys and wherefores of development, what "moves" or facilitates it. What moves a person to take on new challenges, to learn, or to mature socially or cognitively is clearly a question at the heart of each of these papers, more or less explicitly. Some of the authors have emphasized the inner factors associated with this movement—the fundamental motives or experiences that fuel development. Others have emphasized the social context that fosters or inhibits development, either through meeting (or not meeting) these inner needs or through the effects of social context that can direct, shape, or guide development. Thus as a first category of comparison I examine how the contributors to this volume conceive of the variables that underlie the change we refer to as development.

A second theme that both reflects theoretical underpinnings and is relevant to each of the essays concerns the role of the *self* in development. With the possible exception of Carstensen's paper, the concept of self looms large in the presenters' organizing frameworks. But by no means does the term "self" have the same referent throughout. Several essays appealed to an individual's experience as a significant force in shaping development, and they emphasize the self as an agent and initiator of action. Some focus on the self as primarily a representation derived from others' appraisals. I thus will examine what meaning each of our theorists gives to the concept of self and in turn assess how that construct influences their thinking. Along with the focus on self is the issue of *self-esteem*. Under what conditions do people experience a sense of worth and confidence? Each author comments on the role of social context in enhancing or damaging self-esteem and perceived competence.

Finally, after touching ever so briefly on fundamental motives, social contextual forces, the self and self-esteem, I will attempt to excuse myself from further commentary. Any strident critique would seem unfair, given that there is no format for rebuttal or response. Moreover, although there are some places where the present essays disagree in discrete ways, largely I see great convergence between the participants' viewpoints. Since it could only be presumptuous for me to attempt to "resolve" theoretical differences (which I could do only egocentrically, through my own theory), I will be content with bringing into relief some of the reasons for convergence so that we may foster even more continuing dialogue than this well-organized symposium has already afforded.

Motivation in Development and Differentiation

Psychological development is transformation, and it therefore always implies elements of both continuity and change. Werner (1948), for example, defined development in terms of differentiation and hierarchical integration. In differentiation the organism extends its existing skills and capacities to pursue new interests and paths of experience. Much of the focus in the current papers is on the forces that shape such differentiation in psychological development. Integration is less explicitly addressed in the chapters I comment on.

Mihalyi Csikszentmihalyi and Kevin Rathunde explicitly present their conception of how differentiation of skills and interests occurs. They argue that people experience *flow* when they find opportunities for action that match their existing capacities or skills. People enjoy, and therefore continually seek, flow experiences, and in this way the model explains why we are motivated to elaborate existing abilities and engage in ever new challenges. Opportunities for flow ultimately result in the structural elaborations that are the "content" of many developmental theories. The flow model thus offers a description of assimilation (Piaget, 1971) and effectance motivation (White, 1959) in experiential terms.

The very word "flow" evokes the ideas of energy and direction, both essential elements in any theory of motivation. It connotes a force or current that both carries us along and directs us to elaborate and differentiate specific capacities. As Csikszentmihalyi presented it, in this autotelic state we seem to be "flowing down a channel" without need for effort or prodding. Flow experiences make us "inclined" toward an activity; there is a "pull" toward situations that afford such flow experiences. We can see how the metaphor of flow provides these authors with a conception of a natural, dynamic force in the stream of development, continually drawing the individual back to exercise existing skills at ever higher levels of complexity.

The flow model offered by Csikszentmihalyi and Rathunde is remarkably parsimonious. They argue that flow occurs whenever opportunities for action match one's current capabilities, but particularly when both the challenge and the skills are great. Therefore these are the only major factors considered in predicting why people are intrinsically motivated to act and thus to elaborate existing capacities. It is also these two factors that interactively predict enjoyment.

What produces the energy for flow? The authors eschew talk of needs or causes, preferring to stay on what they describe as the "safer grounds" of experiential description, but they suggest that flow may represent an emergent motivation, in two senses. Flow is an emergent motivation in the immediate sense, being the product of interaction between the individual and an environment. It is also an emergent motivation in a second, evolutionary sense. Insofar as those organisms most apt to exercise and therefore develop new skills will undoubtedly glean the selective advantages such skills convey, flow may have emerged as an adaptive elaboration. This evolutionary argument is made more fully by Csikszentmihalyi and Massimini (1985).

Csikszentmihalyi and Rathunde describe their theory as phenomenological rather than functional. A close reading of their chapter suggests, however, that they view certain phenomenological variables as "proximal causes" of intrinsically motivated behaviors, whereas "distal causes" hold less interest for them. Within the flow model the issue is not so much what originally gives impetus to autotelic action as what motivation sustains it. The experiential variable of "enjoyment" is given priority. Thus it seems that developing humans, even if they have no "need" for competence, surely find situations that afford it appealing, and this appeal serves as a proximate cause of much developmental change.

The authors, however, are led beyond their phenomenological stance into a functional one in their attempt to describe environments conducive to intrinsic motivation and creativity. The most obvious prescription we might derive from their flow model of autotelic behavior is that social contexts should provide well-tailored challenges for current skills. But surprisingly, their description of the autotelic environment largely ignores the issue of optimal challenge. Instead, they introduce the theory by considering attachment and family systems. In brief, they characterize autotelic environments as those affording an optimal interplay or balance between interpersonal differentiation and integration. This seems to me a big jump—not intuitively, but theoretically. I was left hanging concerning the specific link between the skill-challenge balance of the flow model and the differentiation-integration dialectic that frames the construct of autotelic environment. For instance, why do people find interpersonal integration with others conducive to flow? Or how does family differentiation enhance the tendency to experience flow? Also, being one of those "functional" types who researches the factors in classrooms, workplaces, and families that facilitate or forestall intrinsic motivation, I am concerned specifically with how to link our literature to this "family systems" conceptualization.

I reason that autotelic family environments as described would offer considerable interpersonal support and a sense of relatedness (integration) as well as a good dose of autonomy support (differentiation). This freedom to differentiate in the context of secure attachments in turn allows a person to find opportunities for flow without the insecurity or threat of contingency a less integrated context might provide. The autotelic family context appears, therefore, to support needs for relatedness and autonomy, which I and my colleagues Wendy Grolnick and Edward Deci have suggested are the primary facilitators of psychological development. I thus find in this concept a great deal of convergence with our own theory and research findings. In either the "autotelic environment" or the autonomy-relatedness conception, we are not simply magnetically drawn to flow; we experience the security and flexibility to swim into its current.

Jacquelynne Eccles's chapter also directly addresses differentiation in development. She presents a well-researched model of what leads children to choose one activity over another. Her model and supporting research emphasize that preferences for the skills we exercise are heavily shaped by social contexts. Children appear to internalize significant adults' perceptions (and biases) concerning their skills and abilities, and this leads them to identify certain domains as optimally challenging, appropriate, and interesting.

Parents, in Eccles's view, are perhaps the most significant "interpreters" of the child's reality, providing messages about appropriate preferences and likely capabilities. For example, mothers' conceptions of their children's ability were shown to directly influence self-perceptions of competence, and accordingly the establishment of confidence and motivation. Furthermore, parents' preconceptions, gender biases, and other beliefs can shape children's self-concepts about abilities and preferences independent of actual competence. Thus, parents who assume that boys are "better" at math than girls may engender more confidence in boys than in girls and accordingly affect their motivation and interest. Similarly, both verbally and behaviorally, parents convey preferences and values about certain activities, again influencing the direction motivation takes. For instance, Eccles presents data suggesting that parents are more likely to be behaviorally involved in boys' athletic events than in girls', and thus reinforce boys' interest in that domain. In Eccles's model we see that social context is strong and the direction motivation takes is relatively mutable. Her work is truly a *social* psychology of development in this respect.

But it is also intriguing that even while stressing the shaping power of the social context, Eccles and her collaborators imply a human nature in their model. Note that the central thesis in the second half of the chapter concerns not the effects of the environment per se, but rather the *match* between the social environment and the internal needs of developing individuals. As she states it, "Optimal development takes place when there is good stage-environment fit between the needs of developing individuals and the opportunities afforded in their social environments." Thus, like Csikszentmihalyi and Rathunde she argues for a match model. But whereas they focus on the match between skills and afforded challenges, she focuses primarily on psychological needs within the individual; and she analyzes social contexts with respect to these inferred needs. For example, the devastating impact of junior high schools stems primarily from the developmental mismatch it engenders for students who have a high need for autonomy. At a time when adolescents are striving to exercise responsibility and self-direction, junior high schools typically offer only greater constraints and controls. This context-need mismatch alienates and demotivates rather than fostering motivation and competence development. Students who experience the mismatch most intensely (e.g., early-maturing girls) are thus turned off from a potential domain of achievement and interest.

Eccles's model and the "flow" model have in common a dialectical approach, in which the developing person spontaneously engages a world that is more or less responsive to, or well tailored for, his or her needs. They both posit a motivation to seek activities and contexts that allow for the expression of inherent developmental propensities, and from this dynamic there results a pattern of differentiation and growth that reflects a synergy of human nature and its nurturing conditions.

Laura Carstensen's chapter focuses on a different phase of development and a different domain of differentiation. She developed her "selectivity theory" through studies of people in late life, and she argues that for them relationships fulfill significant, developmentally specific, psychological needs. Older people perhaps seek fewer relationships, but they desire ones in which they can be meaningfully understood, share intimacy, and express common interests and emotions. Such intimate contacts are only a subset of all possible social contacts, but they are the ones that most prominently enhance well-being in the elderly. Whereas in earlier life relationships carry multiple instrumental values (e.g., gaining information, finding a mate, creating future opportunities), in later life people primarily seek less in the way of instrumental outcomes and are more concerned with intrinsically meaningful aspects of interactions. Thus she suggests that the functions of relationships vary with development.

Carstensen argues that it is not the number of contacts with others but their quality that supports the health and life satisfaction of the elderly. One conclusion to be drawn from her work is that social interaction is not always a positive experience, nor is more of it necessarily a good thing, as many researchers appear to assume. One clear direction for selectivity theory thus appears to be identifying what it is about "meaningful" relationships that promotes well-being in the elderly (and perhaps in the rest of us as well).

Besides clearly articulating a salient developmental need in the aged, Carstensen introduces her own implicit "match" hypothesis. She illustrates how social conditions for the elderly often are not conducive to meaningful contacts, and thus do not foster late adult development. She encourages us to consider the economies of emotion and time that face the aged and to construct social conditions that provide opportunities for interpersonal experiences that enhance the self. Carstensen suggests that providing resources for older people to be with those who can share their experiences, know them as differentiated individuals, and accordingly ensure a sense of continuity and meaning in the waning years of the life span would be a meaningful application of her research. She also suggests that many of our stereotypes and economic arrangements conspire to deprive older adults of meaningful interpersonal contacts at a time when they already face formidable obstacles to intimacy. The humanism and intuitive elegance of her theory were regnant at the symposium.

Casting Carstensen's theory as a model of differentiation within the domain of social relationships raises a number of intriguing questions. She posits that social relationships mean different things across the life span. Early on they have more instrumental significance; later they become more important for their emotional quality. Still, we have to ask *why* emotional salience should carry more weight at this time of life. What human needs motivate people to increasingly weed out nonintimate contacts and focus on intimate ones? Or conversely, why are emotionally salient contacts so much *less* significant in earlier life? Is it that emotional needs are equally salient to young people but they also use relationships to fulfill other needs that drop out with development? Or do the needs for emotional sharing and intimacy themselves grow during adult development? These issues suggest that social selectivity theory may be capable of addressing some very big issues in personality development as it increasingly casts its net downward through the life span.

Susan Harter's chapter presents a theory of development based on symbolic interactionism. Her empirical perspective, as she states it, has for fifteen years been focused on the development of the "Me-self," or "how one's self-concept is constructed, packaged, protected, and enhanced." From this perspective, our self-concept is largely derived from gazing into the looking glass of external social appraisals. We "know" ourselves by internalizing the views and opinions of others, and we pursue directions in development congruent with such appraisals. Although some activity is involved in constructing a self-concept out of the raw materials others provide, the pervasive influence of the social world in development is most salient in this perspective.

Underlying the Coolean looking-glass model of self is, I believe, a human need, or set of needs, for obtaining the regard or approval of others. Insofar as we derive our sense of "goodness" or worth in specific domains by attending to others' appraisals, clearly we must care deeply about such appraisals. Thus the need for what Rogers (1951) called "positive regard" or what I have called "relatedness" plays a central role in Harter's thinking and (implicitly) in the Coolean model more generally.

Interacting with this strong need for regard are the powerful social forces that play on it. In the Coolean model one's self-esteem is fed and fueled by the contingent evaluations of others, which in turn suggests that individuals are largely shaped in their motivation and life direction by the opinions and values of the culture around them. In her presentation of materials from the media and the press Harter vividly illustrates how pervasive a force this is, and how the internalization of certain cultural values is often oppressive and destructive in its effects.

In the Coolean model of development, it appears, cultural forces have the upper hand in shaping interests and motivational propensities. I suggest that such cultural forces thrive primarily on the fundamental need of all individuals to feel related to and esteemed by others. Although the need for relatedness spawns much intrinsically motivated behavior, it is also clear from the research Harter presents here that much of the work of self-development is extrinsically motivated in a specific sense—it is oriented toward gaining approval from others.

The Nature of the Self in Motivated Development

The looking-glass self is the central focus of the research Harter presents. In this model we internalize a sense of self from the appraisals of others, and this internalized conception shapes our behavior throughout development. The internalized appraisals of others also underlie our sense of self-worth in general and our perceived competence in specific domains of activity.

Harking back to the Jamesian formulation, Harter also argues that the influence the domain-specific appraisals of others have on general self-worth depends on the value or importance of that domain. In this regard there is a great deal of convergence between Harter's and Eccles's work. Whereas Eccles's studies highlight the way social context shapes perceived ability and importance, Harter's work demonstrates the powerful impact that such internalized perceptions can have on self-esteem and well-being.

In the most provocative aspect of her essay, Harter asks herself, What is wrong with the looking-glass self as a complete model of the self in development? She suggests that attempting to act "for the other" leads to "false self" behavior. Individuals can become pawns of cultural practices and norms that, though associated with external approval, can ultimately be psychologically damaging. A good example is the approval women receive for physical attractiveness, which leads them to define the self based on external attributes and to dedicate time and energy to appearances rather than inner needs. Harter believes the energies of the self could be, as she puts it, "better spent."

In my own work, I emphasize that being driven by the contingent regard of others can turn people away from intrinsic motivation and self-determination. Thus I have argued that the Coolean framework represents primarily a psychology of conformity and accommodation (see also Ryan, 1991). I was therefore pleased and heartened by Harter's raising the question, What's wrong with this picture? As she presents it, what's wrong is that the looking-glass self can be antagonistic to one's true self. What's right (or accurate) about her model and research is that they demonstrate children's vulnerability in development to seeking positive appraisals from others even at the cost of authentic self-direction. Thus teenage girls spend inordinate amounts of time trying to impress others through their appearance, adults of both genders seek achievement and status, and everyone pursues money—the ultimate stand-in for respect and love from others. These goals often interfere with the fulfillment of more basic, intrinsic needs such as meaningful intimate relationships (Carstensen, Ryan), optimal challenges and flow (Csikszentmihalyi and Rathunde), or autonomy (Eccles, Ryan).

Of course, once we have articulated that the looking-glass self is only one vision of self, the question remains what other self or selves might be beyond it. Harter describes a "true self" and seems to argue that it comes into differentiated awareness around puberty, when adolescents become acutely aware of the discrepancy between their public selves or "being for others" and their not so public inner feelings and desires. But who or what is this real or true self that is so often hidden? I did not find an answer here but instead found a strong sense—drawn from Buddhist thinking—that one might do well to shed self-consciousness altogether. The origins of the true self and its nature were left relatively unaddressed. I found it interesting that Harter chose not to present any of her work on intrinsic motivation, for which she is also well known in developmental circles. I am convinced that as she further investigates the phenomenon of the true self that she introduced in this symposium her research will be deeply informed by what she already knows about intrinsic motivation. It is also my own experience that much of Buddhist thinking can be related to principles of intrinsic motivation.

As I mentioned previously, the metaphor of the looking-glass self that has informed much of Harter's research on self-worth can readily be applied to Eccles's description of how children internalize the appraisals and values of adults as self-perceptions. Parents convey values regarding appropriate goals for their children, which their offspring adopt or internalize during development. The process through which such internalization occurs is not, however, an explicit theoretical aspect of Eccles's presentation. Rather, she primarily demonstrates, particularly through research on gender-laden values, that such perceptions and conveyances *do* shape development, and she cites some specific ways it may happen. She argues, for example, that adults provide their children with varied behavioral opportunities, reinforcements, and levels of involvement, all serving to "influence ontogeny." Although the Coolean approach certainly could be applied as a process explanation of her findings, she does not specifically endorse it or any other model of the self in this essay.

There seems, nonetheless, to be more to Eccles's idea of the developing self than a mere malleable or plastic entity shaped by social forces. She implies at many points that children have an inherent developmental trajectory, either more or less supported by the environment. For example, she suggests, as did Hunt (1975), that there is a developmental continuum of growth toward independence and social maturity. She also suggests that there is a "normal course" for development by which the adequacy of an environment can be gauged. She thus falls short of a wholly social-contextual view of development. Instead, there is a good deal of nature and nurture interacting in her thinking, even if the empirical emphasis is clearly on the nurture.

If the looking-glass self is only partially applicable to Eccles's model of differentiation, it seems particularly foreign to the flow model of Csikszentmihalyi and Rathunde. The self at the core of flow is active and spontaneous. In the state of flow one is typically not self-conscious, or aware of oneself as an object. One is more subject than object, engaged in the world rather than aware of oneself as engaged in the world. The more one is engaged in flow experiences, presumably the more assured and confident this "self as subject" becomes. In fact, through the experience sampling method (ESM) it has apparently been found that the more frequently one experiences flow, the stronger one's self-esteem becomes. Clearly such self-esteem, rather than being derived from the approval of others, is a sign of a robust subject excitedly engaged in an optimally challenging world.

The self described in the flow theory seems to me the same self, or active center, that I attempt to describe in my own chapter. It is this spontaneous self that I argue is phenomenologically linked to autonomy and to intrinsically motivated acts. Harter, similarly, states in her chapter that the true self as she conceives of it is perhaps the self at the center of flow experiences, a viewpoint easily reconciled with a Buddhist approach.

What is clearest in this analysis is that the term "self" has been used in this symposium to refer either to the self as object (or its internalization as self-concept) or to the self as subject, at the core of theories of intrinsic motivation and agency. The gap between these two conceptualizations of self can be as wide as the oceans that divide east and west or as deep as the divergence between behavioristic and organismic accounts of development. The task of developmental theory is not to ignore one for the other but to offer an account in which both are apprehended and dynamically described. The papers in this volume certainly span the range of self-term usages.

The Overall Tenor of the Symposium

I must conclude with some apology to the reader who has endured to this point. I have read many comments sections in edited volumes, and I frequently find them only minimally tolerable. Typically the commentators either restate the authors' points of view less eloquently than in the original presentations or try to "explain" the other papers in terms of their own theories. The first strategy usually leaves me unsated, and the second (affectionately labeled "academic imperialism" by one of the symposium participants) spawns indigestion. I have attempted to navigate this Scylla and Charybdis by focusing on a few issues that I hope have some depth and some relevance to all the thinking presented here.

We should also not overlook the symposium's remarkable convergence in viewpoints at the most fundamental levels. Although each of us took occasion here and there to pick at a thread in another's theoretical fabric, more salient was the appreciation for the tapestries presented, which was expressed in concrete ways. Carstensen was overheard talking with Csikszentmihalyi about his ESM data on interpersonal interactions; Harter nodded affirmatively throughout Eccles's presentation. Despite the grueling pace set by Jan Jacobs and our Nebraska hosts, theoretical discussions broke out in elevators and taxicabs around Lincoln. As the role of intrinsic motivation in evolution was disputed and the "self-in-relation" was contrasted with the agentic self, waiters stood idle and taxi drivers yawned and turned up the radio. The people of Lincoln were patient.

Although one could attribute this sharing and interest merely to good socialization, I thought there might be something deeper at work. For one thing, the metapsychological assumptions of this group largely converged. No one here espoused straight social cognition or behaviorism, nor was there an analytic speaker in the bunch. Rather, this collection of participants shared the tradition of being empiricists, but with a great respect for the functional importance of human motivation and experience. Thus there was a tendency toward sympathy, if not always agreement, among the presenters by virtue of the common ground and meaning of their work.

Furthermore, a good deal of social activism radiated from this group. Csikszentmihalyi and Rathunde are invested in fostering flow in culture; Eccles has strong ideas that could change the structure of schools; Harter stridently presents a feminist critique on socialization and suggests interventions to support adolescents' self-esteem; and Carstensen appeals to us to alter our stereotypes of older adults. It is hard to be critical of such activism in a time when much academic research in psychology lacks any clear relevance or application to human problems. In the current symposium the participants appear to believe that psychological ideas are significant and can lead to change. Let's hope they are right.

NOTE

1. During the 1980s the symposium moved away from the theme of motivation and was organized into topical volumes of some variety. At least for the time being it appears to have resumed its tradition of inviting contributors to relate to the issue of motivation in their presentations.

REFERENCES

Csikszentmihalyi, M., & Massimini, F. (1985). On the psychological selection of bio-cultural information. *New Ideas in Psychology, 3*, 115–138.

Hunt, D. E. (1975). Person-environment interaction: A challenge found wanting before it was tried. *Review of Educational Research, 45*, 209–230.

Piaget, J. (1971). *Biology and knowledge*. Chicago: University of Chicago Press.

Rogers, C. (1951). *Client-centered therapy.* Boston: Houghton-Mifflin.

Ryan, R. M. (1991). The nature of the self in autonomy and relatedness. In J. Strauss & G. R. Goethals (Eds.), *The self: Interdisciplinary approaches* (pp. 208–238). New York: Springer-Verlag.

Werner, H. (1948). *Comparative psychology of mental development.* New York: International Universities Press.

White, R. W. (1959). Motivation reconsidered: The concept of competence. *Psychological Review, 66*, 297–333.

Abstracts for Poster Presentations

Heidi M. Inderbitzen
Coordinator

Elementary Education Majors' Attributions for Personal Failure Experiences in English, Math, Music, and Physical Education Classes

James R. Austin, Ball State University

Attribution theory provides one framework for understanding how motivation develops in academic settings. In this study a retrospective critical incident method was employed to examine college-age elementary education majors' attributional responses to failure in English, math, music, and physical education classes. A total of 419 subjects identified important school-related failures and responded to a series of six-point Likert-scale items designed to assess their relative endorsement of eight causal attributions: ability, effort, task difficulty, luck, strategy, interest, family influence, and teacher influence. Overall, task difficulty was the attribution most consistently endorsed for failure, while family influence, teacher influence, and luck were least endorsed. Significant subject-area differences were found for all attributions except effort and luck. Subject-area differ-

Abstracts only are printed in this volume for each of the poster presentations. Full papers can be obtained by writing to individual authors. Abstracts are included in alphabetical order by last name of the first author.

ences also were evident in terms of the types or proportions of activities and educational levels represented by recalled failures. Within each subject area, responses to items assessing interest, perceived ability, and past achievement were positively correlated with each other but negatively correlated with attributional endorsement, especially the endorsement of ability attributions for failure.

Reasons for Female and Male Adolescents' Positive and Negative Peer Nominations

Robin Beyer, G. Elliot Rivas, and Heidi Inderbitzen, Department of Psychology, University of Nebraska–Lincoln

This study examined 1,142 adolescents' motivations for sociometric nominations through open-ended questions. Raters classified the reasons given for liking a peer most or liking a peer least into 26 positive and 31 negative categories. The most frequently given reasons for liking were companionship and general positive description and, for disliking, arrogance and insensitivity. Results also suggest that male and female adolescents differ somewhat in why they nominate a peer as liked or disliked. Sense of humor and similarity to the nominee were more frequently given as reasons for liking by males, while females frequently gave emotional support as a reason for liking peers. The types of reasons generated in this study appear theoretically consistent with current literature on affiliation motivation in adolescents and have implications for interventions with rejected or neglected adolescents.

High Expectations and Low Appreciation: Academically Gifted Adolescents' Perceived Motivational Context

Pamela Clinkenbeard, Department of Psychology, Yale University

A semester-long qualitative study of motivation patterns was conducted in a middle-school classroom for academically gifted students. The study is part of a plan for constructing grounded theory and developing strategies for more effective organizational structures and teaching methods to foster talent in all students. Data were obtained from classroom observation, student and teacher interviews, student products, and motivation-related instruments.

Students reported feeling more motivated in their gifted class than in other classes and felt that most teachers and students had unfair expectations of them. Students scored higher than norms on intrinsic motivation and most areas of self-competence on Harter scales.

Relations between Ego Development and Motivational Orientations in African American Adolescents

Daria Paul Courtney, School of Human Environmental Sciences, University of Kentucky–Lexington

This study examined relations between ego development and motivational orientations toward academic work in African American adolescents. The influence of gender, anxiety, and achievement on these relations was also tested. Subjects were selected from 10th- and 11th-grade classes in two southern high schools. Results indicate that relations between ego development and motivational orientations are operating differentially according to gender. The patterns of relations for African American girls are consistent with findings from previous studies conducted with predominantly Anglo-American samples. Intrinsic and internalized motivation increases for girls as their ego levels rise. Patterns demonstrated by the African American boys do not reflect the expected relation.

Intrinsic Motivation, Self-Perceived Competence, and Other Factors as Predictors of School Achievement

Eugenia C. Gonzalez, Texas Tech University Health Sciences Center, and Wanda Mayberry, Colorado State University

Children classified as having a learning disability may have neuromotor deficits, particularly in the ocular motor system, in addition to motivational deficits. The physical components of vision, or the maturity of the ocular motor system required to perform school tasks such as reading, were expected to be related to young students' underlying motivation and perceived self-competence. Data were collected for 508 students attending kindergarten through sixth grade in a suburban school. The results indicate that all of the domains (reading, math, and language skills) tapped by the Motivation scale were selected as significant in explaining academic achievement in at least one content area. In addition, the oculomotor area, bilateral use of eyes, quick localization of stimuli, and smoothness of eye pursuit were selected to explain achievement in some content areas. The only other variable selected was number of days absent, which appeared to contribute to performance in school tasks.

Popularity and Friendship: An Investigation of Their Effects on Self-Esteem

Julia A. Groene, and Heidi Inderbitzen, Department of Psychology, University of Nebraska–Lincoln

This study investigated the effects of both peer acceptance and friendship on self-esteem in an adolescent population. A total of 542 ninth-grade students were classified by sociometric group and presence or absence of reciprocal friendships. Results indicate no significant difference in self-esteem scores across sociometric groups. However, subjects with at least one reciprocal friend had higher self-esteem scores than subjects without a reciprocal friend. Furthermore, there did not appear to be a cumulative effect of number of friendships on self-esteem scores. The importance of friendship to the development of the self-concept is discussed.

Factors Affecting the Choice of Comparison Others: Significance versus Similarity

Richard L. Miller, Psychology Department, University of Nebraska at Kearney

This study compared predictions from social comparison theory and symbolic interactionist theory on preferred sources of self-evaluative information. After completing a personality self-assessment and test, subjects were given results that differed from their actual and expected scores in order to create uncertainty. Subjects were then asked to select an individual whose test results they would like to see, as well as someone they would like to talk with about their own results. Subjects then rated the degree of similarity and significance to themselves of the individuals selected. In both cases, the comparison others chosen were rated as more significant to the subjects than similar to them.

A Longitudinal Study of Mastery Motivation in Infants 9 to 25 Months of Age

George Morgan, College of Applied Human Sciences, Colorado State University; Rex Culp, Oklahoma State University; Nancy Busch-Rossnagel, Fordham University; Karen Barrett, Colorado State University; Richard Redding, Washington and Lee University

This study examined, both concurrently and longitudinally, the relationships among three common measures of mastery task behavior (persistence, pleasure, and competence), as well as their relation to goal-directed free play and mother-infant play. The results support the construct validity of the mastery measures and indicate that they can be meaningfully differentiated. Developmental transitions at approximately 9 months and at 15–18 months of age have been postulated. Between 9 and 12 months there was a significant decrease in simple exploration and increase in task-directed persistence, the key measure of mastery motivation. Moreover, exploration in play and task persistence were inversely correlated at both 9 months and 12 months. Low temporal stability for persistence also supported the proposed transformations.

The Role of Experience, Motivation, and Competence in Predicting Self-Worth and Satisfaction of Taekwondo Students

George Morgan, College of Applied Human Sciences, Colorado State University, and Soyeon Shim, University of Arizona

Two samples of Taekwondo students were studied. For the adult students, intrinsic motivation was the main predictor of high motivation for physical activities, which led to high physical competence and, in turn, to high self-worth and satisfaction with the Taekwondo institute. The results for the adults support a proposed model and are generally consistent with the results for children, whose parents answered the questionnaire for them. However, for the children, both satisfaction and physical motivation were predicted by their experiences and goals, suggesting that this type of variable may be more important for children than for adults.

Gender Differences in Adolescent Affiliation Motivation

G. Elliot Rivas, Stephen Bertholf, and Heidi Inderbitzen, Department of Psychology, University of Nebraska–Lincoln

This investigation examined gender differences in adolescent affiliation motivation. In accord with studies that have shown that adult females score higher than adult males on measures of affiliation motivation, adolescent females were expected to be more motivated to engage in specific social provisions indicative of affiliation needs. Self-report and peer-report questionnaires of social behavior were completed by 1,137 ninth-grade students. Two measures were used as indicators of adolescents' motivation to engage in these affiliative behaviors: self-report of one's tendency to engage in these behaviors, and agreement percentages between self-reports and peer reports of one's tendency to engage in them. It was assumed that higher agreement percentages reflected increased attendance to certain behaviors by peers and thus indicated greater salience of that behavior. The hypothesis that females would report a greater tendency to engage in affiliative behaviors, as well as demonstrate higher agreement percentages, was generally supported.

The "Case" against Individualism: Social Orientation in Grade-School Children

Donald Paszek, Department of Psychology, Grand Valley State University

Social orientation (cooperativeness, competitiveness, individualism) and underlying motivations were measured in 221 first- through sixth-grade children using a modified choice game. Children chose among four alternatives offering points to chooser and a peer over 30 problems in which outcomes were varied. Children were most likely to make individualistic choices when combined with a competitive-superiority motive or when the difference between the individualistic outcome and another possible outcome for the chooser was large. If they did not make individualistic choices, children were likely to shift to a competitive alternative. Thus, they were not being truly individualistic. Younger children were more individualistic than older children, who were more competitive.

A Study of the Dimensionality of Beliefs about Intelligence

Terry Roedel and Greg Schraw, Department of Educational Psychology, University of Nebraska–Lincoln

Learners can be characterized by one of two motivational orientations: mastery goals (focus on learning) or performance goals (focus on performing well). Researchers suggest that these orientations arise from implicit theories about intelligence. Other researchers suggest that orientation is related to environmental effects. This study used factor analysis to explore the dimensionality of beliefs about intelligence. A four-factor solution was preferred. Factors 1 and 2 represent the mastery and the performance orientations. The remaining factors represent beliefs about effort and attributions for success and failure. The existence of these separate factors enables researchers to investigate the roles of attributions and beliefs about effort separately from the two basic orientations.

Gender and Age Differences in Attitudes toward Mathematics: Relation to Mathematics Achievement and Mathematics Course-Taking Plans

Tracy Thorndike-Christ, Department of Educational Psychology, University of Nebraska–Lincoln

Attitudes toward mathematics are positively related to, and predictive of, mathematics achievement. When enrollment in mathematics courses becomes optional (in approximately 10th grade), attitudes may also function as a motivational factor in a child's decision to continue or to avoid the further study of mathematics. Lack of adequate mathematical preparation in high school has been advanced as one explanation for the underrepresentation of females in mathematics- and science-related college majors. Gender- and age-related differences in students' attitudes toward mathematics among 1,123 7th through 10th graders were investigated. Overall, females' attitudes were more positive than expected, and no gender differences were found in their intention to continue to take mathematics courses once enrollment became optional. Attitudes were generally less positive among older students and were least positive among 10th graders. In addition, 10th graders were less likely to express plans to continue taking mathematics once they could elect not to than were 7th or 8th graders. Attitudes toward mathematics accounted for 33% of the variability in course-taking plans, confirming that attitudes are at least in part responsible for some of the educational choices a student makes concerning the study of mathematics.

Subject Index

achievement
  children's motivation for, 30,
    259–260
  cultural beliefs regarding, 152
  demographic and economic fac-
    tors of, 147–150
  old age acceptance of, 225
  optimal experience and, 85–91
  parental reinforcement of, 147–
    153, 169–174, 259–260, 265
  poster on predictors of school,
    271–272
  ratio of pretensions to, 101–102
  self-perception theory and, 145–
    146, 157–159
  teacher expectancy of, 177–178
  See also motivation; talent
acquisition of information
  as an interaction goal, 210
  social contact and, 221–223, 239–
    241
activities
  and activity theory described,
    214–215
  adolescent flow, 68–73

age-related drop in, 214–216
emotion-specific ANS and, 231–
  232
flow experience of, 58–65
hierarchy of parent value on,
  157–159
pro-social, 91–93
reinforcement of, 169–174
See also motivation
actualization, 2–3, 65
adolescents
  acquisition of information by,
    222–223, 240–241
  appearance/self-esteem link in,
    117–121
  attachment of, 20–21
  autonomy development of, 15
  autotelic growth in, 89–91
  declining interest in school of,
    178–186
  depression composite of, 114–117
  emergence of false self in, 131–
    133
  environment impact on motiva-
    tion of, 186–191

278

DEVELOPMENTAL PERSPECTIVES ON MOTIVATION

  flow activities of, 68–71
  and imaginary audience phe-
    nomenon, 43
  impact of popularity on self-es-
    teem of, 272
  impact of public vs. private ap-
    proval and, 122–126
  impact of self-esteem on, 111–114
  maturational levels and auton-
    omy in, 191–194
  MSALT, 155–156, 159–161
  multiple Mes conflict in, 129–131
  need for security of, 84
  and need for "zone of comfort,"
    185
  optimal experience study on, 85–
    88
  poster on gender and affiliation
    motivation of, 274
  poster on mathematic attitudes
    of, 275–276
  poster on motivation of African
    American, 271
  poster on motivation of gifted,
    270–271
  poster on peer nominations of, 270
  preoccupation with Me-self in,
    100–101
  and their relationship with
    teachers, 187–189
  social cliques of, 217
  stage-environment fit in, 194–198,
    260
  talent development study on, 76–
    79
  See also children
agency
  role in development of, 46–48
  self-efficacy and, 16–18
aging
  changes in facial expression
    throughout, 233
  and decline of self-enhancing
    contact, 226–228

and emotion during old age, 230–
    243
  emotion as motivating factor dur-
    ing, 211
  life satisfaction and, 235–238
  life-span framework on, 216–220
  research on, 211–212
  and selective optimization with
    compensation model, 212, 244
  social interactions and, 212–216
alienation
  defining, 23
  pawn behavior and, 12–13
appearance. *See* physical appearance
approval
  autonomy and, 37–39
  behavior and, 30, 44, 263
  beliefs conveyed through, 155
  false self and need for, 132–133
  fluctuation of, 127
  from the public domain, 122–126
  impact of conditional, 114–117
  impact of self, 124–126
  women and need for, 45
arousal
  aging and reduced, 237
  ANS emotion-elicited, 231–233
  optimal, 65, 83–84
  self-regulation of, 82–84
  See also stimulation
assimilation
  cultural impact on, 4
  flow model on, 257
  reciprocal, 1–2, 6
  See also internalization
Athletic Competence domain, 103–
    108
attachment
  autonomy and, 20–21, 33–37, 259
  balance between exploration
    and, 35
  optimal arousal theories and, 83–
    84
attribution theory
  on competence perceptions, 162–
    163

familiarity, 174
family
  achievement socialization in the, 147–150
  adolescent relationship with the, 194–196
  autotelic environment of the, 259
  beliefs and child-rearing climate, 150–153
  competence reinforcement by the, 169–174
  contact during old age, 213–214, 218–220
  optimal experience by the complex, 85–91
  role models in the, 153–154
  self-esteem and support of, 110–111
  See also parents
females
  appearance stereotypes and self-esteem in, 118–122
  and being-for-others preoccupation, 45
  and impact of negative social interactions, 226
  implications of false-self for, 133–134
  multiple Mes conflict in, 129–131
  See also gender; males
flow experience
  adolescent, 68–71
  clinical applications of, 79–80
  consequences of, 76–79
  growth of core self and, 73–76, 266
  measurement of, 65–67
  motivation and, 58–61, 257
  pros and cons of, 91–92
  quality of, 71–73, 79, 85–88
  rewards of, 61–65
  See also enjoyment
Flow Questionnaire, 65–66
Flow Scales, 66
Freedom and Nature (Ricoeur), 8

gender
  friendship differences according to, 213–214
  learning contexts and, 176
  maturity levels and motivation and, 191–194
  multiple Mes conflict and, 129–131
  perceived competence and, 159–169, 260, 265
  poster on adolescent affiliation motivation and, 274
  poster on attitudes toward mathematics and, 275–276
  poster presentation on peers and, 270
  self-esteem and, 120–122
  socialization of roles according to, 170
  task encouragement and, 157–158
  See also females; males
gerontology, 210–211
  See also aging
global self-esteem, 104–105
  Global Self-Esteem subscale and, 103–104

heteronomy
  internalization and, 29
  intrinsic motivation for, 26–28
  vs. autonomy, 8–10
  and higher-order reflective appraisal, 10
  homeostatic control and, 231
  and homonomy, 39
  See also relationships

identification, 29–30
  See also internalization
imaginary audience phenomenon, 43
  See also looking-glass self
inauthentic actions, 9
inauthentical self, 44
independence
  allowed by dependence, 84

Author Index

Weinstein, R. S., 177
Weissman, M. M., 215
Wells, A. J., 72, 76
Wentzel, K. R., 172, 173
Werner, H., 1, 257
Wessels, K., 175, 178
Western, D., 7
Whalen, S., 66
Wheeler, L., 66
White, R. W., 19, 21, 22, 65, 255, 257
Whitesell, N. R., 113, 117
Wicklund, R. A., 42
Wigfield, A., 145, 177, 186
Wills, T. A., 224
Winfield-Laird, I., 215
Winnicott, D. W., 6, 35, 40
Winterbottom, M. R., 150
Wisenbaker, J., 175

Wong, M., 72
Wood, J. V., 224
Wylie, R. C., 112

Yarrow, L. J., 234
Yee, D. K., 146, 163, 195, 196
Yerxa, E. J., 80
Yoon, K. S., 172

Zahaykevich, M. K., 4
Zajonc, R. B., 174
Zajonc, R. S., 231, 233
Zanna, M. P., 40
Ziegler, M., 231
Zigler, E., 109
Zuckerman, M., 24, 27, 61
Zumpf, C. L., 117, 120, 121